READERS GUIDES TO ESSENTIAL CRITICISM

CONSULTANT EDITOR: NICOLAS TREDELL

*Published*

| | |
|---|---|
| **Lucie Armitt** | George Eliot: *Adam Bede–The Mill on the Floss –Middlemarch* |
| **Simon Avery** | Thomas Hardy: *The Mayor of Casterbridge – Jude the Obscure* |
| **Paul Baines** | Daniel Defoe: *Robinson Crusoe–Moll Flanders* |
| **Richard Beynon** | D. H. Lawrence: *The Rainbow–Women in Love* |
| **Peter Boxall** | Samuel Beckett: *Waiting for Godot–Endgame* |
| **Claire Brennan** | The Poetry of Sylvia Plath |
| **Susan Bruce** | Shakespeare: *King Lear* |
| **Sandie Byrne** | Jane Austen: *Mansfield Park* |
| **Alison Chapman** | Elizabeth Gaskell: *Mary Barton–North and South* |
| **Peter Childs** | The Fiction of Ian McEwan |
| **Christine Clegg** | Vladimir Nabokov: *Lolita* |
| **John Coyle** | James Joyce: *Ulysses–A Portrait of the Artist as a Young Man* |
| **Martin Coyle** | Shakespeare: *Richard II* |
| **Justin D. Edwards** | Postcolonial Literature |
| **Michael Faherty** | The Poetry of W. B. Yeats |
| **Sarah Gamble** | The Fiction of Angela Carter |
| **Jodi–Anne George** | Chaucer: The General Prologue to *The Canterbury Tales* |
| **Jane Goldman** | Virginia Woolf: *To the Lighthouse–The Waves* |
| **Huw Griffiths** | Shakespeare: *Hamlet* |
| **Vanessa Guignery** | The Fiction of Julian Barnes |
| **Louisa Hadley** | The Fiction of A. S. Byatt |
| **Geoffrey Harvey** | Thomas Hardy: *Tess of the d'Urbervilles* |
| **Paul Hendon** | The Poetry of W. H. Auden |
| **Terry Hodgson** | The Plays of Tom Stoppard for Stage, Radio, TV and Film |
| **William Hughes** | Bram Stoker: *Dracula* |
| **Stuart Hutchinson** | Mark Twain: *Tom Sawyer–Huckleberry Finn* |
| **Stuart Hutchinson** | Edith Wharton: *The House of Mirth – The Custom of the Country* |
| **Betty Jay** | E. M. Forster: *A Passage to India* |
| **Aaron Kelly** | Twentieth-Century Irish Literature |
| **Elmer Kennedy–Andrews** | The Poetry of Seamus Heaney |
| **Elmer Kennedy–Andrews** | Nathaniel Hawthorne: *The Scarlet Letter* |
| **Daniel Lea** | George Orwell: *Animal Farm–Nineteen Eighty-Four* |
| **Sara Lodge** | Charlotte Brontë: *Jane Eyre* |
| **Philippa Lyon** | Twentieth-Century War Poetry |

| | |
|---|---|
| Merja Makinen | The Novels of Jeanette Winterson |
| Matt McGuire | Contemporary Scottish Literature |
| Timothy Milnes | Wordsworth: *The Prelude* |
| Jago Morrison | The Fiction of Chinua Achebe |
| Carl Plasa | Tony Morrison: *Beloved* |
| Carl Plasa | Jean Rhys: *Wide Sargasso Sea* |
| Nicholas Potter | Shakespeare: *Antony and Cleopatra* |
| Nicholas Potter | Shakespeare: *Othello* |
| Nicholas Potter | Shakespeare's Late Plays: *Pericles, Cymbeline, The Winter's Tale, The Tempest* |
| Steven Price | The Plays, Screenplays and Films of David Mamet |
| Andrew Radford | Victorian Sensation Fiction |
| Berthold Schoene–Harwood | Mary Shelley: *Frankenstein* |
| Nick Selby | T. S. Eliot: *The Waste Land* |
| Nick Selby | Herman Melville: *Moby Dick* |
| Nick Selby | The Poetry of Walt Whitman |
| David Smale | Salman Rushdie: *Midnight's Chidren –The Satanic Verses* |
| Patsy Stoneman | Emily Brontë: *Wuthering Heights* |
| Susie Thomas | Hanif Kureishi |
| Nicolas Tredell | F. Scott Fitzgerald: *The Great Gatsby* |
| Nicolas Tredell | Joseph Conrad: *Heart of Darkness* |
| Nicolas Tredell | Charles Dickens: *Great Expectations* |
| Nicolas Tredell | William Faulkner: *The Sound and the Fury–As I Lay Dying* |
| Nicolas Tredell | Shakespeare: *Macbeth* |
| Nicolas Tredell | The Fiction of Martin Amis |
| Matthew Woodcock | Shakespeare: *Henry V* |
| Angela Wright | Gothic Fiction |

*Forthcoming*

| | |
|---|---|
| Pascale Aebischer | Jacobean Drama |
| Annika Bautz | Jane Austen: *Sense and Sensibility – Pride and Prejudice – Emma* |
| Matthew Beedham | The Novels of Kazuo Ishiguro |
| Jodi–Anne George | *Beowulf* |
| Sarah Haggarty & Jon Mee | Willam Blake: *Songs of Innocence and Experience* |
| Matthew Jordan | Milton: *Paradise Lost* |
| Stephen Regan | The Poetry of Philip Larkin |
| Mardi Stewart | Victorian Women's Poetry |
| Michael Whitworth | Virginia Woolf: *Mrs Dalloway* |
| Gina Wisker | The Fiction of Margaret Atwood |

**Readers' Guides to Essential Criticism**
Series Standing Order
ISBN 1–4039–0108–2
*(outside North America only)*

You can receive future titles in this series as they are published by placing a standing order. Please contact your bookseller or, in the case of difficulty, write to us at the address below with your name and address, the title of the series and the ISBN quoted above.

Customer Services Department, Macmillan Distribution Ltd
Houndmills, Basingstoke, Hampshire RG21 6XS, England

# Gothic Fiction

ANGELA WRIGHT

Consultant editor: Nicolas Tredell

palgrave
macmillan

First published 2007 by
PALGRAVE MACMILLAN

Palgrave Macmillan in the UK is an imprint of Macmillan Publishers Limited, registered in England, company number 785998, of Houndmills, Basingstoke, Hampshire RG21 6XS.

Palgrave Macmillan in the US is a division of St Martin's Press LLC, 175 Fifth Avenue, New York, NY 10010.

Palgrave Macmillan is the global academic imprint of the above companies and has companies and representatives throughout the world.

Palgrave® and Macmillan® are registered trademarks in the United States, the United Kingdom, Europe and other countries.

ISBN 978-1-4039-3666-0 hardback
ISBN 978-1-4039-3667-7 paperback

This book is printed on paper suitable for recycling and made from fully managed and sustained forest sources. Logging, pulping and manufacturing processes are expected to conform to the environmental regulations of the country of origin.

A catalogue record for this book is available from the British Library.

Library of Congress Cataloging-in-Publication Data
Wright, Angela, 1969 May 14–
     Gothic fiction / Angela Wright ; consultant editor, Nicolas Tredell.
        p. cm.—(Reader's guides to essential criticism)
     Includes bibliographical references and index.
     ISBN-13: 978–1–4039–3666–0 (cloth)
     ISBN-13: 978–1–4039–3667–7 (pbk.)
     ISBN-10: 1–4039–3666–8 (cloth)
     ISBN-10: 1–4039–3667–6 (pbk.)
        1. Horror tales, English – History and criticism – Guidebooks. 2. Gothic revival (Literature) – Great Britain – Guidebooks. 3. English fiction – 18th century – History and criticism. 4. English fiction – 19th century – History and criticism. I. Tredell, Nicolas. II. Title.

PR830.T3W75 2007
823'.08729—dc22                                                          2006052781

Printed in Great Britain by the MPG Books Group, Bodmin and King's Lynn

For Hamish and Jessica

# CONTENTS

CHAPTER FIVE                                    97

'This narrative resembles a delirious dream': Psychoanalytical
Readings of the Gothic

An appraisal of the differing psychoanalytic approaches that have
been used for reading Gothic fiction.

CHAPTER SIX                                    125

'It is not ours to make election for ourselves': Gender and the
Gothic

An analysis of the anxiety surrounding female authorship; a sample
of the debate surrounding the controversial term 'Female Gothic',
and an analysis of alternative approaches to reading gender in
Gothic.

# ACKNOWLEDGEMENTS

I wish to thank the authors cited in this work who have granted permission for me to do so. Their generosity and swift responses transformed the submission process for this book into a pleasurable experience. I also wish to thank the General Editor, Nicolas Tredell, for his careful and thoughtful suggestions, as well as Sonya Barker at Palgrave Macmillan. The Department of English Literature at the University of Sheffield have been generous in granting me the time, and offering me the encouragement, to complete this book. And finally, I would most particularly like to thank Hamish Mathison for giving me the time and space to complete this, and Jessica, for showing great patience. To these last two people I dedicate this book.

The author and publishers wish to thank the following for permission to reproduce material:

Blackwell Publishing for material from Jerrold E. Hogle, 'The Gothic Ghost of the Counterfeit and the Progress of Abjection', in David Punter (ed.), *Companion to the Gothic* (2000), pp. 293, 295–6.

Cambridge University Press for material from Robert Miles, 'The 1790s: the Effulgence of Gothic', from Jerrold E. Hogle, *The Cambridge Companion to Gothic Fiction* (2002), pp. 60, 48, 48–9; Mark Canuel, *Religion, Toleration and British Writing: 1790–1820* (2002), pp. 55–6, 62, 62–4, 72; and E. J. Clery, *The Rise of Supernatural Fiction, 1762–1800* (1995), pp. 101, 126–7.

David B. Morris for material from his article 'Gothic Sublimity', *New Literary History*, 16 (Winter 1985), pp. 300–1, 306.

Ronald Paulson for material from his book *Representations of Revolution (1789–1820)* (Yale University Press, 1983), pp. 217–18, 221–2, 224–5, 231–2.

Taylor & Francis Books and the University of Nebraska Press for material from J. M. S. Tompkins, *The Popular Novel in England* (1932; Methuen, 1969), pp. 274–6.

Every effort has been made to trace the copyright holders but if any have been inadvertently overlooked the publishers will be pleased to make the necessary arrangement at the first opportunity.

# Introduction

Perhaps the perusal of such works may, without injustice, be compared with the use of opiates, baneful, when habitually and constantly
resorted to, but of most blessed power in those moments of pain and
of languor, when the whole head is sore, and the whole heart sick. If
those who rail indiscriminately at this species of composition, were to
consider the quantity of actual pleasure which it produces, and the
much greater proportion of real sorrow and distress which it alleviates,
their philanthropy ought to moderate their critical pride, or religious
intolerance.

(Sir Walter Scott, 'Ann Radcliffe', *Lives of the Novelists*, from the
*Miscellaneous Prose Works* (1827), in Ioan Williams (ed.),
*On Novelists and Fiction*, London: Routledge, 1968)

What is the Gothic? Few literary genres have attracted so much
critical appetite and opprobrium simultaneously. From its beginnings in 1764 with Walpole's *The Castle of Otranto*, through its production
boom in the 1790s, to its present-day permutations, the Gothic remains
as nebulous a genre as the shadowy veiled figures which haunt its
pages. As E. J. Clery has indicated, 'The attachment of the term *Gothic* to
the literature of terror is quite a recent development – and almost
entirely accidental.'[1] Horace Walpole (1717–97) only attached the
subtitle 'A Gothic Story' to the second edition of his novel, and the term
was rarely used during the late eighteenth and nineteenth centuries.

The word 'Gothic' has been used in many contexts throughout history and culture. Its first usage was to refer to a specific tribe of people,
the Visigoths who invaded and defeated the Roman Empire. Robin
Sowerby notes that 'Throughout history the word "Gothic" has always
been chiefly defined in contrasting juxtaposition to the Roman, and a
constant factor in its various uses ... has continued to be its antithesis
to the Roman or classical.'[2] As an adjective used to describe a people,
then, Gothic came to signify barbarism because of its oppositional position to the Roman Empire. This barbaric association continued
throughout the Renaissance. During the eighteenth century, however,
'Gothic' enjoyed a more positive revival. Its connotations moved from
the historical accounts of barbaric Visigoths to a more fluid aesthetic
association with medieval chivalry. One of the ways in which this

1

revival was effected was through architecture: it is no coincidence that the first 'Gothic' novelist, Horace Walpole, modelled his own home Strawberry Hill upon a Gothic architecture inspired by medievalism. His example was swiftly followed by the author of *Vathek* (1786), William Beckford (1760–1844), who chose a similarly medieval aesthetic for his home, Fonthill Abbey.

One of the early exponents of the aesthetic revaluation of 'Gothic' in the eighteenth century was Bishop Richard Hurd (1720–1808). In his *Letters on Chivalry and Romance* (1762), Hurd associated 'Gothic' with chivalry, feudalism and romance, thus paving the way for Walpole's first 'Gothic Story', *The Castle of Otranto*. In his first letter, Hurd commenced his excavation of 'Gothic' thus:

### ■ LETTER I

The ages, we call barbarous, present us with many a subject of curious speculation. What, for instance, is more remarkable than the Gothic CHIVALRY? or than the spirit of ROMANCE, which took its rise from that singular institution?

Nothing in human nature, my dear friend, is without its reasons. The modes and fashions of different times may appear, at first sight, fantastic and unaccountable. But they, who look nearly into them, discover some latent cause of their production.

'Nature once known, no prodigies remain,'

as sings our philosophical bard; but to come at this knowledge, is the difficulty. Sometimes a close attention to the workings of the human mind is sufficient to lead us to it: sometimes more than that, the diligent observation of what passes without us, is necessary.

This last I take to be the case here. The prodigies, we are now contemplating, had their origin in the barbarous ages. Why then, says the fastidious modern, look any farther for the reason? Why not resolve them at once into the usual caprice and absurdity of barbarians?

This, you see, is a short and commodious philosophy. Yet barbarians have their *own*, such as it is, if they are not enlightened by our reason. Shall we then condemn them unheard, or will it not be fair to let them have the telling of their own story?

Would we know, from what causes the institution of *Chivalry* was derived? The time of its birth, the situation of the barbarians, amongst whom it arose, must be considered: their wants, designs and policies must be explored: we must enquire when, and where, and how it came to pass that the western world became familiarised to this *Prodigy*, which we now start at.

Another thing is full as remarkable, and concerns us more nearly. The spirit of Chivalry, was a fire which soon spent itself: but that of *Romance*, which was kindled at it, burnt long, and continued its light and heat even to the politer ages.

The great geniuses of our own and foreign countries, such as Ariosto [1474–1533] and Tasso [1544–95] in Italy, and Spenser [1552–99] and Milton [1608–74] in England, were seduced by the barbarities of their forefathers; were even charmed by the Gothic Romances. Was this caprice and absurdity in them? Or, may there not be something in the Gothic Romance peculiarly suited to the views of a genius and to the ends of poetry? And may not the philosophic moderns have gone too far, in their perpetual ridicule and contempt of it?

To form a judgment in the case, the rise, progress, and genius of Gothic Chivalry must be explained.

The circumstances in the Gothic fictions and manners, which are proper to the ends of poetry (if any such there be) must be pointed out.

Reasons, for the decline and rejection of the Gothic taste in later times must be given.

You have in these particulars both the SUBJECT, and the PLAN of the following Letters.³ ☐

Hurd's letter challenged the neoclassical principles espoused by Alexander Pope (1688–1744), which retained ascendancy throughout the eighteenth century. He commences an appreciation of the literature of the past by connecting the Italian poets Ariosto and Tasso with Milton and Spenser, admitting that the latter 'were seduced by the barbarities of their forefathers'.

As we shall see in Chapter One of this Guide, Hurd's cultural rescue of Romance, which had fallen into literary disrepute, is of great significance to the rise of the Gothic romance. Clara Reeve (1729–1807), whose romance *The Old English Baron: A Gothic Story* was published in 1778, followed up her Gothic excursion by publishing a sustained literary essay entitled *The Progress of Romance* in 1785. There, she pursued Hurd's revaluation of Romance, and argued that the Romance's ancient and esteemed connections had been overlooked.

Hurd's and Reeve's essays were two of many eighteenth-century attempts to revive both Gothic and Romance from the disrepute into which they had fallen. In terms of literary experimentation, the late eighteenth-century poetry of Thomas Gray (1716–71), James Macpherson (1736–96) and Thomas Chatterton (1752–70) also looked to the past for its sources of literary inspiration. In their turn, they also contributed to the rise of the Gothic Romance.⁴ Hurd's *Letters* indicate that he views Gothic as an ideal that should move between Romance and poetry. And yet, as we will see in Chapter One, the artificial separation of Gothic from poetry began towards the end of the eighteenth century, particularly with the attack by Samuel Taylor Coleridge (1772–1834) on *The Monk* (1796) by Matthew Lewis (1775–1818).

Recent critics of the Gothic genre have problematized the Gothic's separation from Romantic poetry. Anne Williams, for one, in her 1995 study *Art of Darkness*, argues that ' "Gothic" and "Romantic" are not two but one', and Robert Miles, in *Gothic Writing 1750–1820: A Genealogy*, views Gothic writing 'as a discursive site crossing the genres'.[5] More recently, Michael Gamer in his study *Romanticism and the Gothic* agrees with Robert Miles that Gothic is an aesthetic that crosses literary genres, but qualifies this slightly:

> ■ At the very least, if gothic is a site crossing the genres, it is a site that *moves*, and that must be defined in part by its ability to transplant itself *across* forms and media: from narrative into dramatic and poetic modes, and from textual into visual and aural media. I find the conception of gothic as a shifting 'aesthetic' helpful because it corresponds to how late eighteenth-century critical audiences imagined and represented gothic's emergence into British literary culture, except that their own labels for gothic – as foreign invader, as cancer, as enthusiasm, as emasculating disease, or as infantilizing nurse – are more pejorative. The number and intensity of these labels, moreover, demonstrate the range of impressions gothic produced even among its detractors, and give some indication of the extent of the gulf existing between critical and popular audiences.[6] □

Gamer perceptively views Gothic as a nebulous 'protean' entity that both sustains and is sustained by other literary discourses. And crucially, in Gamer's account, its critical reception in the 1790s, also explored in Chapter One of this Guide, also comes to define how we continue to understand the Gothic.

The vibrant debate upon the Gothic and its different generic mutations and implications continues to grow and gather strength. In this Guide, I have chosen to focus primarily upon the prose criticism and fiction which the popularity of the Gothic spawned during the Romantic era. The Guide concentrates upon the 'classic' and widely available Gothic novels from Walpole's *Otranto* in 1764, through the fiction of the 1790s, up to the publication of *Melmoth the Wanderer* (1820) by Charles Robert Maturin (1782–1824).[7] Whilst the majority of the criticism that I refer to throughout the Guide focuses upon the more mainstream Gothic romances of Horace Walpole, Ann Radcliffe (1764–1823), Lewis and Maturin, the contemporary eighteenth-century material that I discuss is less canonical. It makes reference to partially forgotten authors such as Regina Maria Roche (1764–1845), Eleanor Sleath and Francis Lathom (1774–1832) among many others. More recently, the author Charlotte Dacre (?1772–1825) has justifiably received attention, and her romance *Zofloya* (1806) is referred to in Chapter Six. *Northanger*

*Abbey* (1818) by Jane Austen (1775–1817), frequently invoked throughout this Guide as both Gothic critique and Gothic romance, produces a far more heterogeneous and inclusive list of Gothic fiction in the 1790s than many twentieth-century critical accounts. If anything, the eighteenth-century critical reception of Gothic attests to the variety, abundance and terror of the Gothic, and proves that there is yet much critical excavation and evaluation to take place.

I do not subscribe to the belief espoused by Maurice Lévy in his significant critical work *Le roman 'Gothique' Anglais, 1764–1824* (1968) that the Gothic expires in 1824. The vibrancy of the interdisciplinary journal *Gothic Studies*, the internet presence of so many websites devoted to the serious study of the Gothic, and the International Gothic Association's biannual conferences bear testament to the Gothic's endurance well into the twenty-first century. The Gothic is culturally amphibious. As Michael Gamer and others suggest, the Gothic moves across both generic and time boundaries with startling ease, and thrives in contemporary fiction, drama, poetry and film.

In order to explore the richness and vibrancy of the Gothic, however, I have chosen to examine in detail here the Gothic romance from 1764 to 1820 in the hope that the criticism of Gothic in this period alone will give readers an appetite for the wealth of critical accounts on Gothic up to the present day. Gothic criticism is in itself a 'protean' and vibrant field. Over the following six chapters, I examine a range of critical responses to Gothic novels published between 1764 and 1820. I do so by considering six different themes. Chapter One addresses the contemporary response to the Gothic in the eighteenth and early nineteenth centuries. The reception of the Gothic is explored through the lens of both the reviewers and some of the authors. The chapter concludes by considering the continuing critical implications of these early responses. Chapter Two explores the Gothic aesthetic of terror, and its counterpart, horror. The chapter begins by exploring the theory of the sublime through the work of Edmund Burke (1729–97). It then moves on to consider how contemporary commentators such as Anna Laetitia Aikin (later Barbauld, 1743–1825), Nathan Drake (1766–1836) and Ann Radcliffe responded to Burke's theorizing of terror. Then the chapter offers a variety of twentieth-century critical responses to the use of the sublime in the Gothic. In Chapter Three the French Revolution's impact upon the Gothic is examined, again through the lens of both Romantic responses to it as well as twentieth-century responses to the Gothic's engagement with the Revolution. Chapter Four considers the intimate connections between the seemingly profound anti-Catholicism and British nationalism in the Gothic. As the range of criticism and analysis in this chapter proves, the Gothic genre is deeply embedded in discourses of nationalism and religion. In Chapter Five, a range of psychoanalytic approaches to the Gothic genre is explored. We start with Horace Walpole's own analysis of his dream regarding *The Castle of Otranto*, and move through the Surrealists' psychoanalytic appropriation of the Gothic in the early twentieth century. The chapter explores a range of essays and critical analyses through the lens of Sigmund Freud (1859–1939), Jacques Lacan (1901–81) and Julia Kristeva (born 1941). One of the most heated debates currently surrounding the Gothic romance is the issue of 'Female Gothic', a term originally coined by Ellen Moers in *Literary Women* in 1976. Chapter Six, on gender and the Gothic, explores the richness of this debate and just what 'Female Gothic' might imply. It is, however, important to acknowledge that issues of gender in the Gothic are not specifically confined to 'Female Gothic', and the chapter also addresses those Gothic texts which are predominantly male, such as *Caleb Williams* (1794) by William Godwin (1756–1836). Issues of gender, violence, sexuality and desire in the Gothic are explored in this final chapter.

Early twentieth-century critical responses to the Gothic were hesitant and apologetic. In the 'Preface' of her ground-breaking 1932 study *The Popular Novel in England: 1770–1800*, J. M. S. Tompkins began, 'A book devoted to the display of tenth-rate fiction stands in need of justification.'[8] Even as late as 1957, Devendra P. Varma, in *The Gothic Flame*, also perceived the need to excuse his critique: 'A study devoted to the analysis and investigation of a body of fiction that is usually left to moulder in the libraries of the curious, perhaps stands in need of justification.'[9] Thankfully, this former urge to defend study of the Gothic has now evaporated.

The diversity of analyses and criticism explored in the following chapters demonstrates that the Gothic continues to arouse the same critical passions and arguments that it did in the 1790s. As I have also suggested, however, there is yet much work to be done. As Walter Scott suggests in the epigraph to this 'Introduction', the 'actual pleasure' produced in reading and responding to the Gothic ensures its critical survival.

# CHAPTER ONE

# 'Terrorist Novel Writing': the Contemporary Reception of the Gothic

The following work was found in the library of an ancient catholic family in the north of England. It was printed at Naples, in the black letter, in the year 1529. How much sooner it was written does not appear. The principal incidents are such as were believed in the darkest ages of Christianity; but the language and conduct have nothing that favours of barbarism. The style is the purest Italian. If the story was written near the time when it is supposed to have happened, it must have been between 1095, the aera of the first crusade, and 1243, the date of the last, or not long afterwards. ... It is not unlikely that an artful priest might endeavour to turn their own arms on the innovators; and might avail himself of his abilities as an author to confirm the populace in their ancient errors and superstitions.

... Whatever [the author's] views were, or whatever effects the execution of them might have, his work can only be laid before the public at present as a matter of entertainment. Even as such, some apology for it is necessary. Miracles, visions, necromancy, dreams, and other preternatural events, are exploded now even from romances. That was not the case when our author wrote; much less when the story itself is supposed to have happened. Belief in every kind of prodigy was so established in those dark ages, that an author would not be faithful to the *manners* of the times who should omit all mention of them. He is not bound to believe them himself, but he must represent his actors as believing them.

(Horace Walpole, Preface to the first edition of *The Castle of Otranto* (1764), ed. E. J. Clery, Oxford: Oxford University Press, 1996, pp. 5–6)

## Otranto and the uses of 'Romance'

When Horace Walpole first published *The Castle of Otranto* on Christmas Day in 1764, he pretended that the novel was a translation from an obscure Italian work. The first Preface to the novel established this hoax, with the 'translator', one 'William Marshall, Gent.', commenting upon the circumstances under which he discovered the original work, offering some observations on the Romance genre, and arguing for the superior merits of the Italian language.

There are a series of tensions in the opening paragraphs of Walpole's first attempt at a preface to his novel, and it spawns some significant markers for the genre that took after it: the Gothic Romance. The first is in its very first line (see above). Note how the work was allegedly discovered 'in the library of an ancient catholic family in the north of England'. This immediate specificity is not accidental. Whilst the discovery of the work is in Britain, it is distanced – the 'north of England' is far from Walpole's residence to the west of London. This locale enables Walpole to accredit the work's ownership to an 'ancient catholic family' far removed from the Protestant modernities of metropolitan London.

There is a second tension in the opening paragraph of the first Preface. The 'incidents' described belong to systems of thought 'believed in the darkest ages of christianity'. Despite this, though, the language and conduct 'have nothing that favours of barbarism'. 'William Marshall' – the putative translator – speculates that the work's original author could be 'an artful priest', one who could 'avail himself of his abilities as an author to confirm the populace in their ancient errors and superstitions'. The belief system that the novel presents is thus seemingly at odds with the talents and art of its 'author', the 'artful priest'. The supposed author's name is offered on the title-page of the first edition. It is given there as 'Onuphrio Muralto'. We should be suspicious, for this is an Italian approximation of Walpole (*Mur* = wall, 'alto' is literally translated as 'old'). Walpole's literary gag depends on the 'artful' and skilful Catholic priest-author being hard to tell apart from the actual, Protestant and Whig, author.[1]

In his essay 'Europhobia: the Catholic Other in Horace Walpole and Charles Maturin' (2002), Robert Miles relates the tensions of this opening Preface to the ongoing debate on the function of the novel in the eighteenth century:

■ A great deal of anxiety surrounded the invention of the modern novel, which was understood to have been revolutionized by print technology (making the circulating library possible) and by the new writing technology of 'realism'. Walpole's experiment provoked unease, partly because it wilfully interfered with the received Whig progress of literary history, from marvellous tales of adventure (fit for children, Catholics and other primitives) to probable representations of everyday life (fit for those living in a Protestant nation); and partly because he was employing the arms of the novel-writing innovators in support of a tale whose sole aim

appeared to be the undermining of the Protestant rationality of its readers. What was Walpole's game? One answer would be that there wasn't
one. The imposture was meant to be transparent: as a pro-Catholic text
*Otranto* is clearly self-subverting. Indulging in impostures and using the
blessed invention of the novel to inculcate superstition is precisely the
dastardly behaviour one would expect of Catholics, even those from
ancient Northern English families.[2] □

Miles's argument regarding the transparency of the imposture is
persuasive, and helps to account for the parodic nature of the literal
translation of Walpole's name into 'Onuphrio Muralto'.

The contemporary reception of *The Castle of Otranto* in the periodical
press, however, failed to identify this 'transparent subversion'. Writing
for the *Monthly Review*, John Langhorne pronounced the first 'hoax'
edition a 'work of genius, evincing great dramatic powers', clearly written
by 'no common pen'.[3] Buoyed by this successful reception, Walpole
acknowledged his authorship in a second edition. It appeared in April
1765. As E. J. Clery notes in an essay entitled 'The Genesis of "Gothic"
Fiction' (2002), the word 'Gothic' was appended only to this second
Preface.[4] In the first Preface, Walpole ascribed *Otranto*'s use of supernatural apparatus to its apparent authorship by an 'artful' Catholic priest.
'Miracles, visions, necromancy, dreams, and other preternatural
events,' argued Walpole, 'are exploded now even from romances.' This
*apologia* for using the supernatural, though, left Walpole with an even
more pressing need to justify its use, a challenge he met in the Preface
to his second edition:

■ The favourable manner in which this little piece has been received by
the public, calls upon the author to explain the grounds on which he
composed it. But before he opens those motives, it is fit that he should
ask pardon of his readers for having offered his work to them under the
borrowed personage of a translator. As diffidence of his own abilities,
and the novelty of the attempt, were his sole inducements to assume
that disguise, he flatters himself he shall appear excusable. He resigned
his performance to the impartial judgment of the public; determined to let
it perish in obscurity, if disapproved; nor meaning to avow such a trifle,
unless better judges should pronounce that he might own it without
a blush.

It was an attempt to blend the two kinds of romance, the ancient and
the modern. In the former all was imagination and improbability: in the
latter, nature is always intended to be, and sometimes has been, copied
with success. Invention has not been wanting; but the great resources of
fancy have been dammed up, by a strict adherence to common life. But
if in the latter species Nature has cramped imagination, she did but take
her revenge, having been totally excluded from old romances. The actions,

sentiments, conversations, of the heroes and heroines of ancient days were as unnatural as the machines employed to put them in motion. The author of the following pages thought it possible to reconcile the two kinds. Desirous of leaving the powers of fancy at liberty to expatiate through the boundless realms of invention, and thence of creating more interesting situations, he wished to conduct the mortal agents in his drama according to the rules of probability; in short, to make them think, speak and act, as it might be supposed men and women would do in extraordinary positions.[5] □

Here, Walpole finds fault with both the 'ancient' type of romance (too much 'imagination and improbability') and the modern type of romance (too 'strict' an 'adherence to common life'). Essentially, the battle is between supernatural romances characteristic of the Middle Ages, and eighteenth-century romances ('novels') written by the likes of Samuel Richardson (1689–1761) and Tobias Smollett (1721–1771).[6] In 'The Genesis of "Gothic" Fiction' E. J. Clery explains the eighteenth-century struggle between the words 'romance' and 'novel':

■ Novelists quibbled over the boundaries of probability and attempted to balance the demands of instruction and entertainment. Moral messages would be useless if not joined to compelling narratives that stirred the emotions of the reader. Some of the most successful works contained episodes that would not be out of place in Gothic fiction. The imprisonment and madness of Richardson's Clarissa looks back to the melodramatic 'she-tragedies' of Nicholas Rowe [1674–1718] and forward to [The Recess (1783–5) by] Sophia Lee [1750–1824]. The scene from Smollett's Ferdinand Count Fathom (1753) in which the Count finds himself trapped in a bandit's den with a fresh corpse was undoubtedly a source for a similar adventure in The Monk. ... But natural horror was as far as novelists were prepared to go at this stage: there could be no appeal to the imagination that went beyond rational causes.

The Castle of Otranto was presented to the public, especially in the preface to the second edition, as an outright challenge to this orthodoxy. Romances had been called improbable; now Walpole accused modern fiction of being too probable: 'the great resources of fancy have been dammed up, by a strict adherence to common life'. The chief enemy of fancy in his view was Samuel Richardson, whose narrative practices had been raised to the level of absolute moral prescription by Samuel Johnson [1709–84] in a well-known essay in the journal The Rambler (no. 4, 31 March 1750). In order to carry out its true function of instructing the young, fiction should 'exhibit life in its true state, diversified only by accidents that daily happen in the world'. The novel must be exemplary, and 'what we cannot credit we shall never imitate'.[7] □

Walpole's consideration of the relative merits and demerits of 'ancient' and 'modern' romances represents a significant intervention in the debate about the origins of the novel. Clery's argument highlights how *Otranto* is both a departure from the moral prescriptivism of Samuel Richardson's fiction and a revision of ancient (more supernaturally-inclined) romances.

However, when Walpole confessed his hoax in the second Preface to *The Castle of Otranto*, Langhorne (the critic who had initially praised the novel as a work of 'genius') changed his tune. He called it 'preposterous', and excusable only when he thought that it was a 'translation' from a 'gross and unenlightened age'.[8] Of course, Langhorne's personal pride was one reason for his swiftly revised opinion of this now self-titled 'Gothic romance'. More significant, though, was the sense of injury on behalf of the larger British literary community. That a British author felt the need to adapt that most continental of genres, the Romance, and then to masquerade it under the auspices of a translation seemed to go against British ideas of fair play in the literary arena. To Langhorne's dismay, Walpole had found the Romance's modern British counterpart, the novel, wanting. To make matters worse, Walpole had praised some elements of the Romance's structure that had been discarded by other British authors.

The hostility which the second edition encountered was matched only by Walpole's own self-deprecation regarding his literary creation. When writing to the famous dramatist and religious author Hannah More (1745–1833) on 13 November 1784, Walpole protested about the likely effects of his magical romance on readers such as Ann Yearsley, a poet better known as the 'Bristol milkwoman':

> ■ What! if I should go a step farther, dear Madam, and take the liberty of reproving you for putting into this poor woman's hands such a frantic thing as The Castle of Otranto? It was fit for nothing but the age in which it was written, an age in which much was known; that required only to be amused, nor cared whether its amusements were conformable to truth and models of good sense; that could not be spoiled; was in no danger of being too credulous; and rather wanted to be brought back into imagination, than to be led astray by it – but you will have made a hurly-burly in this poor woman's head which it cannot develop and digest.[9] □

Walpole's light dismissal of his own work here was reinforced elsewhere in his correspondence by such words as 'trifle' and 'trifling romance'. In all three descriptions the effect is fundamentally the same: his self-titled 'Gothic romance' was mere froth, designed in 1764 to be digested by careful eighteenth-century readers.

But who believed this? Walpole's own qualification that *Otranto* 'was fit for nothing but the age in which it was written', an age that 'required only to be amused' and did not 'care' about 'truth' and 'good sense' belies the careful consideration that he had so recently bestowed upon modern Romance. Here, perhaps in reaction to the hostile reception of the second, acknowledged edition, Walpole undercuts the arguments made for propriety in fictional realism by Samuel Johnson and others. Walpole contends that the reading public in general had a sufficient amount of scepticism to 'digest' ancient Romance. Of course, his condescending exception of Ann Yearsley in the above letter disables his argument. The letter to More was penned twenty years after the first, anonymous publication of *The Castle of Otranto*. His patronizing pretension of concern about its effects on Yearsley indicates Britain's rising concern about the patriotism, propriety and proper reading habits of young women.

To Walpole's dismay, *The Castle of Otranto* was held to have given birth to a new type of literary discourse in Britain.[10] His original 'trifle' was embraced by the wider reading public. It inspired many novelists (especially women – see Chapter Six below) to take up their pens and write 'Romances'. One novelist in particular made her indebtedness to *The Castle of Otranto* explicit. Clara Reeve, in her Preface to *The Old English Baron: A Gothic Story* (1778), freely admitted that:

■ This story is the literary offspring of the Castle of Otranto, written upon the same plan, with a design to unite the most attractive and interesting circumstances of the ancient Romance and modern Novel, at the same time it assumes a character and manner of its own, that differs from both; it is distinguished by the appellation of a Gothic Story, being a picture of Gothic times and manners. Fictitious Stories have been the delight of all times and all countries, by oral tradition in barbarous, by writing in more civilized ones; and although some persons of wit and learning have condemned them indiscriminately, I would venture to affirm, that even those who so much affect to despise them under one form, will receive and embrace them under another.

Thus, for instance, a man shall admire and almost adore the Epic poems of the Ancients, and yet despise and execrate the ancient Romances, which are only Epics in prose.

History represents human nature as it is in real life; – alas, too often a melancholy retrospect! – Romance displays only the amiable side of the picture; it shews the pleasing features, and throws a veil over the blemishes: Mankind are naturally pleased with what gratifies their vanity; and vanity, like all other passions of the human heart, may be rendered subservient to good and useful purposes.

I confess that it may be abused, and become an instrument to corrupt the manners and morals of mankind; so may poetry, so may plays, so may every kind of composition; but that will prove nothing more than the old saying lately revived by the philosophers the most in fashion, 'that every earthly thing has two handles.'

The business of Romance is, first, to excite the attention; and, secondly, to direct it to some useful, or at least innocent, end; Happy the writer who attains both these points, like Richardson! and not unfortunate, or undeserving praise, he who gains only the latter, and furnishes out an entertainment for the reader![11] ☐

Reeve's preface traces the literary heritage of her own 'Gothic Story' back to *Otranto*. It also serves to put clear blue ideological water between herself and Walpole. She admires Richardson, and admits more of a moral purpose to her tale than Walpole ever did. She does not try to distance her story from conflict through the same geographical devices that Walpole uses: her Gothic story is set in England, around the time of the Crusades.

Reeve's preface to *The Old English Baron* is concerned with tracing the intellectual heritage of the Romance genre. When she argues that 'a man shall admire and almost adore the Epic poems of the Ancients, and yet despise and execrate the ancient Romances', her gendered choice of reader ('a man') is by no means casual. Reeve dramatizes the argument about an incorrect and unnecessary prejudice against Romance in a later significant critical work, *The Progress of Romance* (1785). There she complains in the Preface that 'The learned men of our own country, have in general affected a contempt for this kind of writing, and looked upon Romances, as proper furniture only for a lady's library.'[12] She then proceeds in the body of the essay to reinforce the gendered responses to Romance by imagining a Socratic dialogue upon the topic of Romance between two women, Sophronia and Euphrasia, and a gentleman, Hortensius. Euphrasia, the second woman, marshals a defence of the Romance genre, which she presents to the other two. Hortensius admits that 'By Romance I understand a wild, extravagant, fabulous Story,' while Sophronia, the other woman present, understands it to be 'those kind of stories that are built upon fiction, and have no foundation in truth'.[13] Both definitions by Euphrasia's audience emphasize the Romance's fantastical and incredible qualities, and say nothing about its literary heritage.

But Euphrasia, who aims to 'trace Romance to its Origin' and to show how 'the modern novel sprung out of its ruins', chooses to define Romance from its Latinate origins.[14] She calls it 'simply an *Heroic fable*, – a fabulous Story of such actions as are commonly ascribed to heroes, or men of extraordinary courage and abilities. – Or if you would allow of it, I would say an Epic in prose.'[15] Hortensius immediately disputes this definition, objecting that 'An Epic is a very superior composition.'[16]

This objection from Hortensius (the male character) allows the principal female interlocutor, Euphrasia, to present Reeve's true views on learned gentlemens' contempt of Romance:

■ *Euph.* It is astonishing that men of sense, and of learning, should so strongly imbibe prejudices, and be so loth to part with them. – That they should despise and ridicule Romances, as the most contemptible of all kinds of writing, and yet expatiate in raptures, on the beauties of the fables of the old classic Poets, – on stories far more wild and extravagant, and infinitely more incredible.

*Hort.* It is because we pay due respect to works of true Genius, and disdain the comparison of such weak and paltry imitations, as those you have undertaken to support.

*Euph.* I am no stranger to the charms of Poetry, I have even felt a degree of its enthusiasm, yet I cannot sacrifice the convictions of truth at its shrine. I am of opinion that many of the fine old Historical ballads, are equally entitled to the name of Epic poems. There are examples enough extant, of Romance in verse, and Epics in prose.[17] ☐

Here is the crux of Reeve's argument. Through the mouthpiece of Euphrasia, Reeve insists that educated men are unfavourably biased towards Epic poetry without appreciating its intimate connections with prose Romance. Euphrasia presents a fully researched and learned case in order to prove the worthy heritage of Romance. The arguments that she marshals enable her to affirm that 'there is frequently a striking resemblance between works of high and low estimation, and which when seen, we do not care to acknowledge'.[18] This observation bears significant weight. It refutes an unnecessary male prejudice against Romance. This prejudice has been based upon artificial divisions between 'high' and 'low' cultural works. Euphrasia disputes these divisions. Reeve thus critically positions her own Gothic 'romances' alongside ancient Epic poetry in a continuous literary lineage.

It is important to bear in mind, however, that Reeve's *The Progress of Romance* was published in 1785. In the 1790s, as the Gothic Romance proliferated, so too did its critical detractors. As Robert Miles argues in 'The 1790s: the Effulgence of Gothic':

■ Fashions are ... profound because they key us into movements and changes deep within the culture. One such change was the development of a certain kind of literary snobbery, which for many years blinded critics to the obvious fact that many of the decade's canonical texts were first and foremost tales of terror. Such snobbery was connected to the material fact that for the first time women, at least as readers, were associated with a form that challenged (or was perceived to challenge) traditional literary authority. In other words, much of the tension between 'high' and 'low' literature which has pulsed through the institutionalization of 'literature' over the last 200 years is first generated by the effulgence of the 1790s tale of terror.[19] □

Miles situates the literary snobbery which cropped up around the Gothic Romance firmly in the politically paranoid 1790s. However, Reeve's identification of literary anti-Romance snobbery in *The Progress of Romance* in 1785 detects earlier symptoms. If its gendered argument was perceptive regarding 'learned men's' prejudice against Romance, it was also prophetic. 'Euphrasia's' arguments were increasingly sidelined as the Gothic Romance was tied more securely to 'wild, extravagant and fabulous' narratives and the continent. The increasing military hostilities towards France in the 1790s enabled the Gothic Romance's pernicious effects to be blamed upon the corrupting influence of continental, fantastical imports. As we shall see in Chapter Three in particular, the revolution in literature was swiftly associated with the more violent Revolution taking place across the English Channel.

## Gothic hostilities

The following section will offer a sample of the hostile responses to the Gothic in the literary arena. While the centrality of the 1790s to the Gothic has just been identified, the range of responses offered here is grouped around the year 1797. Why 1797? A glance at a table which details the publication of new novels in Britain between 1770 and 1800 in James Raven's essay 'The Novel Comes of Age' (2000) indicates that novel-production reaches a peak between 1795 and 1800, with the year 1796 in particular producing 91 new titles.[20] Amongst the new titles produced in 1796 was Matthew Lewis's sensational Gothic novel *The Monk*, which drew hostile responses from the pen of Samuel Taylor Coleridge among others.

If Clara Reeve had already identified the genesis of the anti-Gothic impulse in *The Progress of Romance* in 1785, this impulse reached its apogee in the 1790s. In particular, Lewis's *The Monk*, with its tale of incest, seduction, matricide and Catholic hypocrisy, outraged its reviewers to such an extent that critics began to reflect upon the pernicious effects of the Gothic genre *en masse*. Samuel Taylor Coleridge led the charge against *The Monk*. In the *Critical Review* he began his response to it by summarizing the national critical antipathy towards Gothic Romance:

■ The horrible and the preternatural have usually seized on the popular taste, at the rise and decline of literature. Most powerful stimulants, they can never be required except by the torpor of an unawakened, or the languor of an exhausted, appetite. The same phaenomenon, therefore, which we hail as a favourable omen in the belles lettres of Germany, impresses a degree of gloom in the compositions of our countrymen. We trust, however, that satiety will banish what good sense should have prevented; and that, wearied with fiends, incomprehensible characters, with shrieks, murders, and subterraneous dungeons, the public will learn, by the multitude of the manufacturers, with how little expense of thought or imagination this species of composition is manufactured. But, cheaply as we estimate romances in general, we acknowledge, in the work before us, the offspring of no common genius. [Coleridge then proceeds to praise the narrative skills exhibited in the management of the central tale of Ambrosio and Matilda, and the subplot of Raymond and Agnes.]

... As far, therefore, as the story is concerned, the praise which a romance can claim, is simply that of having given pleasure during its perusal; and so many are the calamities of life, that he who has done this, has not written uselessly. The children of sickness and solitude thank him. – To this praise, however, our author has not entitled himself. The sufferings which he describes are so frightful and intolerable, that we break with abruptness from the delusion, and indignantly suspect the man of a species of brutality, who could find a pleasure in wantonly imagining them; and the abominations which he pourtrays with no hurrying pencil, are such as the observation of character by no means demanded, such as 'no observation of character can justify, because no good man would willingly suffer them to pass, however transiently, through his own mind.' The merit of a novelist is in proportion (not simply to the effect, but) to the *pleasurable* effect which he produces. Situations of torment, and images of naked horror, are easily conceived; and a writer in whose works they abound, deserves our gratitude almost equally with him who should drag us by way of sport through a military hospital, or force us to sit at the dissecting-table of a natural philosopher. ... Figures that shock the imagination, and narratives that mangle the feelings, rarely discover *genius*, and always betray a low and vulgar *taste*.[21] □

Coleridge begins his review of *The Monk* by making general observations upon the status of Romance. He argues that those which use horror and the supernatural (see Chapter Two for further exploration of the differences between terror and horror) indicate a state of literary torpor in the nation in which they appear. Coleridge thus almost immediately links the use of Romance to national concerns. After dismissing the Romance genre as a form of light entertainment at best, he then proceeds to attack Lewis upon aesthetic grounds, arguing that the shock tactics Lewis deploys in his graphic descriptions of rape and murder are too brutal to exhibit any true 'genius'. But Coleridge reserves his most stern censure for the scene in *The Monk* when Elvira bowdlerizes her daughter Antonia's Bible, and compares the Bible's 'blasphemies' to some scenes depicted in ancient romance. On Lewis's insertion of this passage, Coleridge unleashes his full wrath:

■ Mildness of censure would here be criminally misplaced, and silence would make us accomplices. Not without reluctance then, but in full conviction that we are performing a duty, we declare it to be our opinion, that the Monk is a romance, which if a parent saw in the hands of a son or daughter, he might reasonably turn pale. The temptations of Ambrosio are described with a libidinous minuteness, which, we sincerely hope, will receive its best and only adequate censure from the offended conscience of the author himself. The shameless harlotry of Matilda, and the trembling innocence of Antonia, are seized with equal avidity, as vehicles of the most voluptuous images; and though the tale is indeed a tale of horror, yet the most painful impression which the work left on our minds was that of great acquirements and splendid genius employed to furnish a *mormo* [bugbear] for children, a poison for youth, and a provocative for the debauchee. Tales of enchantment and witchcraft can never be *useful*: our author has contrived to make them *pernicious*, by blending, with an irreverent negligence, all that is most awfully true in religion with all that is most ridiculously absurd in superstition.[22] □

Coleridge's outrage over Lewis's fictional consideration of the lewdness of the Bible hinged upon Lewis's simultaneous consideration of the relative merits of stories in the Bible and stories of romance. Superstitious romance was being used to question the relative morality of the Bible, and for Coleridge, this was Lewis's grave sin: 'We believe it not absolutely impossible that a mind may be so deeply depraved by the habit of reading lewd and voluptuous tales, as to use even the Bible in conjuring up the spirit of uncleanness.'[23]

Whereas previously the Gothic Romance was a genre deemed too low to attract true critical censure, such censure became an urgent and patriotic critical measure, designed to prevent the wholesale corruption of a young British readership. One of the most famous critical works, written between the years 1794 and 1797 in the form of four dialogues, was the excoriating lampoon *The Pursuits of Literature* by the Reverend Thomas James Mathias (1754?–1835). In it, Mathias defended the classic Augustan tradition of British poetry (represented by authors such as Alexander Pope) against the encroachment of Gothic Romance. *The Pursuits* spoke to much more than straightforward literary prejudice, however. In the preface to his fourth dialogue, Mathias linked Matthew Lewis's biblical blasphemy (the passage that had offended Coleridge) to Lewis's position as an MP:

■ But there is one publication of the time too peculiar, and too important to be passed over in a general reprehension. [This is after Mathias has asserted (first in Dialogue Three, and then repeated in the preface to Dialogue Four) that, 'Literature, well or ill conducted, IS THE GREAT ENGINE by which, I am fully persuaded, ALL CIVILIZED STATES must ultimately be supported or overthrown.'] There is nothing with which it may be compared. A legislator in our own parliament, a member of the House of Commons of Great-Britain, an elected guardian and defender of the laws, the religion, and the good manners of the country, has neither scrupled nor blushed to depict, and to publish to the world, the arts of lewd and systematic seduction, and to thrust upon the nation the most open and unqualified blasphemy against the very code and volume of our religion. And all this, with his name, style, and title, prefixed to the novel or romance called 'THE MONK.' ... I consider this as a new species of legislative or state parricide [the killing of a father]. What is it to the kingdom at large, or what is it to all those whose office it is to maintain truth, and to instruct the rising abilities and hopes of England, that the author of it is *a very young man*? That forsooth he is a man of genius and fancy? So much the worse. That there are very poetical descriptions of castles and abbies in this novel? so much the worse again, the novel is *more alluring* on that account. Is it a time to poison the waters of our land in their springs and fountains? Are we to add incitement to incitement, and corruption to corruption, till there neither is, nor can be, a return to virtuous action and to regulated life? Who knows the *age* of this author? I presume very few. *Who does not know*, that he is a Member of Parliament? ... we can feel that it is an object of moral and of national reprehension, when a Senator openly and daringly violates his first duty to his country. There are wounds, and obstructions, and diseases in the political, as well as in the natural, body, for which the removal of the part affected is alone efficacious. At an hour like this, are we to stand in consultation on the remedy, when not only the disease is ascertained, but the very stage of the disease, and its specific symptoms? Are we to spare the sharpest instruments of authority and of censure, when public establishments are gangrened in the life-organs?[24] □

Mathias's hyperbolic indictment of Lewis goes much further than Coleridge's. He accuses Lewis, a young MP, of 'state parricide' and of corrupting the body politic of Britain with his 'blasphemous' novel. For Mathias, Lewis's creation is rendered all the more dangerous because it contains 'poetical descriptions of castles and abbies'. This may lead unsuspecting females to read *The Monk* in the expectation that it participates in the same vein of Romance that Reeve's and Radcliffe's fiction does. Thus, in the fourth dialogue of the poem, Mathias lays the blame for the parricidal monster of the Gothic firmly with Walpole. Referring specifically to Walpole's counterfeit preface, Mathias pleads:

> Shall nought but ghosts and trinkets be display'd,
> Since Walpole play'd the virtuoso's trade,

> Bade sober truth revers'd for fiction pass,
> And mus'd o'er Gothic toys through Gothic glass?[25]

According to Mathias, Walpole's 'trifling' with a 'virtuoso's trade' (by contrast, Pope and Johnson are spoken of favourably) has transformed the literary landscape of Britain irrevocably. Mathias expresses the same prejudices as Reeve's male character Hortensius; truth and fiction must never mingle. The Gothic trinkets that Walpole impassively selects have transformed Britain's literary arena into one large Gothic display case.

Elsewhere, Mathias distances his own poetic endeavours from what he views as the Gothic contamination:

> Is it for me to creep, or soar, or doze,
> In modish song, or fashionable prose?
> To pen with garreteers obscure and shabby,
> Inscriptive nonsense in a fancied Abbey?[26]

Coupling 'fashionable prose' with 'doze' and 'shabby' with 'fancied Abbey' is in itself sufficiently incriminatory of the Gothic romance's perceived tendencies towards a well-tried fashionable formula. None the less, Mathias persists in his condemnation by targeting in particular female authors of the Gothic romance, naming in a footnote Charlotte Smith (1749–1806), Elizabeth Inchbald (1753–1821), Mary Robinson (1758–1800) and 'Mrs. &c. &c.' who are 'too frequently *whining* or *frisking* in novels, till our girls' heads turn wild with impossible adventures, and now and then are tainted with democracy'.[27] The use of 'democracy' here is crucial. As Fred Botting argues in relation to this word in his book *Gothic* (1996), 'Departing from the strictures of reason and morality, novels are seen to cause violent frenzy as terrifying as that exhibited in France. By touching on political subjects women writers "unsex" themselves: they enter with impunity and impropriety a male domain of writing instead of remaining within the domesticated limits of fiction.'[28] Mathias's reference to the 'unsex'd females', however, is relatively light-hearted in contrast to the venality of his attack on Lewis and Walpole. These are the authors who 'should know better' because they are 'legislators', both MPs (at different times) and therefore answerable to their country.[29]

While the blame for the rise of Gothic romance is more difficult to apportion along gender lines, the effects of reading Gothic romances are undoubtedly associated with women (see also Chapter Six for further exploration of this). In a tradition of criticism of the genre that began in the 1780s and endured throughout the Romantic era, critical concern focused upon the pernicious effects of Gothic romances on young, female readers. Young women, it was argued, were the untutored readers of romances who might try and mimic some of the lewd scenes or escapes that they read about or, in Mathias's words, become 'tainted with democracy'.[30]

The potential effects of Gothic romances on young women were spelled out in the 1790s in a number of satirical articles that appeared in the periodical press. Whilst appearing to be light-hearted, and providing some edifying recipes for writing Gothic romances, they none the less passed serious comment upon the consequent evils of over-consumption of Gothic romance by young women. One of the most interesting articles, which strengthened the links between the events in France and the pernicious effects of reading Gothic fiction, appeared in the *Monthly Magazine* in 1797. The events in France, of course, were those of the French Revolution, which, it is generally believed, gathered impetus with the fall of the Parisian prison the Bastille in 1789. One of the chief spokesmen of the French Revolution and its eventual beheading, in January 1793, of King Louis XVI (1754–93) and Queen Marie Antoinette (1755–93) was Maximilien Robespierre (1785–94), who, from being a hero for supporters of the Revolution, rapidly declined in everyone's estimation to being a figure of universal terror. This transition from hero to tyrant in the public imagination was due to the era of paranoia and execution that accompanied his membership of the twelve-man committee of public safety which ran France from April 1793 to July 1794. 'The Terrorist System of Novel Writing', the open letter to the editor of the *Monthly Magazine*, began by making specific references to the political events taking place on the European continent:

■ SIR,
ALBEIT you may wish to avoid the dryness and dullness of political discussion in your Magazine, yet you must be sensible that in an age of *quidnunkery* [appetite for news and gossip] like the present, it is not always possible to disregard the passing events of Europe. It has long, for example, been the fashion to advert to the horrid massacres which disgraced France during the tyranny of Robespierre; and, whatever a good and loyal subject happens to write, whether a history, a life, a sermon, or a posting bill, he thinks it his duty to introduce a due portion of his abhorrence and indignation against all such bloody proceedings. Happy, sir, would it be, if we could contemplate barbarity without adopting it; if we could meditate upon cruelty without learning it; and if we could paint a man without a head, without supposing what would be the case if some of our friends were without their heads. But, alas! so prone are we to imitation, that we have exactly and faithfully copied the SYSTEM OF TERROR, if not in our streets, and in our fields, at least in our circulating libraries, and in our closets. Need I say that I am adverting to the wonderful revolution that has taken place in the *art* of novel-writing, in which the only exercise for the fancy is now upon the most frightful subjects, and in which we reverse the petition in the litany, and riot upon 'battle, murder, and sudden death.'

Good, indeed, it must be confessed, arises out of evil. If, by this revolution, we have attained the art of frightening young people, and reviving the age of ghosts, hobgoblins, and spirits, we have, at the same time, simplified genius, and shown by what easy process a writer may attain great celebrity in circulating libraries, boarding schools, and watering places. What has he to do but build a castle in the air, and furnish it with dead bodies and departed spirits, and he obtains the character of a man of a most 'wonderful imagination, rich in imagery, and who has the wonderful talent of conducting his reader in a cold sweat through five or six volumes.'

Perhaps necessity, the plea for all revolutions, may have occasioned the present. A novel used to be a description of human life and manners; but human life and manners *always* described, must become tiresome; all the difficulties attending upon the tender passion have been exhausted; maiden aunts have become stale; gallant colonels are so common, that we meet with them in every volunteer *corps*. There are but few ways of running away with a lady, and not many more of breaking the hearts of her parents. Clumsy citizens are no longer to be seen in horse-chaises, and their *villas* are removed from the bottom of Gray's Inn Lane, to the most delightful and picturesque situations, twelve or fifteen miles from London. Footmen and ladies' maids are no longer trusted with intrigues, and letters are conveyed with care, expedition, and secrecy, by the mail coach, and the penny-post. In a word, the affairs and business of common life are so perfectly understood, that elopements are practised by girls almost before they have learned to read; and all the incidents which have decorated our *old* novels, come easy and natural to the parties, without the assistance of a circulating library, or the least occasion to draw upon the invention of a writer of novels.

It was high time, therefore, to contrive some other way of interesting these numerous readers, to whom the stationers and trunk-makers are so deeply indebted, and just at the time when we were threatened with a stagnation of fancy, arose Maximilian Robespierre [*sic*], with his system of terror, and taught our novelists that *fear* is the only passion they ought to cultivate, that to frighten and instruct were one and the same thing, and that none of the productions of genius could be compared to the production of an ague. From that time we have never ceased to 'believe and tremble'; our genius has become hysterical, and our taste epileptic.

Good, I have observed, arises out of evil, or apparent evil: it is now much easier to write a novel adapted to the prevailing taste than it was. The manners and customs of common life being no longer an object for curiosity or description, we have nothing to do but launch out on the main ocean of improbability and extravagant romance, and we acquire a high reputation. It having fallen to my lot to peruse many of these wonderful publications, previously to my daughters reading them (who, by the bye, would read them whether I pleased or not) I think I can lay down a few plain and simple rules, by observing which any man or maid,

I mean, ladies' maid, may be able to compose from four to six uncommonly interesting volumes, that shall claim the admiration of all true believers in the marvellous.

In the first place, then, trembling reader, I would advise you to construct an *old* castle, *formerly* of great magnitude and extent, built in the Gothic manner, with a great number of hanging towers, turrets, and pinnacles. One half, at least, of it must be in ruins; dreadful chasms and gaping crevices must be hid only by the clinging ivy; the doors must be so old, and so little used to open, as to grate tremendously on the hinges; and there must be in every passage an echo, and as many reverberations as there are partitions. As to the furniture, it is absolutely necessary that it should be nearly as old as the house, and in a more decayed state, if a more decayed state be possible. The principal rooms must be hung with pictures, of which the damps have very nearly effaced the colours; only you must preserve such a degree of likeness in one or two of them, as to incline your heroine to be very much affected by the sight of them, and to imagine that she has seen a face, or faces, very like them, or very like something else, but where, or when, she cannot *just now* remember. It will be necessary, also, that one of those very old and very decayed portraits shall seem to frown most cruelly, while another seems to smile most lovingly.

Great attention must be paid to the tapestry hangings. They are to be very old, and tattered, and blown about with the wind. There is a great deal in the wind. Indeed, it is one of the principal objects of terror, for it may be taken for almost any terrific object, from a banditti of cut-throats to a single ghost. The tapestry, therefore, must give signs of moving, so as to make the heroine believe, there is something behind it, although, not being *at that time* very desirous to examine, she concludes very naturally and logically, that it can be nothing but the wind. This same wind is of infinite service to our modern castle-builders. Sometimes it *whistles*, and then it shows how sound may be conveyed through the crevices of a Baron's castle. Sometimes it *rushes*, and then there is reason to believe the Baron's great grandfather does not lie quiet in his grave; and sometimes it *howls*, and, if accompanied with rain, generally induces some weary traveller, perhaps a robber, and perhaps a lover, or both, to take up their residence in this *very same castle* where virgins, and virtuous wives, were locked up before the invention of a *habeas corpus*. It is, indeed, not wonderful, that so much use is made of the wind, for it is the principal ingredient in that sentimentality of constitution, to which romances are admirabl[y] adapted.

Having thus provided such a decayed stock of furniture as may be easily affected by the wind, you must take care that the battlements and towers are remarkably *populous* in *owls* and *bats*. The *hooting* of the one, and the *flitting* of the other, are excellent engines in the system of terror, particularly if the candle goes out, which is very often the case in damp caverns.

And the mention of caverns brings me to the essential qualities inherent in a castle. The rooms *upstairs* may be just habitable, and no more; but the principal incidents must be carried on in *subterraneous* passages. These, in general, wind round the whole extent of the building; but that is not very material, as the heroine never goes through above half without meeting with a door, which she has neither strength nor resolution to open, although she has found a rusty key, very happily fitted to as rusty a lock, and would give the world to know what it leads to, and yet she can give no reason for her curiosity.

The building now being completely finished, and furnished with all desirable imperfections, the next and only requisite is a heroine, with all the weakness of body and mind that appertains to her sex; but, endowed with all the curiosity of a spy, and all the courage of a troop of horse. Whatever she hears, sees, or thinks of, that is horrible and terrible, she must enquire into it again and again. All alone, for she cannot prevail on the timid *Janetta* to go with her *a second time*; all alone she sets out, in the dead of the night, when nothing but the aforesaid owls and bats are *hooting and flitting*, to resolve the horrid mystery of the moving tapestry, which threw her into a swoon the preceding night, and in which she knows her fate is awfully involved, though she cannot tell why. With cautious tread, and glimmering taper, she proceeds to descend a long flight of steps, which bring her to a door she had not observed before. It is opened with great difficulty; but, alas! a rush of wind puts out the glimmering taper, and while Matilda, Gloriana, Rosalba, or any other name, is deliberating whether she shall proceed or return, without knowing how to do either, a groan is heard, a second groan, and a fearful crash. A dimness now comes over her eyes (which in the *dark* must be terrible) and she swoons away. How long she may have remained in this swoon, no one can tell; but when she awakes, the sun peeps through the crevices, for all subterraneous passages must have crevices, and shows her such a collection of skulls and bones as would do credit to a parish-burying-ground.

She now finds her way back, determined to make a farther search next night, which she accomplishes by means of a better light, and behold! having gained the fatal spot where the mystery is concealed, the tapestry moves again! Assuming courage, she boldly lifts up a corner, but immediately lets it drop, a cold sweat pervades her whole body, and she sinks to the ground; after having discovered behind this dreadful tapestry, the tremendous solution of all her difficulties, the awful word.

HONORIFICABILITATUDINIBUSQUE!!!

Mr. Editor, if thy soul is not harrowed up, *I* am glad to escape from this scene of horror, and am,
Your humble servant,<br>
A JACOBIN NOVELIST.
*Greenwich, Aug. 19, 1797.*[31] □

'The Terrorist System of Novel Writing' satirically pinpoints the formulaic nature of the Gothic novel, and laments its effects upon female readers. The article seemingly mourns for the passing of realism in the novel, and the revival of the ancient romance features in the form of the Gothic. It strongly links these concerns to the French Revolution, charging Maximilien de Robespierre and his reign of terror quite specifically with the horrible 'revolution' in fiction.[32]

The narrative 'recipe' that the satirist suggests is highly reminiscent of Ann Radcliffe's *The Mysteries of Udolpho* (1794) with the humorously pantomimic relationship between the heroine, Emily St Aubert, and her servant, Annette, being targeted in particular. The satirist highlights the incongruities between the Radcliffean heroine's bodily weakness and superstition and her indomitable curiosity and 'courage of a troop of horse'.

This article spawned many imitations. The most similarly titled, 'Terrorist Novel Writing', evinced even stronger concerns over women's reading habits, and their links with fashion:

■ Sir,

I never complain of fashion, when it is confined to externals – to the form of a cap, or the cut of a lapelle; to the colour of a wig, or the tune of a ballad; but when I perceive that there is such a thing as fashion even in composing books, it is, perhaps, full time that some attempt should be made to recall writers to the old boundaries of common sense.

I allude, Sir, principally to the great quantity of novels with which our circulating libraries are filled, and our parlour tables covered, in which it has been the fashion to make *terror the order of the day*, by confining the heroes and heroines in old gloomy castles, full of spectres, apparitions, ghosts and dead men's bones. This is now so common, that a Novelist blushes to bring about a marriage by ordinary means, but conducts the happy pair through long and dangerous galleries, where the light burns blue, the thunder rattles, and the great window at the end presents the hideous visage of a *murdered* man, *uttering* piercing groans, and developing shocking mysteries. If a curtain is withdrawn, there is a bleeding body behind it; if a chest is opened, it contains a skeleton; if a noise is heard, somebody is receiving a deadly blow; and if a candle goes out, its place is sure to be supplied by a flash of lightning. Cold hands grasp us in the dark, statues are seen to move, and suits of armour walk off their pegs, while the wind whistles louder than one of Handel's choruses, and the still air is more melancholy than the dead march in Saul.

A novel, if at all useful, ought to be a representation of human life and manners, with a view to direct the conduct in the most important duties of life, and to correct its follies. But what instruction is to be reaped from the distorted ideas of lunatics, I am at a loss to conceive. Are we come to such a pass, that the only commandment necessary to be repeated is, 'Thou shalt do no murder?' Are the duties of life so changed, that all the instructions necessary for a young person is to learn to walk at night upon the battlements of an old castle, to creep hands and feet along a narrow passage, and meet the devil at the end of it? Is the corporeal frame of the female sex so masculine and hardy, that it must be softened down by the touch of dead bodies, clay-cold hands, and damp sweats? Can a young lady be taught nothing more necessary in life, than to sleep in a dungeon with venomous reptiles, walk through a ward with assassins, and carry bloody daggers in their pockets, instead of pin-cushions and needle-books?

Every absurdity has an end, and as I observe that almost all novels are of the terrific cast, I hope the insipid repetition of the same bugbears will at length work a cure. In the mean time, should any of your female readers be desirous of catching the season of terrors, she may compose two or three very pretty volumes from the following recipe:

*Take* – An old castle, half of it ruinous.
A long gallery, with a great many doors, some secret ones.
Three murdered bodies, quite fresh.
As many skeletons, in chests and presses.
An old woman hanging by the neck; with her throat cut.
Assassins and desperados '*quant suff.*'
Noise, whispers and groans, threescore at least.

Mix them together, in the form of three volumes to be taken at any of the watering places, before going to bed.
PROBATUM EST.[33] □

'Terrorist Novel Writing' is clearly concerned with the lack of instruction in Gothic fiction, and laments the disappearance of the eighteenth-century conduct-book tradition from the Gothic. Its concern with the 'female sex' becoming 'masculine and hardy' is similar to that of 'The Terrorist System of Novel Writing', and strikingly resembles Mathias's 'unsex'd female writers'. Clearly, for these writers, the Gothic does not set good examples for young female readers, nor is its predominantly female authorship endowed with 'genius' or originality.

The recipe that 'Terrorist Novel Writing' concocts for the successful production of a Gothic novel struck a chord amongst its readership. This recipe created what Eugenia C. DeLamotte has described effectively, in *Perils of the Night* (1990), as the 'laundry-list approach' to eighteenth-century Gothic fiction.[34]

Interestingly, however, the editor of the journal in which 'Terrorist Novel Writing' appeared, chose to name specifically Ann Radcliffe as the chief perpetrator who contributed to this terrorist school. In an added footnote, he wrote:

■ It is easy to see that the satire of this letter is particularly levelled at a literary lady of considerable talents, who has presented the world with three novels, in which she has found out the secret of making us 'fall in love with what we fear to look on.' – The *system of terror* which she has adopted is not the only reproach to which she is liable. Besides the tedious monotony of her descriptions, she affects in the most disgusting manner a knowledge of languages, countries, customs, and objects of art of which she is lamentably ignorant.[35] □

The editor lambasts Radcliffe's descriptions in a particularly vicious critique, later noting the 'gross violation of language' in her Italian vocabulary. His insistence regarding Radcliffe's inaccuracies is part of his overall concern about the realistic functions of a novel. When later he complains that 'she covers the kingdom of Naples with India figs because *St Pierre* has introduced these tropical plants in his tales', he suggests that Radcliffe is both imitative of the French novel, and indebted to the unrealistic Romance tradition.[36]

This targeting of Radcliffe was, however, fairly exceptional. Elsewhere, she was singled out as the unique 'terrorist' author in possession of genius, with even Mathias excepting her from his satire with the words 'Not so the mighty magician of THE MYSTERIES OF UDOLPHO'.[37] The *Critical Review* summarized the general critical exoneration of Radcliffe when reviewing a novel called *Austenburn Castle* by an 'unpatronized [i.e. anonymous] female' in 1796. The reviewer complained that 'Since Mrs Radcliffe's justly admired and successful romances, the press has teemed with stories of haunted castles and visionary terrors; the incidents of which are so little diversified, that criticism is at a loss to vary its remarks.'[38] For this reviewer, Radcliffe's romances were 'justly admired', but had sadly spawned a number of poor imitations which adapted the motifs (or 'laundry list' in DeLamotte's tempting phrase) with little variation and no originality.

In his *Lives of the Novelists* (1827), Sir Walter Scott (1771–1832) offered a lengthy assessment which took an attitude towards Radcliffe similar to that of the *Critical Review*. He acknowledged her genius, and appraised her literary corpus conscientiously and thoroughly, whilst regretting the poor imitations that her romances inspired:

■ The species of romance which Mrs. Radcliffe introduced, bears nearly the same relation to the novel that the modern anomaly entitled a melodrame does to the proper drama. It does not appeal to the judgment by deep delineations of human feeling, or stir the passions by scenes of deep pathos, or awaken the fancy by tracing out, with spirit and vivacity, the lighter marks of life and manners, or excite mirth by strong representations of the ludicrous or humorous. In other words, it attains its interest neither by the path of comedy nor of tragedy; and yet it has, notwithstanding, a deep and powerful effect, gained by means independent of both – by an appeal, in one word, to the passion of fear, whether excited by natural dangers, or by the suggestions of superstition. The force, therefore, of the production, lies in the delineation of external incident, while the characters of the agents, like the figures in many landscapes, are entirely subordinate to the scenes in which they are placed; and are only distinguished by such outlines as make them seem appropriate to the rocks and trees, which have been the artist's principal objects. The persons introduced – and here also the correspondence holds betwixt the melo-drame and the romantic novel – bear the features, not of individuals, but of the class to which they belong. A dark and tyrannical count; an aged crone of a housekeeper, the depositary of many a family legend; a garrulous waiting-maid; a gay and light-hearted valet; a villain or two of all work; and a heroine, fulfilled with all perfections, and subjected to all manner of hazards, form the stock-in-trade of a romancer or a melo-dramatist; and if these personages be dressed in proper costume, and converse in language sufficiently appropriate to their stations and qualities, it is not expected that the audience shall shake their sides at the humour of the dialogue, or weep over its pathos.[39] □

Scott's assessment of Radcliffe here is balanced and judicious. He acknowledges her as the 'founder' of the Gothic Romance tradition, and defends her fiction on the basis of the functions of Gothic Romance. Again, we have careful distinctions forged between the modern novel and the 'Romance'. Scott argues that Radcliffe's delineation of character is 'entirely subordinate to the scenes in which they are placed'. He thus defends her use of Romance by arguing that her characters are not significant in themselves. Instead, it is the 'delineation of external incident' which arouses 'the passion of fear'.

## Novelistic satire of the Gothic

Sir Walter Scott's 'Introduction' to his own first novel, *Waverley, Or 'tis sixty years since* (1814), emphasizes the centrality of the Gothic romance empire to fiction during the Romantic era. Here, Scott is careful to distance himself from Radcliffe's reign of romance. His choice of subtitle, 'Or, 'tis sixty years since', suggests a specific temporal location for his novel which is seemingly in direct contrast to the Gothic romance's lack of temporal specificity. In Chapter One Scott took care to emphasize that his subtitle bore little relation to those of Gothic romances:

■ Had I, for example, announced in my frontispiece, 'Waverley, a Tale of other Days', must not every novel reader have anticipated a castle scarce less than that of Udolpho, of which the eastern wing had long been uninhabited, and the keys either lost, or consigned to the care of some aged butler or housekeeper, whose trembling steps, about the middle of the second volume, were doomed to guide the hero, or heroine, to the ruinous precincts? Would not the owl have shrieked and the cricket cried in my very title-page? And could it have been possible for me, with a moderate attention to decorum, to introduce any scene more lively than might be produced by the jocularity of a clownish but faithful valet, or the garrulous narrative of the heroine's fille-de-chambre, when rehearsing the stories of blood and horror which she had heard in the servants' hall? Again, had my title borne 'Waverley, a Romance from the German,' what head so obtuse as not to image forth a profligate abbot, an oppressive duke, a secret and mysterious association of Rosicrucians and Illuminati, with all their properties of black cowls, caverns, daggers, electrical machines, trap-doors and dark lanterns? Or if I had rather chosen to call my work a 'Sentimental Tale,' would it not have been a sufficient presage of a heroine with a profusion of auburn hair, and a harp, the soft solace of her solitary hours, which she fortunately finds always the means of transporting from castle to cottage, although she herself be sometimes obliged to jump out of a two-pair-of-stairs window, and is more than once bewildered on her journey, alone and on foot, without any guide but a blowsy peasant girl, whose jargon she hardly can understand? ...
... From this my choice of an era the understanding critic may farther presage, that the object of my tale is more a description of men than manners. A tale of manners, to be interesting, must either refer to antiquity so great as to have become venerable, or it must bear a vivid reflection of those scenes which are passing daily before our eyes, and are interesting from their novelty. Thus the coat-of-mail of our ancestors, and the triple-furred pelisse of our modern beaux, may, though for very different reasons, be equally fit for the array of a fictitious character; but who, meaning the costume of his hero to be impressive, would willingly attire him in the court dress of George the Second's reign, with its no collar, large sleeves, and low pocket-holes? The same may be urged, with equal truth, of the Gothic hall, which, with its darkened and tinted windows, its elevated and gloomy roof, and massive oaken table garnished with boar's-head and rosemary, pheasants and peacocks, cranes and cygnets, has an excellent effect in fictitious description.[40] □

Scott here emphasizes that his novel, in contrast specifically to Gothic romances, will be more a tale of 'men than manners'. He humorously appeals to his reader regarding his own temporal setting of *Waverley*, arguing 'who ... would willingly attire [the hero] in the court dress of George the Second's reign, with its no collar, large sleeves, and low pocket-holes?' The desired effect on the reader is that we believe that Scott remains faithful to 'men' and realism above all else, even when that authorial fidelity demands concessions in terms of fashion.

Scott distances his fiction from the Radcliffean romance tradition, the German Romance tradition,[41] and the sentimental tradition. The parodic plot summaries of these three traditions provided by Scott suggest that this 'Introduction' to Waverley is anti-Gothic, and yet he qualifies his self-distancing from the 'tale of manners' by claiming that it must 'either refer to antiquity so great as to have become venerable, or ... bear a vivid reflection of those scenes which are passing daily before our eyes, and are interesting from their novelty'. In itself, this is *not* as stern a critique of the Gothic as one initially anticipates from this chapter; it is, rather, a qualifier regarding the appropriate temporal settings for Gothic romances. Scott's choice, to set his tale around the time of the Jacobite uprising in Scotland in 1745, disqualifies him from deploying Gothic tropes because the tale is set neither in 'antiquity' nor in the immediate present.[42]

The same qualification applies to the most famous satire of the Gothic, the posthumously published *Northanger Abbey* by Jane Austen. It is undoubtedly the 'inventory of linen' which Catherine Morland mistakes for an ancient manuscript that prompted Eugenia DeLamotte's characterization of the 'laundry list approach' to Gothic fiction. Like Scott, Austen certainly satirizes the recurrent tropes of Gothic fiction through Catherine's ardent engagement with them. However, Catherine Morland's voracious consumption of Gothic fiction only becomes questionable when she attempts to transfer the plots to present-day England. Her Gothic quest provokes Henry Tilney to admonish her, 'Remember the country and the age in which we live. Remember that we are English, that we are Christians. Consult your own understanding, your own sense of the probable, your own observation of what is passing around you.'[43] Henry Tilney's timely reminder suggests that for Austen it is not so much Gothic romance itself that is inappropriate, but rather its wholesale transportation to the everyday reality of the 1790s and 1800s.[44]

None the less, the evident pleasure with which Catherine and Isabella Thorpe discuss their 'Gothic' reading list is suggestive of the pleasurable terror which Gothic romance provokes. It is significant that Catherine and Isabella do not discuss character portrayal in Gothic fiction. As Scott also suggests above, character is subordinated in Radcliffean Gothic romance to the effects of terror, a phenomenon which will be further explored in Chapter Two. Isabella's withholding of the plot of *The Mysteries of Udolpho* prolongs the frisson of anticipation for Catherine:

■ '... my dearest Catherine, what have you been doing with yourself all this morning? – Have you gone on with Udolpho?'

'Yes, I have been reading it ever since I woke; and I am got to the black veil.'

'Are you, indeed? How delightful! Oh! I would not tell you what is behind the black veil for the world! Are you not wild to know?'

'Oh! yes, quite; what can it be? – But do not tell me – I would not be told upon any account. I know it must be a skeleton, I am sure it is Laurentina's skeleton. Oh! I am delighted with the book! I should like to spend my whole life in reading it. I assure you, if it had not been to meet you, I would not have come away from it for all the world.'

'Dear creature! how much I am obliged to you; and when you have finished Udolpho, we will read the Italian together; and I have made out a list of ten or twelve more of the same kind for you.'

'Have you, indeed! How glad I am! – What are they all?'

'I will read you their names directly; here they are, in my pocket-book. Castle of Wolfenbach, Clermont, Mysterious Warning, Necromancer of the Black Forest, Midnight Bell, Orphan of the Rhine, and Horrid Mysteries. Those will last us some time.'

'Yes, pretty well; but are they all horrid, are you sure they are all horrid?'[45] □

Isabella's creation of a Gothic 'reading list' for Catherine is not simply an anti-Gothic jibe. If we recall, Mathias and many other anonymous authors in the 1790s worried about female readerships of Gothic fiction, and the possible effects that they might have upon the propriety, politics and chastity of British women. If anything, Austen's intervention here might further provoke these concerns as she portrays an exclusively female reading circle between Isabella and Catherine. It is Isabella Thorpe who establishes the 'canon' of Gothic romance for Catherine, based upon notes made in her pocket-book.

Besides the references to Ann Radcliffe's two best known novels, *The Mysteries of Udolpho* and *The Italian* (1797), all of the novels listed by Isabella Thorpe in *Northanger Abbey* are Gothic romances: Eliza Parsons published *Castle of Wolfenbach; a German Story* in 1793; Regina Maria Roche published *Clermont. A Tale* in 1798; Peter Teuthold translated *The Necromancer: or the Tale of the Black Forest* from the German of 'Lawrence Flammenberg' in 1794; Francis Lathom published *The Midnight Bell* anonymously in 1798; Eleanor Sleath published *The Orphan of the Rhine* in 1798; and Peter Will adapted *Horrid Mysteries* from the German of Karl Grosse in 1796.

With the exception of Radcliffe's fiction, these novels have now been out of print for some time. Despite this, Michael Sadleir's 1927 excavation of them in 'The Northanger Novels: a Footnote to Jane Austen' has guaranteed them some level of critical recognition. In this early essay (the dating partly accounts for the condescension in tone to Austen), Sadleir defends the Gothic romance's reputation from the charges seemingly levelled against it in such contemporary parodies as *Northanger Abbey*:

■ It may be presumptuous to claim for such an investigation that it provides a 'footnote to Jane Austen'. Admittedly – save during its actual pause beneath the Gothic porch of Northanger Abbey – the argument must travel roads which, so far as historical evidence is concerned, Miss Austen herself was content to leave unexplored. And yet it seems probable that the spinster-genius had in her time actually more pleasure and even profit from the Gothic romance than she saw occasion to record; and certainly a woman of her sympathy and perception – however ready she may have been publicly to make fun of the excesses of a prevailing *chic* – would in her heart have given to that *chic* as much credit for its qualities as mockery for its absurdities.

For qualities it had, and good historical and psychological justification also. The Gothic romance was not by any means – as it is now generally regarded – a mere crazy extravagance. Like most artistic movements, it had its primitive impotence and its over-ripe elaboration; but it sprang from a genuine spiritual impulse, and during its period of florescence produced work of real and permanent beauty.[46] □

Sadleir makes the important point that Austen's critique of the Gothic probably concealed a much more deep-seated affection for the genre, quoting her own admission in a letter: 'Our family are great novel readers and not ashamed of being so.' From Austen's presumed literacy in the Gothic romance, Sadleir infers of Isabella Thorpe's reading list that:

■ Within the limits of that brief selection are found three or four distinct 'make-ups', assumed by novelists of the day for the greater popularity of their work. And this fact strengthens the suspicion that Jane Austen's pick of Gothic novels was rather deliberate than random, was made for the stories' rather than for their titles' sake. Chance alone could hardly have achieved so representative a choice; the chooser, had she merely wished to startle by violence or absurdity of title, could have improved without difficulty on more than one of her selection.[47] □

Sadleir divides the seven named titles in *Northanger Abbey* into three different critical categories. He first cites Roche's *Clermont* as an example of 'the rhapsodical sensibility romance in its finest form' before placing *The Castle of Wolfenbach*, *The Mysterious Warning*, *The Orphan of the Rhine* and *The Midnight Bell* in the terror category because they *pretend* to be translations from the German 'for fashion's sake'.[48] Sadleir excludes *The Necromancer* from this category, however, because 'it probably represents the manipulation of genuine German material to create something to English taste'. This early critical division of the Gothic romance into three categories is significant. Sadleir's categorization of the *Northanger* novels mirrors the three categories that Sir Walter Scott used to define prose fiction in the 'Introduction' to *Waverley*. His excavation of these novels thus suggests that both Austen and Scott were extremely well-read in Gothic romances, and were able to subdivide the genre critically into three discrete categories.

In particular, Michael Sadleir's detection of the first two 'Gothic' categories (the romance of sensibility and the German horror romance) has survived the critical developments of the intervening decades almost intact. The debate on the relative merits of terror as opposed to horror has been ongoing since the inception of the Gothic romance in the 1760s, and created an early critical defence of the works of Radcliffe and others who subscribed to the school of terror. For every critical detractor of terror that we have thus far explored from contemporary criticism of the Gothic, there was an equally vigorous defence of the uses of terror in the 1790s and 1800s, as Chapter Two demonstrates. Likewise, as Chapters Three, Four and Five demonstrate, the Gothic's position vis-à-vis the French Revolution, nationalism and anti-Catholicism, dreams and psychology, and gender have also been defended contemporaneously and to the present day.

## The justifications of terror

In 1987, Elizabeth R. Napier published the provocatively titled *The Failure of Gothic: Problems of Disjunction in an Eighteenth-Century Literary Form*. Returning to the satires and 'laundry lists' of the Gothic that were so ubiquitous in the 1790s, Napier argued that:

■ Th[e] essentially decorative effect of the Gothic has repeatedly been condemned by critics and has made the form particularly vulnerable to satire. Most of the novels gain resonance and continuity by making use of the same devices: ruined castles, secret panels, concealed portraits, underground passageways. There is surprisingly little variation on this design. Even in more sophisticated examples of the genre, such as the novels of Maturin, where the devices, bolstered by other aspects of the narrative, become more psychologically suggestive, they occupy an undeniably prominent position. In extreme cases – those of Reeve or Lee, for example – the essential 'Gothicness' of the work attaches almost exclusively to these properties. An attempt to isolate the distinctive qualities of Gothic narrative brings the reader repeatedly back to this characteristic: Gothicism is finally much less about evil, 'the fascination of the abomination',[49] than it is a standardized, absolutely formulaic system of creating a certain kind of atmosphere in which a reader's sensibility toward fear and horror is exercised in predictable ways. ... This is not a popular stand to take towards the Gothic because much of the more spirited recent criticism of the genre has been explicitly directed towards denying that it is 'a collection of ghost-story devices'. ... The devices ... become necessarily signifiers of some deeper meaning.[50] ☐

Napier continues to contend that despite the fact that the Gothic novel raised serious political issues during the Romantic period, it addressed these issues weakly, resorting to the set collection of motifs upon which all examples of the genre relied. Her critique is reminiscent of the suggestions made in the articles 'The Terrorist System of Novel Writing' and 'Terrorist Novel Writing' that we examined earlier in this chapter. Whilst both of those articles suggested that the Gothic romance toyed with the politics of the French Revolution, they implied that the genre did little beyond playing with those motifs. Napier's charge is similar. She argues that the aesthetic devices of the Gothic romance override any serious attempt at political critique in the form.

The Failure of Gothic offers a provocative if somewhat unfair continuation of the debate over the aesthetics and 'value' of the Gothic genre: unfair, because her emphasis on Reeve's and Lee's romances as Gothic solely due to their adoption of specific Gothic tropes is misleading. Whilst Clara Reeve and Sophia Lee may have been working within the historical romance tradition, we cannot argue that their works were Gothic simply because of their deployment of Gothic aesthetics. The grouping of Gothic aesthetics had been neither acknowledged nor reworked in the 1780s when Reeve and Lee wrote The Old English Baron and The Recess respectively. And, in fact, whilst Reeve acknowledged her indebtedness to Walpole's The Castle of Otranto, the origins of Sophia Lee's The Recess are less easy to discern. Lee's poetical and psychological exploration of two displaced twin sisters cannot be condensed to a reworking of certain Gothic tropes.

In a review of The Failure of Gothic, David Punter queries the aesthetic emphasis of Napier's account. Instead, he argues that the Gothic's carefully papered narrative cracks; the artificial closures address a 'deeper wound' in the social self.[51] Whilst Napier may not deny this, her account does not acknowledge, as Punter indicates, that the aesthetics of the Gothic romance recognize and celebrate fracture and disjunction. In Love, Mystery and Misery (1978), Coral Ann Howells has identified the genre's preoccupation with external conventions as 'the peculiar quality and the contemporary appeal of Gothic fiction'.[52] Howells argues that the Gothic's essentially visual nature is suggestive of its affinities with drama as it was between 1790 and 1820.

The predominant focus of this chapter upon the contemporary reception of the Gothic in the 1790s and 1800s has revealed that the Gothic romance's identification by a stable number of external tropes was secured during the height of its popularity in the 1790s. Despite this recognition, there remained a contemporaneous unease with the Gothic's origins in the genre of romance (as discussed by Walpole and Reeve in particular), its subsequent bifurcation into sentimental terror narratives (as exemplified in Radcliffe's fiction) and German-influenced tales of horror (like Lewis's), and its connections with drama, poetry and contemporary politics. As the following chapters testify, the external conventions of the Gothic cannot be divorced from these other concerns and traditions.

By way of conclusion to this chapter, Maggie Kilgour provides us with a suitably 'Gothic' metaphor to analyse the plurality of traditions that foment the Gothic romance. In *The Rise of the Gothic Novel* (1995), Kilgour argues that:

■ ... one of the factors that makes the gothic so shadowy and nebulous a genre, as difficult to define as any gothic ghost, is that it cannot be seen in abstraction from the other literary forms from whose grave it arises, or from its later descendants who survive after its demise, such as the detective novel and horror movie. It feeds upon and mixes the wide range of literary sources out of which it emerges and from which it never fully disentangles itself: British folklore, ballads, romance, Elizabethan and Jacobean tragedy (especially Shakespeare), Spenser, Milton, Renaissance ideas of melancholy, the graveyard poets, Ossian, the sublime, sentimental novelists (notably [Abbé] Prevost [1697–1763], [Samuel] Richardson, and [Jean-Jacques] Rousseau [1712–78]), and German traditions (especially [*The Robbers* (1781) *and Ghost-Seer* (1789), by Friedrich] Schiller [1759–1805]). The form is thus itself a Frankenstein's monster, assembled out of the bits and pieces of the past. While it therefore can at times seem hopelessly naïve and simple, it is, at its best, a highly wrought artificial form which is extremely self-conscious of its artificiality and creation out of old material and traditions.[53] □

The anatomy of Mary Shelley's monster, sewn together from different bodies which have been obtained through occasionally illegitimate means, provides a good way of thinking around the concerns and literary genres from which the Gothic romance is born in the late eighteenth century. The following chapters examine the critical appraisals of both the aesthetic sources and the political and psychological concerns which give life blood to the Gothic romance on the cusp of the eighteenth and nineteenth centuries.

# CHAPTER TWO

# 'Terror and Horror': Gothic Struggles

Towards the close of day, the road wound into a deep valley. Mountains, whose shaggy steeps appeared to be inaccessible, almost surrounded it. To the east, a vista opened, that exhibited the Appennines in their darkest horrors; and the long perspective of retiring summits, rising over each other, their ridges clothed with pines, exhibited a stronger image of grandeur, than any that Emily had yet seen. The sun had just sunk below the top of the mountains she was descending, whose long shadow stretched athwart the valley, but his sloping rays, shooting through an opening of the cliffs, touched with a yellow gleam the summits of the forest, that hung upon the opposite steeps, and streamed in full splendour upon the towers and battlements of a castle, that spread its extensive ramparts along the brow of a precipice above. The splendour of these illumined objects was heightened by the contrasted shade, which involved the valley below.

'There,' said Montoni, speaking for the first time in several hours, 'is Udolpho.'

Emily gazed with melancholy awe upon the castle, which she understood to be Montoni's; for, though it was now lighted up by the setting sun, the gothic greatness of its features, and its mouldering walls of dark grey stone, rendered it a gloomy and sublime object. As she gazed, the light died away on its walls, leaving a melancholy purple tint, which spread deeper and deeper, as the thin vapour crept up the mountain, while the battlements above were still tipped with splendour. From those too, the rays soon faded, and the whole edifice was invested with the solemn duskiness of evening. Silent, lonely and sublime, it seemed to stand the sovereign of the scene, and to frown defiance on all, who dared to invade its solitary reign. As the twilight deepened, its features became more awful in obscurity, and Emily continued to gaze, till its clustering towers were alone seen, rising over the tops of the woods, beneath whose thick shade the carriages soon after began to ascend.

(Ann Radcliffe, *The Mysteries of Udolpho* (1794), ed. Bonamy Dobrée, Oxford: Oxford University Press, 1980, pp. 226–7)

One of the first words that we associate with Gothic fiction is 'terror'. As we saw in the previous chapter in the satirical letters 'Terrorist Novel Writing' and 'The Terrorist System of Novel Writing', the Gothic romance was in fact more often identified by the word 'terror' than by the word 'Gothic' during the late eighteenth century.[1] But what does terror stand for, and why was it such a ubiquitous signifier for Gothic at the end of the eighteenth century? This is the question that this chapter will engage with through an exploration of contemporaneous critical writings on terror and its counterpart, horror, as well as twentieth-century critical responses to these terms.

In Chapter One, we noted that Michael Sadleir's 1927 excavation of the 'horrid novels' in Austen's *Northanger Abbey* subdivides the romances that Isabella and Catherine discuss into two aesthetic subgroups; those novels which use horror, and those which engage with the aesthetic of terror. The fundamental schism between terror and horror has haunted Gothic criticism from the eighteenth century itself to the present day. Why? Because underneath the arch of 'Gothic', we continue to assemble a disparate collection of texts which share a fascination with persecuted heroines, gloomy villains, castles and monasteries.

If we recall from Chapter One, in his assessment of the Gothic romance in relation to Radcliffe, as early as 1827 Sir Walter Scott noted that the 'characters of the agents, like the figures in many landscapes, are entirely subordinate to the scenes in which they are placed'.[2] The buildings are as important as the protagonists in Gothic romance. From the oppressive castles in Walpole's and Radcliffe's fiction, to the extensive exploration of monasteries and the Inquisition in Lewis's and Maturin's work, the Gothic building as a symbol of fear and unyielding power is ubiquitous. Perhaps this is rendered most explicit in the opening to Ann Radcliffe's second novel, *A Sicilian Romance* (1790). Its very opening page – which establishes the conceit of a curious traveller who is permitted to read an old manuscript – embarks upon the exploration of an ancient edifice:

■ On the northern shore of Sicily are still to be seen the magnificent remains of a castle, which formerly belonged to the noble house of Mazzini. It stands in the centre of a small bay, and upon a gentle acclivity, which, on one side, slopes towards the sea, and on the other rises into an eminence crowned by dark woods. The situation is admirably beautiful and picturesque, and the ruins have an air of ancient grandeur, which, contrasted with the present solitude of the scene, impresses the traveller with awe and curiosity. During my travels abroad I visited this spot. As I walked over the loose fragments of stone, which lay scattered through the immense area of the fabrick, and surveyed the sublimity and grandeur of the ruins, I recurred, by a natural association of ideas, to the times when these walls stood proudly in their original splendour, when the halls were the scenes of hospitality and festive magnificence, and when they resounded with the voices of those whom death had long since swept from the earth. 'Thus,' said I, 'shall the present generation – he who now sinks in misery – and he who now swims in pleasure, alike pass away and be forgotten.' My heart swelled with the reflection; and, as I turned from the scene with a sigh, I fixed my eyes upon a friar, whose venerable figure, gently bending towards the earth, formed no uninteresting object in the picture. He observed my emotion; and, as my eye met his, shook his head and pointed to the ruin. 'These walls,' said he, 'were once the seat of luxury and vice.'³ ☐

Radcliffe's second novel thus commences with a frame where an unnamed traveller surveys the ruins of a castle. His identity is not important. Instead, we are compelled to focus upon what the castle comes to represent through his perspective. The traveller pays a great deal of attention to the landscape – the ruined fabric of the castle is contrasted with its 'beautiful and picturesque' location.⁴ This location inspires the traveller with 'awe and curiosity', and thereby stimulates his imaginative faculties. Imagination re-creates the castle and its former scenes of splendour for the traveller, and imagination allows him to meditate upon the inevitable mortality of the 'present generation'.

In this picturesque opening description, then, we find the key elements of a particular aesthetic that is used in some Gothic romances. The combination of landscape and ruined castle, which the traveller frames in a 'picture' as an artist might, provokes a meditation from both the traveller and the friar regarding the transient nature of power. Thus a castle – even a ruined one – becomes the imaginative catalyst for contemplating power. In his early critical work *The Gothic Flame* (1957), Devendra P. Varma commented enthusiastically upon the aesthetic and political implications of the Gothic's sustained use of castles:

■ Imagination inspires the Gothic mind to carry itself back to the past and observe the artistic effect of the truly mysterious. The cathedrals or castles look like spectres of ancient times, and permit indulgence in a melancholic nostalgia. ... Besides the 'gloom' and 'delightful horrors' of a castle, there are a number of pleasing elements linked with a Gothic mansion. Castles are traditionally associated with childhood stories of magic, and the Gothic romances are themselves in the nature of adult fairy-tales. Moreover, an antique edifice satisfied the craving for something strange, emotional, and mysterious. Antiquity inspires us with veneration, almost with a religious awe, and the Gothic mind loves to brood over the hallowed glory of the past.

The element of terror is inseparably associated with the Gothic castle, which is an image of power, dark, isolated and impenetrable. No light penetrating its impermeable walls, high and strengthened by bastions, it stands silent, lonely and sublime, frowning defiance on all who dare to invade its solitary reign. Through its dim corridors now prowl armed bandits; its halls ring with hideous revelry or anon are silent as the grave. Even when presented in decay, the castle is majestic and threatening: a spot where we encounter the mysterious and demoniac beings of romance.[5] □

Here, Varma had Radcliffe's fourth novel *The Mysteries of Udolpho* in mind in his characterization of the Gothic castle. Indeed, his lexis in this final paragraph is taken (without acknowledgement) from the heroine Emily's first view of the castle of Udolpho (as I have quoted in the epigraph to this chapter). 'Silent, lonely and sublime', 'frowning defiance', the Gothic castle simultaneously invokes terror (through its high walls and solitary position) and veneration.

In the epigraph that I have chosen from *The Mysteries of Udolpho* by way of introduction to the themes of this chapter, the heroine Emily St Aubert and company reach Udolpho through a wild landscape. This is far removed from the bucolic pastoral descriptions of her childhood home La Vallée. It is a landscape that is punctuated with terror: the mountains are guarded by 'inaccessible' 'shaggy steeps' and are exhibited in their 'darkest horrors', their summits are concealed but exhibit 'a stronger image of grandeur, than any that Emily had yet seen.'

The first glimpse of the castle unites it with the cliffs that the sun's rays dare to touch. Udolpho, the embodiment of 'Gothic' terror, seems to grow out of the terrifying natural landscape which surrounds it. This is one of Ann Radcliffe's most magisterial descriptions and crucially, it conjoins the natural (the landscape) with the cultural (the castle). Emily's imagination is at its most alert. The partial obscurity of the landscape and castle awaken a 'melancholy awe' which permits her to endow the castle with supernatural powers.

The potent combination of imagination and fear that *The Mysteries of Udolpho* describes here is symptomatic of the Gothic romance's intimate engagement with the theory of the sublime. As an idea, the sublime has been debated since the classical scholar Longinus (c. 213–73) wrote a treatise entitled 'On the Sublime' (date unknown) where he advocated a 'limitless' literature.[6] With the publication in 1757 of Edmund Burke's *A Philosophical Enquiry into the Sublime and Beautiful*, the concept of the sublime gained considerable critical currency in the eighteenth century. Burke's work proved to be of great significance to Gothic literature due to its theorization of terror and sublimity. In one of its central sections, 'Of the sublime', Burke first made the connections between terror and sublimity explicit:

■ Whatever is fitted in any sort to excite the ideas of pain, and danger, that is to say, whatever is in any sort terrible, or is conversant about terrible objects, or operates in a manner analogous to terror, is a source of the sublime; that is, it is productive of the strongest emotion which the mind is capable of feeling. I say the strongest emotion, because I am satisfied the ideas of pain are much more powerful than those which enter on the part of pleasure.[7] □

Burke embarks upon his lengthy and dilatory exploration of the sublime powers of terror and pain by asserting that terror is 'the strongest emotion'. He later asserts that this 'strongest emotion' is produced through 'Astonishment' where 'the mind is so entirely filled with its object, that it cannot entertain any other, nor by consequence reason on that which employs it'.[8] Burke's description of this 'astonishment' corresponds with Radcliffe's later descriptions of her heroine's 'melancholy awe' when gazing upon the castle of Udolpho. The castle engrosses Emily's visual and mental landscape to such an extent that she pays no attention to her fellow travellers and gaolers. In his *Philosophical Enquiry*, Burke theorizes the connections between terror, fear and pain in the following way:

■ No passion so effectually robs the mind of all its powers of acting and reasoning as fear. For fear being an apprehension of pain or death, it operates in a manner that resembles actual pain. Whatever therefore is terrible, with regard to sight, is sublime too, whether this cause of terror, be endued with greatness of dimensions or not; for it is impossible to look on any thing as trifling, or contemptible, that may be dangerous. There are many animals, who though far from being large, are yet capable of raising ideas of the sublime, because they are considered as objects of terror. As serpents and poisonous animals of almost all kinds. And to things of great dimensions, if we annex an adventitious idea of terror, they become without comparison greater. A level plain of a vast extent on land, is certainly no mean idea; the prospect of such a plain may be as extensive as a prospect of the ocean; but can it ever fill the mind with anything so great as the ocean itself? This is owing to several causes, but it is owing to none more than this, that the ocean is an object of no small terror. Indeed terror is in all cases whatsoever, either more openly or latently the ruling principle of the sublime.[9] □

Here, Burke demonstrates with force that terror, intimately connected with the fear of subjection and death, is the 'ruling principle of the sublime'. Terror is primarily evoked through sight; if we contemplate, for example, an immeasurably vast ocean which exceeds our visual boundaries, then we will experience terror. But, Burke contends, this can also be the case for smaller objects that we view. Because of its threatening and dangerous nature, for example, a snake can evoke terror.

In order to explain his hesitancy in definition, Burke then proceeds to qualify his view of terror in the following section, 'Obscurity':

■ To make any thing very terrible, obscurity seems in general to be necessary. When we know the full extent of any danger, when we can accustom our eyes to it, a great deal of the apprehension vanishes. Every one will be sensible of this, who considers how greatly night adds to our dread, in all cases of danger, and how much the notions of ghosts and goblins, of which none can form clear ideas, affect minds, which give credit to the popular tales concerning such sorts of beings. Those despotic governments, which are founded on the passions of men, and principally upon the passion of fear, keep their chief as much as may be from the public eye. The policy has been the same in many cases of religion. Almost all the heathen temples were dark. Even in the barbarous temples of the Americans at this day, they keep their idol in a dark part of the hut, which is consecrated to his worship. For this purpose too the druids performed all their ceremonies in the bosom of the darkest woods, and in the shade of the oldest and most spreading oaks. No person seems better to have understood the secret of heightening, or of setting terrible things, if I may use the expression, in their strongest light by the force of a judicious obscurity, than Milton. His description of Death in the second book [Burke here refers to Book II of Milton's *Paradise Lost* (1667)] is admirably studied; it is astonishing with what a gloomy pomp, with what a significant and expressive uncertainty of strokes and colouring he has finished the portrait of the king of terrors.

> The other shape,
> If shape it might be called that shape had none
> Distinguishable, in member, joint, or limb;
> Or substance might be called that shadow seemed,
> For each seemed either; black he stood as night;
> Fierce as ten furies; terrible as hell;
> And shook a deadly dart. What seemed his head
> The likeness of a kingly crown had on.
> (Milton, *Paradise Lost*, II, ll. 666–73)

In this description all is dark, uncertain, confused, terrible, and sublime to the last degree.[10] □

In essence, Burke argues here that a degree of obscurity reinforces terror. The passage that he selects from Book II of Milton's *Paradise Lost* illustrates his point extremely well. Milton's description of Death here does not provide us with a clear picture. Instead, the repetition of 'seemed', and the appeals to similes ('terrible as hell', 'black as night'), provide the reader with only the vaguest and most uncertain idea of Death's stature. But by invoking uncertainty in this manner, Burke maintains, Milton heightens the sense of terror, and hence sublimity, that his readers experience. As we can see from this passage 'On Obscurity' from the *Philosophical Enquiry*, Burke's own argument lacks clarity in places. As David Punter remarks, Burke's lengthy accretion of random examples 'tend[s] sometimes towards the ludicrous' and thus risks losing the reader at times.[11]

Following this section of Burke's *Philosophical Enquiry*, we can also see how the effect of terror in Radcliffe's fiction is dependent upon precisely the same condition of obscurity. Returning to the epigraph that I have chosen from *Udolpho*, we can see that as the night begins to fall upon the castle, it becomes an object of increasing terror. The narrative remarks that 'As the twilight deepened, its features became more awful in obscurity' and later, that 'The extent and darkness of these tall woods awakened terrific images in [Emily's] mind.' Radcliffe clearly follows Burke's prescription of obscurity and darkness as a precondition for the sublime in literature.

Burke's *Philosophical Enquiry* is undoubtedly one of the most significant works on aesthetics in the eighteenth century. As we have seen, his linkage of terror with obscurity exercised great influence upon Gothic writers in particular. Gothic romance relies upon uncertainty and obscurity. In some examples, such as Radcliffe, this is immediately evident through the writer's focalization of a character's responses to a landscape; in other places, the sublime can be seen to operate at the narratological level where the very obscurity and uncertainty of the plot takes the form of the terror that we and the characters experience. In Radcliffe's earlier novel *A Sicilian Romance*, for example, the governess Madame de Menon experiences anxiety over the disappearance of her young charge Julia. We gain an insight into Madame de Menon's anxiety: 'Wild and terrific images arose to her imagination. Fancy drew the scene; – she deepened the shades; and the terrific aspect of the objects she presented was heightened by the obscurity which involved them.'[12] It is the very obscurity that envelops Julia's fate which causes Madame de Menon so much anxiety. As Burke argues, obscurity expands the imaginative faculties and enables us to create darker and more dangerous pictures of situations that lack certainty.

What Madame de Menon is described as experiencing in *A Sicilian Romance* also corresponds to the emotional potential involved in reading a Gothic romance. As the epigraph to *A Sicilian Romance*, Radcliffe uses part of a line from a speech by the Ghost of Hamlet's Father in Act 1, Scene 4 of *Hamlet* (about 1601) by William Shakespeare (1544–1616); 'I could a tale unfold'. As Alison Milbanke argues in her edition of the novel, first and foremost this 'indicates its intention of arousing suspense and terror in its readers, of disarranging them physically in the manner of the sublime effect'.[13] Gothic romance is intimately concerned with prolonging suspense and evoking terror in its readership. By delaying the explanation of a mystery for as long as possible, the romance allows its reader to experience obscurity and its attendant sublimity because, like Madame de Menon, the readers stretch their imaginative faculties.

Many examples of this narrative uncertainty spring to mind besides that of Radcliffe. The embedded lengthy story of Raymond and Agnes within Lewis's *The Monk* contributes to the uncertain direction of the story, and shrouds us in mystery for a long time. It is only towards the romance's conclusion that the connection between the two plot strands becomes clear. Later, this is raised to an art form by Charles Robert Maturin in *Melmoth the Wanderer*, where its convoluted, uncertain narrative structure participates in the creation of terror. As readers, we thus participate in one of the central paradoxes of the Gothic. We are forced to explore the labyrinthine nature of the Gothic romance, and yet we gain pleasure from this very compulsion. In the following section, we will examine some later eighteenth-century critical responses to the potent combination of terror and pleasure offered by the Gothic romance.

## Gothic paradoxes: terror, pain and pleasure

One of the most important contemporary essays on the correspondence between the sublime and terror was written by Anna Laetitia Aikin (later Barbauld). In a 1773 collection of essays which she composed with her brother John, Anna Laetitia Aikin wrote a piece entitled 'On the Pleasure Derived from Objects of Terror' where she embarked upon an exploration of a 'paradox of the heart', namely 'the apparent delight with which we dwell upon objects of pure terror'.[14] This delight, in Aikin's view, seems to be in tension with the benevolent feelings, inherent in 'the moral and natural system of man', which are aroused when we see another in distress. The paradox resides in the seemingly immoral pleasure gained from terror, experienced even by virtuous, benevolent readers. Referring to the public's appetite for terror, Aikin goes on to argue:

■ The reality of this source of pleasure seems evident from daily obser-vation. The greediness with which the tales of ghosts and goblins, or murders, earthquakes, fires, shipwrecks, and all the most terrible disas-ters attending human life, are devoured by every ear, must have been generally remarked. ...
How are we then to account for the pleasure derived from such objects? I have often been led to imagine that there is a deception in these cases; and that the avidity with which we attend is not a proof of our receiving real pleasure. The pain of suspense, and the irresistible desire of satisfying curiosity, when once raised, will account for our eagerness to go quite through an adventure, though we suffer actual pain during the whole course of it. We rather chuse [sic] to suffer the smart pang of a violent emotion than the uneasy craving for an unsatis-fied desire. That this principle, in many instances, may involuntarily carry us through what we dislike, I am convinced from experience. This is the impulse which renders the poorest and most insipid narrative interesting when once we get fairly into it; and I have frequently felt it with regard to our modern novels, which, if lying on my table, and taken up in an idle hour, have led me through the most tedious and disgusting pages, while, like Pistol eating his leek, I have swallowed and execrated to the end.[15] And it will not only force us through dullness, but through actual torture – through the relation of a Damien's execution, or an inquisitor's act of faith.[16] □

Aikin draws our attention to the perceived 'dullness' of contemporary novels whilst excusing her own reading of them by referring to the compulsion of curiosity. She embarks upon an exploration of the rea-sons why we endure torture and violence within a narrative, and links the pleasure that we derive from such tales with the violence inherent in curiosity.

According to Aikin, curiosity is the determining factor in our reading which will propel us through any narrative, however dull, in order to reach closure. Once suspense has been created, the readers must satisfy their curiosity. The state of *not knowing* the outcome of a narrative is more painful than the tedium of discovering the conclusion to a bad narrative.

The connections that Aikin forges between pleasure and terror are later self-consciously affirmed in Maturin's *Melmoth the Wanderer*. At one point in this novel, the unwilling novice Monçada is astonished at his own mechanical compulsion when watching a crowd execution. He accounts for the 'horrid trance' that compels him to spectate the crowd violence by admitting 'I actually for a moment believed myself the object of their cruelty. The drama of terror has the irresistible power of converting its audience into its victims.'[17] Imagination enables Monçada to participate in the 'drama of terror' and to become its victim too. This imaginative absorption, which is far from pleasurable, is symptomatic of the attendant pain that accompanies the sublime.

In her essay, Aikin chooses to dwell on the reader's compulsion to endure torture in order to reach the end of a narrative. Although this may appear to be similar to Burke's discovery of terror in *unfamiliar* objects, Aikin is careful to reconcile the pleasure of terror with *actual* violence in narratives, emphasizing the importance of repetition to our experiences of terror and pleasure: 'Here, though we know beforehand what to expect, we enter into them with eagerness, in quest of a pleasure already experienced.'[18]

Aikin's essay is both literary criticism and a psychological insightful exploration of the 'paradox of the heart'. The essay continues by distinguishing between good and bad narratives of terror. Aikin argues that 'well-wrought scenes of artificial terror which are formed by a sublime and vigorous imagination' will eradicate the pain inherent in reading through narratives of torture in order to satisfy curiosity:

■ This is the pleasure constantly attached to the excitement of surprise from new and wonderful objects. A strange and unexpected event awakens the mind, and keeps it on the stretch; and where the agency of invisible beings is introduced, of 'forms unseen and mightier far than we'[19] our imagination, darting forth, explores with rapture the new world which is laid open to its view, and rejoices in the expansion of its powers. Power and fancy co-operating elevate the soul to its highest pitch; and the pain of terror is lost in amazement.[20] □

The importance of Aikin's essay is its location of pleasure in 'new and wonderful objects'. According to Aikin, our desire to experience terror is connected to our desire to discover a 'new world ... laid open to its view' which stimulates the imagination, and causes the 'pain of terror' to be subsumed by awe.

It is evident both from her fiction and from a later critical essay that she wrote that Ann Radcliffe in particular was strongly influenced by Aikin's refinement of Burke's argument. Radcliffe's heroines often find themselves in perilous situations which allow their imaginations to expand and obliterate the 'pain of terror' through amazement. In her penultimate novel *The Italian*, for example, the heroine Ellena is able to forget about her imprisonment in a convent by contemplating the scenery outside:

■ [Ellena] ascended the winding steps hastily, and found they led only to a door, opening into a small room, where nothing remarkable appeared, till she approached the windows, and beheld thence an horizon, and a land-scape spread below, whose grandeur awakened all her heart. The con-sciousness of her prison was lost, while her eyes ranged over the wide and freely-sublime scene without. She perceived that this chamber was within a small turret, projecting from an angle of the convent over the walls, and suspended, as in air, above the vast precipices of granite, that formed part of the mountain. These precipices were broken into cliffs, which, in some places, impended far above their base, and, in others, rose, in nearly-perpendicular lines, to the walls of the monastery, which they supported. Ellena, with a dreadful pleasure, looked down them ...[21] □

The scene depicted is dangerous to the heroine Ellena, with the room she occupies hanging perilously over the sides of her prison. However, as Aikin argues, the 'new world' laid open to Ellena's view compensates for the terror that she experiences.

One contemporary commentator in particular, Nathan Drake, celebrated Ann Radcliffe's balancing of terror with natural beauty. In *Literary Hours* (1798), Drake first established his critical precepts on ter-ror before proceeding to praise Radcliffe's penultimate novel, *The Italian*:

■ Terror ... requires no small degree of skill and arrangement to prevent its operating more pain than pleasure. Unaccompanied by those mysteri-ous incidents which indicate the ministration of beings mightier far than we, and which induce that thrilling sensation of mingled astonishment, apprehension and delight so irresistably [sic] captivating to the general-ity of mankind, it will be apt to create rather horror and disgust than the grateful emotion intended. To obviate this result, it is necessary either to interpose picturesque description, or sublime and pathetic sentiment, or so to stimulate curiosity by the artful texture of the fable, or by the uncertain and suspended fate of an interesting personage, that the mind shall receive such a degree of artificial pleasure as may mitigate and subdue what, if naked of decoration and skilful accompaniment, would shock and appal every feeling heart. ...

In the productions of Mrs. Radcliffe, the Shakspeare [sic] of Romance Writers, and who to the wild landscape of Salvator Rosa [Neapolitan painter, 1615–73], has added the softer graces of a Claude [Claude Sellér, or Lorraine Claude, French painter, 1600–82], may be found many scenes truly terrific in their conception, yet so softened down, and the mind so much relieved, by the intermixture of beautiful description, or pathetic incident, that the impression of the whole never becomes too strong, never degenerates into horror, but pleasurable emotion is ever the domi-nating result. In her last piece, termed *The Italian*, the attempt of Schedoni to assassinate the amiable and innocent Ellena whilst confined with Banditti in a lone house on the sea shore, is wrought up in so masterly a manner that every nerve vibrates with pity and terror, especially at the moment when about to plunge a dagger into her bosom he discovers her to be his daughter: every word, every action of the shocked and self-accusing Confessor, whose character is marked with traits almost super-human, appal yet delight the reader, and it is difficult to ascertain whether ardent curiosity, intense commiseration, or apprehension that suspends almost the faculty of breathing, be, in the progress of this well-written story, most powerfully excited.[22] □

Drake analyses a protracted later scene from Volume II of *The Italian* where Schedoni, on the brink of assassinating Ellena to prevent her marriage to Vivaldi, discovers a miniature upon his intended victim which suggests that Ellena is his daughter. The poise with which the scene moves between Schedoni's conscience and his self-interest creates, as Drake rightly argues, a convincingly terrifying scene:

■ [Schedoni's] agitation and repugnance to strike encreased with every moment of delay, and, as often as he prepared to plunge the poniard in her bosom, a shuddering horror restrained him. Astonished at his own feelings, and indignant at what he termed a dastardly weakness, he found it necessary to argue with himself, and his rapid thoughts said, 'Do I not feel the necessity of this act? Does not what is dearer to me than existence – does not my consequence depend on the execution of it? Is she not also beloved by the young Vivaldi? ...' This consideration reani-mated him; vengeance nerved his arm, and drawing aside the lawn from her bosom, he once more raised it to strike; when, after gazing for an instant, some new cause of horror seemed to seize his frame, and he stood for some moments, aghast and motionless like a statue. His respi-ration was short and laborious, chilly drops stood on his forehead, and all his faculties of mind seemed suspended. When he recovered, he stooped to examine again the miniature, which had occasioned this revolution, and which had lain concealed beneath the lawn that he withdrew.[23] □

The terror created in this scene is dependent upon Schedoni's own uncertainty over the justice of his actions, and the way in which this uncertainty is transmitted to the reader. Schedoni is undoubtedly Radcliffe's most convincing anti-hero, and the success of his characteri-zation is derived in part from the hesitations of his conscience. These hesitations, alongside the obscurity concerning his origins, create the suspense and terror for which Radcliffe became justifiably renowned.

Radcliffe's own later critical essay 'On the Supernatural in Poetry' further refines Aikin's aesthetic arguments on terror by drawing a strong distinction between it and its counterpart, horror. It is presented as a dialogue between two gentlemen travellers, the rational and unimaginative Mr Simpson (Mr. S—), and the more emotional and imaginative Mr Willoughton (Mr. W—). The travellers are journeying towards Kenilworth Castle, and Willoughton is animated by the prospect of rediscovering Shakespeare's Arden. The characters reappear and are enlarged upon in the lengthy prefatory essay to Radcliffe's final, posthumously published romance *Gaston de Blondeville* (1826), but this particular essay, published in the *New Monthly Magazine*, contains different material from that romance's preface despite the fact that both use the same characters and scenario.

'On the Supernatural in Poetry' is, in essence, a manifesto which confirms and celebrates Radcliffe's use of terror and obscurity. It defends Radcliffe's use of terror rather than horror, and, through the mouthpiece of one of the gentlemen, Mr. W., defends Shakespeare, Milton and Burke in their use of obscurity. Mr. S., the more down-to-earth of the two travellers, refers to those contemporaries of Radcliffe who disagreed with Burke's addition of the obscure to his discussion of the sublime.[24] Mr. W. appears to defend Radcliffe's views on the sublime and warmly endorses the sublime value of obscurity. The majority of the debate refers to the tragedies of Shakespeare which make use of the supernatural, with many references in particular to *Macbeth* and *Hamlet*. The debate on obscurity begins by Mr. S. wondering about the effects of the supernatural when it appears in scenes of gaiety:

■ 'How happens it then,' said Mr. S—, 'that objects of terror sometimes strike us so very forcibly, when introduced into scenes of gaiety and splendour, as, for instance, in the Banquet scene in Macbeth?'

'They strike, then, chiefly by the force of contrast,' replied W—; 'but the effect, though sudden and strong, is also transient; it is the thrill of horror and surprise, which they then communicate rather than the deep and solemn feelings excited under more accordant circumstances and left long upon the mind. Who ever suffered for the ghost of Banquo, the gloomy and sublime kind of terror, which Hamlet calls forth? Though the appearance of Banquo, at the high festival of Macbeth, not only tells us that he is murdered, but recalls to our minds the fate of the gracious Duncan, laid in silence and death by those who, in this very scene, are revelling in his spoils. There, though deep pity mingles with our surprise and horror, we experience a far less degree of interest, and that interest too of an inferior kind. The union of grandeur and obscurity, which Mr. Burke describes as a sort of tranquillity tinged with terror, and which causes the sublime, is to be found only in Hamlet; or in scenes where circumstances of the same kind prevail.'

'That may be,' said Mr. S—, 'and I perceive you are not one of those who contend that obscurity does not make any part of the sublime.'

'They must be men of very cold imaginations,' said W—, 'with whom certainty is more terrible than surmise. Terror and horror are so far opposite, that the first expands the soul, and awakens the faculties to a high degree of life; the other contracts, freezes, and nearly annihilates them. I apprehend, that neither Shakespeare nor Milton by their fictions, nor

Mr. Burke by his reasoning, anywhere looked to positive horror as a source of the sublime, though they all agree that terror is a very high one; and where lies the great difference between horror and terror, but in the uncertainty and obscurity, that accompany the first, respecting the dreaded evil?

'But what say you to Milton's image –
"On his brows sat horror plumed."'

'As an image, it is certainly sublime; it fills the mind with an idea of power, but it does not follow that Milton intended to declare the feeling of horror to be sublime; and after all, his image imparts more of terror than of horror; for it is not distinctly pictured forth, but is seen in glimpses through obscuring shades, the great outlines only appearing, which excite the imagination to complete the rest; he only says, "sat horror plumed"; you will observe, that the look of horror and the other characteristics are left to the imagination of the reader; and according to the strength of that, he will feel Milton's image to be either sublime or otherwise. Milton, when he sketched it, probably felt, that not even his art could fill up the outline, and present to other eyes the countenance which his "mind's eye" gave to him. Now, if obscurity has so much effect on fiction, what must it have in real life, when to ascertain the object of our terror, is frequently to acquire the means of escaping it. You will observe, that this image though indistinct or obscure, is not confused.'

'How can any thing be indistinct and not confused?' said Mr. S—.

'Ay, that question is from the new school,' replied W—; 'but recollect, that obscurity, or indistinctness, is only a negative, which leaves the imagination to act upon the few hints that truth reveals to it; confusion is a thing as positive as distinctness, though not necessarily so palpable; and it may, by mingling and confounding one image with another, absolutely counteract the imagination, instead of exciting it. Obscurity leaves something for the imagination to exaggerate; confusion, by blurring one image into another, leaves only a chaos in which the mind can find nothing to be magnificent, nothing to nourish its fears or doubts, or to act upon in any way; yet confusion and obscurity are terms used indiscriminately by those, who would prove, that Shakspeare and Milton were wrong when they employed obscurity as a cause of the sublime, that Mr. Burke was equally mistaken in his reasoning upon the subject, and that mankind have been equally in error, as to the nature of their own feelings, when they were acted upon by the illusions of those great masters of the imagination, at whose so potent bidding, the passions have been awakened from their sleep, and by whose magic a crowded Theatre has been changed to a lonely shore, to a witch's cave, to an enchanted island, to a murderer's castle, to the ramparts of an usurper, to the battle, to the midnight carousal of the camp or the tavern, to every various scene of the living world.'[25] □

The argument over Milton's use of the word 'horror' is useful as a retrospective on Radcliffe's earlier fiction where, in places, she uses the terms 'terror' and 'horror' almost interchangeably.[26] Here, drawing inspiration from Milton, she suggests that the word 'horror', if used discriminately to signify partial obscurity, is more indebted to the terror aesthetic of the sublime rather than its counterpart, horror. The distinctions that she forges between confusion and obscurity, however, are important to her aesthetic mission. Clearly, like Burke, she views obscurity as far superior to the confusion that Mr. S. refers to.

The attack on horror that Radcliffe launches here under the critical protection of Shakespeare, Milton and Burke can be read as an implicit attack on Matthew Lewis's use of horror in *The Monk*. Whereas Radcliffe's narratives only hinted at physical threats such as incest and rape for her heroines, Lewis graphically depicted physical and mental tortures in his Gothic romance. *The Monk's* vivid descriptions of rape and putrefying death are disturbing even to a modern reader. When Radcliffe, through the mouthpiece of 'Mr. W.', argues that horror 'contracts' and 'freezes' the imaginative faculties, she undoubtedly has Lewis's romance in mind. By contrast, the uncertainty and obscurity of the threats in Radcliffes' fiction are an attempt to stimulate the reader's curiosity and to expand their imaginations.

In *Gothic Bodies: The Politics of Pain in Romantic Fiction* (1994), Steven Bruhm links Radcliffe's aesthetic distancing from horror back to Burke's arguments, comparing their uses of horror, terror and self-preservation in particular:

> ■ Terror, then, is that carefully regulated aesthetic experience that can use intense feeling to seek objects in the world, objects which can include people in distress. Conversely, horror 'contracts, freezes and nearly annihilates' the passions which lead to community, and forces the horrified spectator to enclose and protect the self. 'Positive horror' behaves for Radcliffe in the same way that absolute pain behaves for Burke: both render us anti-social and self-protecting. Radcliffe's distinction between terror and horror, then, is analogous to Burke's distinction between society and self-preservation. Terror situates us in the social world, the world of the outside, while horror freezes us within the self.[27] □

Here, Bruhm refers to the precise definition of horror invoked by Radcliffe in her essay 'On the Supernatural' in order to drive home the comparisons between the terms used by both Burke and Radcliffe. He emphasizes that Radcliffe's aesthetic of terror 'invoke[s] physical mutilation, suffering and even death to stimulate great emotional activity, but to emphasize that this emotion is *imaginatively* generated'.[28] The connection between terror and the imagination, then, confirms the links between the individual who experiences this and the outside world.

By contrast, Bruhm explains, horror is connected to physical, tangible experiences of pain. He explains the differences between imagined and real pain by examining the dreams of Adeline, the heroine of Radcliffe's third novel *The Romance of the Forest* (1791):

> ■ At precisely the moment in which imagined pain threatens to become physical – it impinges on the physicality of the imaginer rather than the imagined, and the perceiving consciousness halts its own projective capabilities – the heroine swoons or wakes up, depending on the medium of the imagined body. The socializing force which constitutes the construction of community ... is halted at the moment of the perceiving subject's threatened violation and danger.[29] □

Bruhm rightly detects a paradox in Radcliffe's aesthetic of terror that she did not herself acknowledge in her critical essay. He explores how Radcliffe's heroines effectively shield themselves from the horrible fates that befall other female characters in the novels through their very sensibility, arguing that Radcliffe's aesthetic 'took the form of a dialectic of imagination, in which one sympathetically identified with a community of sufferers in order to isolate oneself more fully from them'.[30] What Bruhm describes is Radcliffe's renegotiation of Burke's arguments on self-preservation.[31] When confronted with scenes of extreme distress, her heroines effect an imaginative escape through swooning. By so doing, they avoid having to attempt to articulate these emotions.

Bruhm's account of self-preservation in relation to Radcliffe's swooning heroines is a useful point at which to consider other theories of the Gothic sublime that are less indebted to Burke. Although his account above takes as its starting point Burke's arguments on self-preservation, Bruhm acknowledges that swooning and escaping are, in effect, a refusal to frame an experience linguistically. Other theories of the Gothic sublime also pursue this refusal of language, and use it to demonstrate the limitations of Burke's theories of the sublime.

## The Gothic sublime and narrative

Burke's attempt to unite the psychological with the physical in the *Philosophical Enquiry* is a strand of argument that David B. Morris also queries in his 1985 essay 'Gothic Sublimity'. Here, Morris reads Walpole's 1764 *The Castle of Otranto* against Burke's 1757 *Enquiry* in order to demonstrate what he perceives to be the Gothic's overarching revision of eighteenth-century theories of the sublime. Morris argues for a specific Gothic sublime which occupies a recognizable space between the eighteenth-century and Romantic sublimes. While acknowledging the plurality of theories of the sublime, Morris proceeds to argue against the centrality of Burke's *Enquiry* to the Gothic:

■ Burke's account of the sublime is clearly relevant to the almost simultaneous Gothic explorations of terror. Walpole, for example, in his preface to *The Castle of Otranto*, describes terror as his 'principal engine' and writers committed to explorations of terror found obvious uses for the sublime.[32] Thus scholars of the Gothic novel – no doubt following the steps of many Gothic novelists – regularly consult Burke's *Philosophical Enquiry* as if it were a storehouse of approved and guaranteed terrors. His illustrations of the sublime have provided something like a reader's guide to the Gothic novel: vast cataracts, raging storms, lofty towers, dark nights, ghosts and goblins, serpents, madmen; mountains, precipices, dazzling light; low, tremulous, intermittent sounds, such as moans, sighs, or whispers; immense, gloomy buildings; tyranny, incarceration, torture.[33] Certainly it is true that some unusually artless Gothic novels seem patched together as a sampler of Burkean terrors. Yet there are serious drawbacks to the standard critical reading which interprets Gothic sublimity as merely instrumental, something to be used, a repertoire of terrifying devices. A critical approach which reduces Gothic sublimity to the familiar inventory of ghosts and dark passageways cannot help us understand what was both profoundly innovative and yet also deeply inadequate in Burke's account.

Burke's strengths lie in the far-reaching implications which his theory held for an unprecedented 'poeticizing' of the British novel. Gothic writers, in pursuing Burke's alliance between terror and sublimity, contribute to a new mixing of the previously separate conventions associated with verse and with prose, and this mixing of conventions opens fruitful possibilities for the development of plot, character, setting and language. Gothic sublimity in *The Castle of Otranto* thus belongs to Walpole's conscious protest against the Richardsonian model in fiction, with its realist techniques of narrative and its bourgeois attitudes toward marriage and social relations. ... In its marvels and terrors, *The Castle of Otranto* actively subverts the prosaic vision of the world implicit in novelistic conventions of probability and verisimilitude. The sublime in effect recaptures for the Gothic novel the same emotional intensities and narrative freedoms which belonged to poetry and to the poetic province of romance. Yet the vastly important implications of a 'poeticizing' of the novel – which we cannot trace to Burke alone – must not prevent us from understanding a major defect of the *Philosophical Enquiry*, a defect especially pertinent to the Gothic novel. This is its account of terror.[34] □

Morris argues here that in order to move beyond a listing of sublime effects in the Gothic, we need to consider the overarching influences that the sublime offered to it. These he locates in a generic fluidity which enabled Gothic writers to move between the conventions and themes of verse and prose. The emotional intensity more often associated with poetry (particularly, in the eighteenth century, with the graveyard poetry of Thomas Gray and William Collins, 1721–59) became available to Gothic writing through the theorization of the sublime. As did, according to Morris, the 'poetic province of the romance', which, as we saw in the previous chapter, was warmly debated and criticized thanks to its 'Gothic' revival.

Morris maintains, however, that to consider the sublime offered by Burke as the bedrock of the Gothic romance is misleading because Burke rests his theory of terror on a 'narrow, mechanical account of bodily processes' which privileges the visual.[35] As an argument, however, this risks overlooking Burke's theorization of obscurity, which, as we have seen with Radcliffe, was crucial to her descriptions of terror which cannot be seen. Morris's theorization of Gothic sublimity is none the less significant because of the different aspects of the sublime that he considers throughout his essay. Taking Walpole's *The Castle of Otranto*, which he claims is the beginning of the Gothic's revision of the sublime, he argues that Walpole's subversion of neoclassical literary properties resides in his unashamed use of supernatural props such as the gigantic knight's helmet and the bleeding statues. But according to Morris, Walpole's joyful salvage of Gothic props is only paralleled by his 'figures of speech long associated with the sublime style'.[36] He transforms these into a narrative principle.

For Morris, then, the Gothic sublime is not a series of recognizable visual stimuli – what he questionably views as the foundation of the Burkean sublime – but a narrative form based on repetition. Morris identifies exaggeration and repetition as the two predominant figures of speech in *Otranto*, arguing that the only type of discourse that the novel lacks is, in fact, ordinary speech. Exaggeration, for Morris, lies in the excesses of villainy and innocence that the novel displays, and repetition is located in the 'strange patterns of desire revealed in this family drama', figures of speech which are constantly repeated, and actions which are repeated (such as the imprisonment of Theodore by Manfred three times).[37] For Morris, such repetitions become a 'narrative principle' which 'challenges the concept of a world where everything and everyone is unique'.[38] The uncanny structures of repetition in *Otranto* also govern the pairing of the characters, Matilda and Isabella, Duke Frederic and Manfred, and so forth. These 'mirror images', according to Morris, are suggestive of incest and become the 'new and often unspoken terror at the heart of Gothic sublimity'.[39] Thus terror, for Morris, comes to reside in the unspeakable of a Gothic text.

As Morris proceeds to argue, *The Castle of Otranto* never entirely resolves the threat of incest, even with the resolution of Isabella and

Theodore's marriage at the end of the novel. Incest threatens the entire social order of the novel, through the crumbling walls of Otranto to Manfred's ardent pursuit of his daughter-in-law Isabella. Thus, for Morris:

■ Gothic sublimity – by releasing into fiction images and desires long suppressed, deeply hidden, forced into silence – greatly intensifies the dangers of an uncontrollable release from restraint. Such dangers no doubt help to explain why censorship and swooning were amongst the most common social responses to Gothic texts. Terror was a liberating – hence dangerous – force. ... In its excessive violations of excess sense, Gothic sublimity demonstrates the possibilities of terror in opening the mind to its own hidden and irrational powers.[40] □

Morris invokes Freud's 1919 essay 'The Uncanny' where Freud explored the very familiarity of the source of our terrors (see Chapter Five for further explanation and exploration of this essay). 'The Uncanny' emphasizes the distinctions that Morris perceives between Burke's wild and alien sources of terror and the very familiarity of the tropes of incest and (as he later argues) death in *The Castle of Otranto*. The repetitional structure of the novel emphasizes the familiarity of the themes which invoke terror. For Morris, 'Repetition is the essential structure of the uncanny. Borrowing Freud's language, we might describe Gothic sublimity as drawing its deepest terrors from a return of the repressed.'[41]

Morris confines his argument to Walpole's *Otranto* and Burke's specific interpretation of the sublime, taking Walpole's romance as indicative of how the Gothic sublime both interacts with, and reacts against, the Burkean sublime. It is, of course, difficult to disagree with his conclusion that 'It is not Walpole's ghosts who inspire terror, but the ghosts we carry within us.'[42] But he does not explore the ways in which other eighteenth-century essayists, such as Aikin, Drake, Radcliffe and other Gothic novelists, engaged with Burke and tested his conclusions. To take two texts (Burke and Walpole) written within a decade of each other as symptomatic of Gothic sublimity is limited. Likewise, in his insistence upon Burke's visual prioritization, there is a neglect of Burke's qualifications on 'obscurity'.

None the less, 'Gothic Sublimity' is both innovative and significant because Morris demonstrates that discussions of sublimity should not be confined uniquely to a Burkean checklist of natural sources and physical effects. The essay moves the debate on the sublime and the Gothic towards the unnameable, invoking the psychoanalytic theories of Freud and Lacan. In so doing, it provides an alternative view of the sublime's relevance to the eighteenth century.

In *Gothic Writing 1750–1820: A Genealogy* (1993), Robert Miles agrees with Morris's narratological repositioning of the Gothic sublime, and extends this thesis. He begins by reinforcing the generic differences between three versions of the sublime: eighteenth-century, Gothic and Romantic:

> ■ The Gothic sublime, as Morris defines it, is self-evidently narrative, as the tag 'return of the repressed' makes clear, while focusing on vagaries of signification tends to narrow down discussion of the Romantic sublime to considerations of the vexed pursuit, in poetry, of the 'Romantic Image'. These generic lines will appear rational ones to draw if the focus is hermeneutic: we encounter distinctions between the eighteenth-century sublime, where meaning is relatively stable, the 'sublime' crises of Romantic poetry, where it is no longer so, and Gothic novels, where crises are primarily psychological.[43] □

However, Miles then identifies a problem with this taxonomy when considering Female Gothic novels such as Radcliffe's *The Italian* and Charlotte Dacre's *Zofloya*. Such texts, he argues, share characteristics of both the Gothic and the Romantic sublime. This occurs 'as the failure of the natural sublime, where scenery ceases, transcendentally, to signify. The Gothic and Romantic sublimes here are distinguished, less by difference and more by similarity.'[44] In turn, Miles argues, this leads to a binary tension that exists between the eighteenth-century sublime 'with its stable meanings' and the 'Gothic and Romantic sublimes with their moments of terrifying defamiliarity'.[45]

Miles uses the term the 'Female Gothic sublime' to suggest a form of the Gothic sublime that moves between the eighteenth-century Burkean and the narrative-driven sublime that Morris argues for. Focusing upon the doubling that occurs in Radcliffe's *The Mysteries of Udolpho*, Miles refers to the 'supernatural moments' of uncanny coincidence within the novel (the doubles of Emily St Aubert and Laurentini; St Aubert and Montoni). He argues that the contagion of superstition that permeates *Udolpho* revolves around the troubling of boundaries between these doubled characters. This invokes the Female Gothic sublime:

> ■ To focus exclusively on the eighteenth-century sublime in a Radcliffe text – the heroine dilated with the natural sublime – is to miss much. Conversely, to note Morris's Gothic sublime in Radcliffe is helpful, but it tends to ignore the discursive character of the uncanny moment on which it is based.
>
> The 'Female Gothic sublime' is necessary because it alerts us to a recurring, complex textual interaction, but this is not the same as saying it is generically fixed. On the contrary, as an enabling structure the female Gothic sublime produces meaning in the manner of all complex

interactions between culture and literary form where power is at issue. The female Gothic sublime begins with discontents inherent in a uniformly defined subjectivity, one written into the sublime: the female Gothic explores, rather than resolves, these discontents. It would be wrong to say that the power inherent in the nexus of patriarchal values surrounding the sublime is deliberately and habitually subverted in the female Gothic. It is rather that, in the dialogical environment of the novel naming alone has a subversive potential. Radcliffe does not simply name, nor does she simply subvert. The tension between an orthodox representation of the 'female' subject (the eighteenth-century sublime) and a heterodox one (visible in the textual instabilities produced by the contagion of superstition) resulted in the expression of a more complex 'female' subjectivity than was otherwise envisaged, or was otherwise possible to envisage; and it was this that challenged.[46] ☐

Thus Miles argues that in the fiction of Radcliffe in particular, the hesitancies explored above, over whether the sublime invoked is a natural Burkean eighteenth-century sublime or a more complex narratological sublimity are, if not intended, then certainly manifest expressions of the tensions in female subjectivity. The irreconcilable differences between the two forms of sublime demonstrate if anything that the language of the sublime cannot be regulated or controlled. Its ghostly resurfacing in unexpected places is testament to the Gothic's troubling of boundaries and discourse.

In *Gothic Writing*, Miles uses a specific theoretical model built upon the notion of genealogy proffered by the French thinker Michel Foucault (1926–84) in order to demonstrate the plural vibrancy of the Gothic. In *The Gothic Sublime* (1994), Vijay Mishra takes a more specifically postmodern approach to his subject. Essentially, Mishra proposes a departure from historical theories of the sublime (such as Edmund Burke's eighteenth-century account) in favour of a more linguistically directed analysis of how the Gothic sublime exceeds language. Like Morris, Mishra advocates a radical break from the original eighteenth-century connection between terror and the sublime:

■ To shift from Gothic terror (a critical dominant for so long) to the Gothic sublime means that we can intervene into the Gothic through a much more pervasive and contradictory aesthetic. In other words, we now break the boundaries of the Gothic by using it to challenge the received wisdom of the sublime itself. The bold claim that we would want to make is that no sublime, not even the Gothic sublime, is pure in terms of either discursivity or phenomenality. All sublimes are contaminated, though some sublimes are less contaminated (but equally contaminable) than others. Our working definition would then take some such form as the following. The Gothic sublime is not a definitive form in its own right; it is a symbolic structure, historically determined though not rigidly constrained by the dawn of capitalism, around which a host of other sublimes intersect. The Gothic tropes the sublime as the unthinkable, and the unspeakable, always making it, the sublime, and its basic forms (the rhetorical and the natural) both incommensurable with each other and in excess of language. The phantasmagoria of the Gothic sublime, as the projection of a psychic terror, finally leads to the unpresentability of death itself. It is not what the Gothic sublime is that is crucial, it is what it effects that is its essence.[47] □

Mishra's enthusiastic vision of the Gothic sublime here (like Miles's category of the Female Gothic sublime) repositions the Gothic sublime as a crossroads through which all other versions of the sublime (the natural and the narratological) must pass. The Gothic sublime thus becomes something that remains in the imagination as a constant presence, inexpressible, seeking to haunt alternative representations of reality.

By challenging the certainties of representation, the Gothic sublime continues to challenge the essence of representability. Perhaps, after all, Vijay Mishra's account here is not so far removed from Radcliffe's own theorization of terror in 'On the Supernatural in Poetry'. On the value of obscurity, Mr. W. challenges his interlocutor, 'Now, if obscurity has so much effect on fiction, what must it have in real life, when to ascertain the object of our terror, is frequently to acquire the means of escaping it.' For Radcliffe, terror and its attendant pre-requisite obscurity awaken the imagination and enable it to transcend the petty fears that imprison it. It *effects* change just as much as Mishra's more sophisticated version of the Gothic sublime.

The critical explorations of sublimity and obscurity that we have considered in this chapter, from both contemporary eighteenth-century sources and present-day accounts, agree on one thing. Terror is an emotion that stimulates the imaginative faculties through its very association with the unknown. It is somewhat surprising, then, to discover that during the 1790s, across the English Channel in France, terror acquired both a pronoun and a capital letter – 'The Terror' – in order to signify the regime of fear created during the French Revolution. As the following chapter demonstrates, Edmund Burke's denigration of that revolutionary 'Terror' assumed Gothic overtones that would unite the political debate on the Revolution in Britain with the literary form of terror, the Gothic romance.

# CHAPTER THREE

# 'our hearths, our sepulchres':
# the Gothic and the French Revolution

But when [St Ursula] related the inhuman murder of Agnes, the indignation of the Mob was so audibly testified, that it was scarcely possible to hear the conclusion. The confusion increased with every moment: At length a multitude of voices exclaimed, that the Prioress should be given up to their fury. To this Don Ramirez refused to consent positively. Even Lorenzo bade the People remember, that She had undergone no trial, and advised them to leave her punishment to the Inquisition. All representations were fruitless: The disturbance grew still more violent, and the Populace more exasperated. In vain did Ramirez attempt to convey his Prisoner out of the Throng. Wherever He turned, a band of rioters barred his passage, and demanded her being delivered over to them more loudly than before. Ramirez ordered his Attendants to cut their way through the multitude: Oppressed by numbers, it was impossible for them to draw their swords. He threatened the Mob with the vengeance of the Inquisition: But in this moment of popular phrenzy even this dreadful name had lost its effect. ... They forced a passage through the Guards who protected their destined Victim, dragged her from her shelter, and proceeded to take upon her a most summary and cruel vengeance. Wild with terror, and scarcely knowing what She said, the wretched Woman shrieked for a moment's mercy: She protested that She was innocent of the death of Agnes, and could clear herself from the suspicion beyond the power of doubt. The Rioters heeded nothing but the gratification of their barbarous vengeance. They refused to listen to her: They showed her every sort of insult, loaded her with mud and filth, and called her by the most opprobrious appellations. They tore her one from another, and each new Tormentor was more savage than the former. They stifled with howls and execrations her shrill cries for mercy; and dragged her through the Streets, spurning her, trampling her, and treating her with every species of cruelty which hate or vindictive fury could invent.

(Matthew Lewis, *The Monk* (1796), ed. Howard Anderson, Oxford: Oxford University Press, 1980, pp. 355–6)

## Gothic receptions and perceptions: Edmund Burke and Mary Wollstonecraft

As we have already seen in both Chapters One and Two, Gothic fiction was often referred to in its heyday as 'Terrorist Writing'. In Chapter Two we explored the links of terror with eighteenth-century theories of the sublime. However, as 'The Terrorist System of Novel Writing' cited in Chapter One suggests, the term 'terrorism' was also equated with the emergent events of the French Revolution in the 1790s.[1] In 'The Terrorist System of Novel Writing', the anonymous 'Jacobin Novelist' specifically linked the rise of the Gothic romance with the rise of the tyrannical and over-reaching Robespierre, who, by the late 1790s, had become infamous for his 'reign of terror' in Paris. The letter complained: 'just at the time when we were threatened with a stagnation of fancy, arose Maximilian [sic] Robespierre, with his system of terror, and taught our novelists that *fear* is the only passion they ought to cultivate, that to frighten and instruct were one and the same thing ...'.[2] 'Terror' as an aesthetic Burkean concept (as explored in Chapter Two) was summarily stripped of its intellectual credentials in relation to Gothic fiction, and became a synecdoche – a part standing for the whole – for a more specifically threatening literary movement. This literary revolution was compared unflatteringly with the violent events of the French Revolution in the late 1790s.

A brief contextualization of the French Revolution may prove helpful here. While mutual suspicion between Britain and France had been rising since the Seven Years War (1756–63), the events of the Revolution in France crystallized British hostility towards the French in many conservative quarters. The Revolution is often dated from the fall of the Parisian prison the Bastille in 1789. Thereafter, events quickly succeeded one another, and in 1793 the French King, Louis XVI, was beheaded. After this, France was run by a Committee of Public Safety and the most eloquent of its twelve members, Maximilien Robespierre, became widely associated with the 'reign of Terror' referred to in 'The Terrorist System of Novel Writing'. Political paranoia created a rise in mob violence and executions became widespread. The ideals of *liberté, égalité* and *fraternité* that inaugurated the French Revolution were swiftly undermined by this 'Terror'. By 1799 the country was in such chaos that Napoleon Bonaparte was made Consul in France. His appointment formally marked the conclusion to the French Revolution.

The decade of the 1790s, then, was a time of intense political turmoil across the Channel. This turmoil swiftly invaded Britain with the detractors and supporters of the French Revolution in Britain launching their own war of words. The critic, essayist and journalist William

Hazlitt (1778–1830), for one, remarked of the political unrest in Britain that 'Our pens and our swords have been alike drawn' in defence of the King (George III) and his government, and that 'the manufacture of newspapers and parliamentary speeches, have exceeded all former example'.[3] The intense political debate generated by 'the supposed tottering state of all old structures at the time', Hazlitt then speculated, no doubt contributed to the universal interest in Ann Radcliffe's fiction.[4] Again, a strong link was forged between the revolutionary events in France and the rise of the Gothic romance in the 1790s.

Of particular note in the political debates upon the French Revolution was the exchange that occurred between the MP Edmund Burke (the same who wrote the *Philosophical Enquiry* that we examined in the previous chapter), who deplored the events of the Revolution, and the novelist, essayist and educational writer Mary Wollstonecraft (1759–97), who (initially, at least) supported the principles of the French Revolution. What is of particular interest in their political debate is the peculiarly 'Gothic' language used by Edmund Burke and then critiqued by Wollstonecraft. The timing of this war of ideas and words in 1790 suggests that this particular political row may well have influenced the continued proliferation of the Gothic romance in the 1790s.[5]

Burke published the *Reflections on the Revolution in France, and on the proceedings in certain societies in London relative to that event* in the form of an open letter in 1790.[6] He used his letter to condemn the events of the French Revolution and attack the warm reception given them by some of his peers. In particular, Burke criticized a sermon by Dr Richard Price (1723–91), delivered as the 'Discourse on the Love of our Country' at the Old Jewry on 4 November 1789. There, Price had given thanks for the spread of democracy which the events of the French Revolution promised at that time. In the *Reflections*, Burke recast Price's sermon as a devious and dangerous recipe, of which 'the revolution in France is the grand ingredient in the cauldron'.[7] 'For my part,' said Burke, 'I looked on that sermon as the public declaration of a man much connected with literary caballers, and intriguing philosophers; with political theologians, and theological politicians, both at home and abroad.'[8] Burke's rendition of 'literary caballers', 'political theologians' and so forth conveys his horror at what he perceives as the topsy-turviness engendered by the Revolution. For Burke, literary men and women should remain uncontaminated by 'cabal', and theologians like Price should not meddle in politics. Literature, politics and theology should remain discrete enterprises, a surprising volte-face from the aspirant lawyer and politician who had written the *Philosophical Enquiry into the Sublime and Beautiful* in 1756.[9]

In one section, Burke curiously refers to the Revolution as 'this monstrous tragic-comic scene'. Such an epithet, which mingles the dramatic with the melodramatic, the barbaric with the performative, in many ways describes the Gothic genre itself, with its blend of tragedy, comedy and monstrosity. Burke then goes on to connect the liberties offered by the English constitution with an *'entailed inheritance* derived to us from our forefathers' and 'transmitted to our posterity'.[10] Thus he ties the present-day liberties of Britain irrevocably to its past in a particularly Gothic manner:

> ■ A spirit of innovation is generally the result of a selfish temper and confined views. People will not look forward to posterity, who never look backward to their ancestors. Besides, the people of England well know, that the idea of inheritance furnishes a sure principle of conservation, and a sure principle of transmission; without at all excluding a principle of improvement. It leaves acquisition free; but it secures what it acquires. Whatever advantages are obtained by a state proceeding on these maxims, are locked fast as in a sort of family settlement; grasped as in a kind of mortmain for ever. By a constitutional policy, working after the pattern of nature, we receive, we hold, we transmit our government and our privileges, in the same manner in which we enjoy and transmit our property and our lives. The institutions of policy, the goods of fortune, the gifts of Providence, are handed down, to us and from us, in the same course and order. Our political system is placed in a just corre-spondence and symmetry with the order of the world, and with the mode of existence decreed to a permanent body composed of transitory parts; wherein, by the disposition of a stupendous wisdom, moulding together the great mysterious incorporation of the human race, the whole at one time, is never old, or middle-aged, or young, but in a condition of unchangeable constancy, moves on through the varied tenour of per-petual decay, fall, renovation, and progression. Thus, by preserving the method of nature in the conduct of the state, in what we improve we are never wholly new; in what we retain we are never wholly obsolete. By adhering in the manner and on those principles to our forefathers, we are guided not by the superstition of antiquaries, but by the spirit of philo-sophic analogy. In this choice of inheritance we have given to our frame of polity the image of a relation in blood; binding up the constitution of our country with our dearest domestic ties; adopting our fundamental laws into the bosom of family affections; keeping inseparable, and cherishing with the warmth of all their combined and mutually reflected charities, our state, our hearths, our sepulchres, and our altars.[11] □

Here, Burke reflects upon Britain's achievements, and argues that the principle of 'entailed inheritance' is the glue of British society. He argues for a society that is beholden to its ancestors, and is content to respect its past rather than embrace the future. But Burke's language sends a tremor down the spine. At the conclusion to this particular passage, he envisions a Britain which combines the social (state), the domestic (hearths) with death (sepulchres) and religion (altars). The overarching thrust of this comparison is towards a peculiarly Gothic vision of Britain, populated by tombs and churches. Likewise, further up in this passage, Burke envisages Britain's inheritance 'grasped as in a kind of mortmain for ever'. Burke views 'mortmain', a legal term which literally translates as a 'dead hand' and which in the eighteenth century guaranteed entailed inheritances, as a positive force, and yet his imagery suggests otherwise: 'mortmain' embraces Britain in a suffocating grasp.

Mary Wollstonecraft identified the peculiarly Gothic thrust of Burke's critique immediately. In her 'Letter to the right honourable Edmund Burke', published as *A Vindication of the Rights of Men* (1790), Wollstonecraft defends the events in France and attacks Burke's conservative position and the language that he deploys to convey it. Responding in particular to his Gothic rendition of 'entailed inheritance' Wollstonecraft argues:

> ■ I perceive, from the whole tenor of your Reflections, that you have a mortal antipathy to reason; but, if there is anything like argument, or first principles, in your wild declamation, behold the result: – that we are to reverence the rust of antiquity, and term the unnatural customs, which ignorance and mistaken self-interest have consolidated, the sage fruit of experience: and that if we do discover some errors, our *feelings* should lead us to excuse, with blind love, or unprincipled filial affection, the venerable vestiges of ancient days. These are gothic notions of beauty – the ivy is beautiful, but, when it insidiously destroys the trunk from which it receives support, who would not grub it up?[12] ☐

In the very opening pages of her response to Burke, Wollstonecraft views the illogic of Burke's hereditary argument in relation to 'gothic notions of beauty'. Thus, Gothic as an aesthetic is immediately pitched against progress and reason. Wollstonecraft then proceeds to juxtapose the new constitutional Assembly of France against Burke's entrenchment in the past:

> ■ But, in settling a constitution that involved the happiness of millions, that stretch beyond the computation of science, it was, perhaps, necessary for the Assembly to have a higher model in view than the *imagined* virtues of their forefathers; and wise to deduce their respect for themselves from the only legitimate source, respect for justice. Why was it a duty to repair an ancient castle, built in barbarous ages, of Gothic materials? Why were the legislators obliged to rake amongst heterogeneous ruins; to rebuild old walls, whose foundations could scarcely be explored, when a simple structure might be raised on the foundation of experience, the only valuable inheritance our forefathers could bequeath?[13] ☐

The Gothic castle here is pitted against the new rational materials that have been used to create the French Assembly. For Wollstonecraft, ancient ruins should remain unrepaired and unreconstructed because it is difficult to discern the bases of their foundations. Her metaphorizing of the Gothic castle is comparable to the opening scene in Radcliffe's contemporaneous novel *A Sicilian Romance*, which we examined in the previous chapter. There, if we recall, the unnamed narrator contemplates the ruins of the castle of Mazzini on the shores of Northern Sicily. He walks 'over the loose fragments of stone' and recalls 'the times when these walls stood proudly in their original splendour'.[14] Crucially, however, these recollections do not serve to venerate the past, but to execrate the luxury and vice exhibited during the castle's heyday. The rhetoric employed by Wollstonecraft here has a remarkably similar effect: she can admire the 'Gothic beauty' of the past, but she cannot regret its passing.

In his *Reflections*, Burke almost raised Marie Antoinette to the level of a deity, 'glittering like the morning-star, full of life, and splendour, and joy'.[15] Lamenting the Queen's lack of champions to defend her from insult, Burke then mourned that 'the age of chivalry is gone'.[16] In the *Vindication of the Rights of Men*, Wollstonecraft's attack on this particular angle of Burke's letter was brutal and unambiguous:

■ What were the outrages of a day to these continual miseries? Let these sorrows hide their diminished head before the tremendous mountain of woe that thus defaces our globe! Man preys on man; and you mourn for the idle tapestry that decorated a gothic pile, and the dronish bell that summoned the fat priest to prayer. You mourn for the empty pageant of a name, when slavery flaps her wing, and the sick heart retires to die in lonely wilds, far from the abodes of men. Did the pangs you felt for insulted nobility, the anguish that rent your heart when the gorgeous robes were torn off the idol human weakness had set up, deserve to be compared with the long-drawn sigh of melancholy reflection, when misery and vice are thus seen to haunt our steps, and swim on the top of every cheering prospect? Why is our fancy to be appalled by terrific perspectives of a hell beyond the grave? – Hell stalks abroad; – the lash resounds on the slave's naked sides; and the sick wretch, who can no longer earn the sour bread of unremitting labour, steals to a ditch to bid the world a long good night – or, neglected in some ostentatious hospital, breathes his last amidst the laugh of mercenary attendants.[17] □

Here, Wollstonecraft attacks Burke's indulgent, melodramatic and sentimental eulogy of the Queen of France. She invokes images that we now associate with the classic Gothic romances of Radcliffe and Lewis – the 'idle tapestry', the 'gothic pile' and the 'fat priest'. Significantly, however, Wollstonecraft does so prior to the publication of Radcliffe's most famous novels, and Lewis's *The Monk*.

The controversy over the French Revolution, explored here through the works of Wollstonecraft and Burke, inevitably had an impact upon how the Gothic novel was received and viewed at the time. In the prose of Mary Wollstonecraft, 'Gothic' became a derogatory epithet to describe Burke's regressive conservatism. As Robert Miles notes in 'The 1790s: the Effulgence of Gothic' (2002), Wollstonecraft's demonization of 'Gothic' in response to Burke was surprising and innovative:

■ Prior to the French Revolution, for any of those subscribing to Whiggism in its many varieties, 'Gothic' possessed a positive rather than negative political valence. It was a common belief among Whigs and radicals alike that the English Parliament traced its origins to an ancient, or Gothic, constitution brought to England by the Saxons. ... Chivalry, in turn, was considered to be the cultural expression of Saxon manners, just as the Witangemot, or parliament, was its political one. Burke's high-profile ideological capture of chivalry and the widespread radical condemnation of it fundamentally transformed the semantic field of the word *Gothic*.[18] □

Miles views the exchange between Burke and Wollstonecraft as a turning point in the history of the term 'Gothic'. Inevitably, as he also suggests, Burke and Wollstonecraft's trading of insults had an impact upon the subsequent reception and consumption of Gothic romance in the 1790s.

By way of illustrating how this political argument affected the reception of the Gothic, we can look again at T. J. Mathias's *The Pursuits of Literature*, which we examined in Chapter One. In the first dialogue (1794), Mathias forged a connection between the Gothic romance's ability to rouse passion and fervour, and the influence of revolutionary zeal from France, arguing that 'our girls' heads turn wild with impossible adventures, and now and then are tainted with democracy'.[19] Mathias's critical trend became widespread. As we have already noted, the critical conjunction of the Gothic with the French Revolution was satirically remarked upon in the open letters 'Terrorist Novel Writing' and 'The Terrorist System of Novel Writing'.[20] To a significant extent, the hostile reaction in the British periodical press to the Gothic genre was created by Wollstonecraft's radical attack upon Burke's conservative use of Gothic imagery. Paradoxically, however, many of the attacks on the Gothic romance also issued from the conservative spectrum of the periodical press, which with Burke, expressed anxiety over events in France. The critical reception of the Gothic in the 1790s demonstrates that the Gothic as a recognizable genre was forged in the crucible of the French Revolution. In spite of its existence well before the 1790s, Wollstonecraft's disdainful recognition of the Gothic discourse at work in Burke's *Reflections* created the circumstances for the cementing of the Gothic romance with the French Revolution during the Romantic era.

## Revolution within the Gothic

One of the first critical writers to speculate upon the reasons for the Gothic romance's seeming engagement with the events of the French Revolution was a Frenchman himself, the Marquis de Sade (1740–1814). A former inmate of the Bastille, in 1800 de Sade wrote a critical essay entitled 'Ideas on the Novel' ('Idée sur les romans'). Speaking of the audacity of the 1790s, he speculated in the essay on whether the eighteenth-century man was exactly the same as the eleventh-century man in terms of passions, foolhardiness and bravery. De Sade then proceeded to analyse the Gothic romance's contributions to this debate:

■ Perhaps it is here that we should analyse these new novels in which sorcery and phantasmagoria constitute almost their entire merit, by placing at their head *The Monk*, superior in all respects to the bizarre flights of Mrs. Radcliffe's imagination. But this dissertation would be too long; let us agree that this style, whatever may be said about it, is undoubtedly not without merit. It was the inevitable fruit of the revolutionary shocks felt by the whole of Europe. For one who knew all the miseries with which the wicked can afflict humanity the novel became as difficult to create as it was monotonous to read. There was not a single individual who had not experienced more misfortune in four or five years than the most famous novelist in literature could paint in a century. It was therefore necessary to call Hell to one's aid in order to draw up a title to our interest and to find in the country of chimeras that which we are only too easily acquainted with when we scan the history of man alone in this age of iron.[21] □

De Sade's preference for Lewis's *The Monk* over Radcliffe's fiction is not as significant as his legitimation of the Gothic romance's engagement with the supernatural. He argues that the modern romance's recourse to the supernatural was not only justified, but also 'inevitable' because of the 'revolutionary shocks felt by the whole of Europe'. De Sade claims that during this 'age of iron', the reading population required more violent shocks because of the everyday horrors which confronted them in newspapers.

In *The Literature of Terror* (2 vols, 1996) David Punter identifies Radcliffe's and Lewis's fiction in 'The classic Gothic novels' as the epitome of the Revolutionary themes that the Gothic exhibits. He makes a good point about the 1790s Gothic novel's stylistic reflection of political turmoil, arguing that 'Within the Gothic we can find a very intense, if displaced, engagement with political and social problems, the difficulty of negotiating these problems being precisely reflected in the Gothic's central stylistic conventions.'[22] In *The Rise of the Gothic Novel* (1995) Maggie Kilgour goes further by relating the anxiety surrounding the French Revolution to Britain's anxiety about the seventeenth-century English Civil War (1642–51) and Glorious Revolution (1688) – the overthrow of James II (1633–1701) of England and his replacement by his daughter Mary (1662–94) and her husband William III (1650–1702), better known as 'William of Orange'. Kilgour boldly (and rightly, I think) claims that the Gothic as a genre might have died out before its generic recognition were it not for the political turmoil of the 1790s:

■ As a literary species it certainly looked at first like one which, like poor Conrad [in *The Castle of Otranto*], was nipped in the bud; with few exceptions, notably Clara Reeve who claimed Walpole as her rightful, if somewhat erring, literary father, the gothic looked as though it rose and fell at the same time. Despite its engagement of contemporary issues, it might have been an aesthetic dead end, a one-shot eccentric mutation on the literary evolutionary line, if the terrifying events of the 1790s had not made it an appropriate vehicle for embodying relevant political and aesthetic questions. While the nature of the past, and its relation to the present, was debated throughout the eighteenth century, it gained new life with the French Revolution, as the Terror proved fertile for a literature of terror. In an England obsessed with the question of parliamentary reform and agitation for social changes, the abrupt and total change that occurred in France seemed both exhilarating and terrifying, and to require a complete rethinking of the basis of all systems of order. This was partially because this spectacle, as well as raising the danger of contamination from abroad, raised again and more pressingly the spectre of its own past: the Civil War and Glorious Revolution. The gothic displaced anxieties at home onto places geographically and temporally remote, at the very time that, inversely, the British were reading the Revolution of 1789 through the Revolution of 1688, understanding the foreign present in terms of the domestic past.[23] □

For Kilgour, then, the Gothic romance's displacement of domestic anxieties onto a remote Catholic continent where unrest was fomented by political intrigue acts as both therapy and challenge to the political status quo at home.

We can apply Kilgour's argument regarding temporal and locational displacement to the majority of (but not all) Gothic romances in the 1790s.[24] The opening to Matthew Lewis's *The Monk* (1796) offers a particularly apposite metaphor for the consideration of this. *The Monk* begins in the Church of the Capuchins in Madrid, where a congregation assembles for a sermon to be preached by the famously austere monk Ambrosio. The audience's reasons for attending are described as 'foreign to the ostensible motive'.[25] The church congregation can be read as representative of the range of religious, political and sovereign anxieties freighted onto the Gothic romance's remote location. The external, 'ostensible' generic conventions of the Gothic – the persecuted heroines, evil monks and ruined abbeys – become detectable signifiers for a range of other motives.

In his 1983 monograph *Representations of Revolution*, Ronald Paulson goes so far as to equate particular Gothic tropes with particular revolutionary events. Like Punter, Paulson addresses the 'classic' Gothics of Radcliffe and Lewis in order to argue that:

■ The Gothic did in fact serve as a metaphor with which some contemporaries in England tried to understand what was happening across the channel in the 1790s. The first Revolutionary emblem was the castle-prison, the Bastille and its destruction by an angry mob, which was fitted by the English into the model of the Gordon Riots.[26] But if one way of dealing with the Revolution (in its earliest stages) was to see the castle-prison through the eyes of a sensitive young girl who responds to terror in the form of forced marriage and stolen property, another was to see it through the case history of her threatening oppressor, Horace Walpole's Manfred or M. G. Lewis's Ambrosio. ... In Lewis's *The Monk* (1795)[27] the two striking phenomena dramatized are first the explosion – the bursting out of his bonds – of a repressed monk imprisoned from earliest childhood in a monastery, with the havoc wreaked by his self-liberation on the Church and his own family, who were indirectly (through the father) responsible for his being immured; and second, the bloodthirsty mob that lynches – literally grinds into a bloody pulp – the wicked prioress who has murdered those of her nuns who succumb to sexual temptation (and who represents the Church that locked away Ambrosio). Both are cases of justification followed by horrible excess. Ambrosio deserves to break out and the mob is justified in punishing the evil prioress, but Ambrosio's liberty leads him to the shattering of his vow of celibacy, to repression, murder, and rape not unlike the ecclesiastical compulsion against which he was reacting; the mob not only destroys the prioress but ... the whole community and the convent itself.[28] □

While Ronald Paulson views the storming of the Bastille in Paris in 1789 as the central metaphor used in Gothic romance to describe scenes of tyranny and mob violence, André Parreaux, on the other hand, suggests that the destruction of the convent in *The Monk* offers 'an echo of the French September Massacres' of 1792.[29] Both interpretations refer to the section of Lewis's *The Monk* which I have chosen as the epigraph for this chapter, the moment towards the end of the novel where the 'mob' destroys the tyrannical Prioress of St Clare.

The destruction of the Prioress and her convent in *The Monk* has been a much-discussed emblem of the French revolutionary crowds. Lewis's specific repetition in this passage of 'Mob' and 'popular phrenzy' is so marked that it suggests a strong degree of discomfort with this dark prototype of revolutionary democracy. The destruction of the Prioress is so visceral that it is suggestive of the subconscious, irrational violence of the mob. Lorenzo's rational and measured pleas to the mob for justice and fair trials fall on deaf ears as the 'populace' moves towards the Prioress with a collective will. Critics make much of the fact that Lewis's residence in Paris in 1791 made him a direct witness of revolutionary events. As Markman Ellis notes in *The History of Gothic Fiction* (2000), Lewis's 'view of these events is that of a loyal Briton, to some extent distanced from, and critical of, the unfolding events'.[30] He qualifies this, however, by adding that 'Lewis was not simply writing an allegory of revolution, nor propaganda for one of its factions' and that this 'engagement with the revolution might better be understood at the level of language and tone in the deployment of revolutionary symbols'.[31]

In the earlier *Representations of Revolution*, Ronald Paulson also refrains from imputing political commentary to any of the Gothic novelists under discussion: 'I do not mean to suggest that Ann Radcliffe or "Monk" Lewis was producing propaganda either for or against the French Revolution.'[32] Kilgour, Paulson, Ellis and Miles are all careful to point out that 'the fad for Gothic romances predates the French Revolution, or at any rate, the fall of the Bastille in July 1789'.[33] By way of caution against the Marquis de Sade's one-dimensional reading of the rise of the Gothic as a direct response to the French Revolution, Paulson reminds us of the earlier manifestation of Horace Walpole's *Castle of Otranto* in order to strengthen his argument about a specific development in 1790s fiction:

■ However, the Gothic had existed from the 1760s onward. The castle as prison was already implicit in *The Castle of Otranto* and Radcliffe's *Castles of Athlin and Dunbayne* (1789), and it may only have been this image and this frame of mind that made the fall of the Bastille an automatic image of revolution for French as well as English writers.[34] By the time *The Mysteries of Udolpho* appeared (1794), the castle, prison, tyrant, and sensitive young girl could no longer be presented naively; they had all been familiarized and sophisticated by events in France.

We are talking about a particular development in the 1790s, a specific plot that was either at hand for writers to use in the light of the French Revolution, or was in some sense projected by the Revolution and borrowed by writers who may or may not have wished to express anything specifically about the troubles in France. For example, Ambrosio has to be seen as a more sympathetic descendant of Walpole's Manfred, another conflation of rebelling son and tyrant father, but notably unconcerned with property. Although his pact with the devil introduces the Faustus story, he is not seeking the intellectual, spiritual, or specifically political power called for by the Enlightenment. He wants only sexual liberty and fulfilment. The Revolution, in Burke's as in Lewis's terms, exposed the reality under the intellectual and social knowledge of the Enlightenment to be unrestrained sexual 'knowledge'. Faustus's Mephistopheles becomes Ambrosio's Matilda. It is Ambrosio's desire for her that draws him in deeper and the unleashing of repressed sexual desires that shatters the barrier between the natural and supernatural worlds in The Monk. (In the subplot Raymond's passion for Agnes permits the supernatural to penetrate the human world, for it is as he waits to elope with her and consummate his desire that the Bleeding Nun appears to him in her place.)

This overtly sexual passion is what makes Ambrosio sympathetic in a way Manfred is not, even given Walpole's assurance to the reader that Manfred is otherwise a great soul. The Monk is about the act of liberation whereas The Castle of Otranto was about a man's attempt to hold together his crumbling estate and cheat others of their rightful inheritance. One is a fable of revolution, the other of the ancient regime.[35] □

Paulson's argument for the revolutionary potential of The Monk revolves around the prison, but it is less a specific prison (the Bastille) than the wider motif of imprisonment, confinement and immurement. Repressed sexual desires in The Monk unleash the supernatural, and serve as a large critique of the stern Catholicism depicted in the novel. This stern Catholicism, as both Paulson and Ellis point out, was itself challenged effectively during the Revolution in France by the curtailment of clerical powers. Here, Lewis's noted anti-clericalism is not as pointed as one might be led to suspect. Instead, Lewis chooses to critique the sexual ignorance and intolerance that Catholicism still espoused in the eighteenth century. Paulson is thus able to argue that:

■ The fact that Lewis does not stress the cruelty of the master, only the effect of repression and immurement, does not alter the general point that Ambrosio's revolt is understood in terms of the oppression against which he reacts. For if from one point of view he is the cruel hypocrite, matricide, and incestuous rapist, whose hypocrisy and aggression he had learned from his master the Church, from another he is still – at every step of his way – the helpless, passive, victim of his repressive environment, and this is allegorized in the story of his Satanic persecution.[36] □

Paulson also compares the mystery which surrounds sexual motivation for Ambrosio to the Gothic romance's stylistic engagement with 'unresolved mystery' where both protagonist and reader are enveloped in obscurity. The notion of obscurity brings us back to Burke's notion of 'terror' in his *Philosophical Enquiry*, and Paulson unites the Gothic's aesthetic engagement with terror to the Revolutionary terror:

■ Behind all this obscurity, however, is the elaborate plot, masterminded but slipping out of control, which involves the overthrow of a property owner. When the Revolution itself came, and as it progressed, it was precisely this inability to make out the events on a day-to-day basis, but with the suspicion of personal skulduggery beneath each new changing-hands of property, that made the gothic novel a roughly equivalent narrative form. Depending on what stage a spectator looked back from, he saw a different structure, but one increasingly colored on the dark side by the Terror. The standard features of the rebellion were the vast possibilities and the hopes it opened up, followed by delusions, dangerous and unforeseen contingencies, horrible consequences, and disillusionment. Behind all was a new sense of history, of what could or should happen in history, and what history was in fact about. From being about the kings, it became, in certain ways, about larger groups of subjects and their attempts to come to terms with, or create a new order from, the disorder consequent upon the overthrow of an old established order.[37] □

Paulson concludes this section of his argument by differentiating between Radcliffe and Lewis in terms of the victim position. Distinguishing between Radcliffe's 1794 *The Mysteries of Udolpho* and Lewis's 1796 *The Monk*, Paulson argues that 'If Radcliffe produces a fiction about a spectator of revolutionary activity who can be confused by her experience, whose response though virtuous is both ambivalent and liable to the temptation to misperceive, then Lewis's *The Monk* reproduces the exhilarating but ultimately depressing experience of the revolutionary himself.'[38]

## Revolutionary figures: *Caleb Williams* and the uses of romance

In addition to the classic 1790s Gothic novels by Radcliffe and Lewis that the Marquis de Sade first identified for praise in the genre, Paulson, Miles and Kilgour also discuss in their studies different generic examples of Gothic fiction in relation to the Revolution. All three explore William Godwin's 1794 novel *Caleb Williams, or Things as they are*. Godwin wrote this novel as a dramatization of his political thinking, from his 1793 political text *An Enquiry Concerning Political Justice*. His *Enquiry* was also written in part as a response to Burke's *Reflections on the Revolution in*

*France*, but it is through *Caleb Williams* that Godwin issues the most direct challenge to Burke's arguments on chivalry and inheritance.

Godwin effects this critique through a complex narrative of persecution and obsession. Caleb Williams, a working-class boy elevated by his employer Falkland to become a private secretary, aspires to become his master's confidant. When he gains his master Falkland's confidence, however, it is not through earned respect, but through discovering that Falkland has broken his own adherence to the chivalric code by stabbing his adversary Tyrrel in the back. In *Representations of Revolution*, Paulson justifies his introduction of the novel of reform, or the Jacobin novel, by correctly arguing that as a genre, it 'joins the Gothic in the representation of tyranny and revolution'. Under the generic heading of 'Jacobin Novel' he unites the fiction of William Godwin, Thomas Holcroft, Robert Bage, Elizabeth Inchbald and Charlotte Smith, but reserves most of his critical attention for Godwin's *Caleb Williams, or Things as they are*. Paulson compares the eponymous Caleb of Godwin's novel to Lewis's Ambrosio. For him, both are revolutionary figures because they attempt to end secrecy:

■ Caleb is, like Ambrosio, a Faustus figure who describes his 'crime' or 'offence' as 'a mistaken thirst of knowledge' (knowledge of his master's crime) but couches his obsessive quest in sexual terms. He feels a 'thrill' in his 'very vitals' when he approaches the secret, and Falkland responds by insisting that Caleb 'shall not watch my privacies with impunity' and threatening him with a pistol. ... When Caleb realizes that Falkland is a murderer, he says, 'My blood boiled within me' – as we are told that Ambrosio's 'blood boiled in his veins' when he looked upon Rosario–Matilda's bosom. 'I was conscious of a kind of rapture for which I could not account,' Caleb goes on. 'I was solemn, yet full of rapid emotion, burning with indignation and energy.' Based on Godwin's insight into the nature of the servant–master relationship for both parties, Caleb's almost sexual curiosity releases all the darker potentialities of Falkland's inner self and so lays Caleb open to both inhuman pursuit and persecution by his master and the corruption of his own nature.

If the *sexual* urge is implied, however, there is no Matilda, Marie Antoinette, or Sin present as its object. The object of desire – the invisible figure of Sin in the Satan–Death confrontation – is Falkland's box and its secret. Only because the chest is so precious to Falkland (in the manner of Bluebeard's locked closet) does it take on for Caleb the attributes of a sacred object.[39] □

Paulson's linkage of the sexual with the quest for knowledge is entirely apposite in relation to this novel. His later focus upon Bluebeard is in part derived from Godwin himself. In his preface to the later 'Standard

Novels Edition' issued by Bentley, Godwin himself traced his source
back to the Bluebeard of the French poet, polemicist and fairy-tale
writer Charles Perrault (1628–1703). With its representation of the
ferocious punishment endured by Bluebeard's wives for their transgressive curiosity, Perrault's tale could in fact be read as a dominating motif
behind many Gothic romances, particularly those of Radcliffe. Godwin
states in his 'Introduction':

■ I rather amused myself with tracing a certain similitude between the
story of Caleb Williams and the tale of Bluebeard, than derived any hints
from that admirable specimen of the terrific. Falkland was my Bluebeard,
who had perpetrated atrocious crimes, which if discovered, he might
expect to have all the world roused to revenge against him. Caleb
Williams was the wife, who in spite of warning, persisted in his attempts
to discover the forbidden secret; and when he had succeeded, struggled
as fruitlessly to escape the consequences, as the wife of Bluebeard in
washing the key of the ensanguined chamber, who, as often as she
cleared the stain of blood from the one side, found it showing itself with
frightful distinctness on the other.[40] □

Godwin himself draws attention to the representation of Falkland as the
*ancien régime* tyrant, while Caleb represents the revolutionary figure in
his attempt to challenge that tyrannical authority by discovering
Falkland's secret. In the novel, Caleb himself admits that 'I was desirous
of tracing the variety of effects which might be produced from given
causes. It was this that made me a sort of natural philosopher; I could
not rest till I had acquainted myself with the solutions that had been
invented for the phenomena of the universe.'[41] For Maggie Kilgour,
Caleb's curiosity, his desire to discover the *variety* of effects, comes from
Godwin's insight that 'self-scrutiny can make us free'.[42]

In 'The 1790s: the Effulgence of Gothic' Robert Miles explores
further the reasons why the decade which immediately followed the
French Revolution witnessed such a proliferation of the Gothic genre.
In this essay, Miles identifies 1794 as the 'pivotal year' in which the
romance structure which hitherto dominated the Gothic genre was
supplanted by what he calls 'Jacobin Gothic' through *Caleb Williams*.
Miles's use of 'Jacobin Gothic', similarly to Paulson and Kilgour, unites
the Jacobin and Gothic genres through Godwin's 1794 novel. He
strengthens the critical equation of the Burke and Falkland strand of the
novel by quoting from John Thelwall (1764–1834):

■ [Godwin's] underlying premise is neatly explained by John Thelwall,
one of the accused in Pitt's treason trials and a fellow radical. Thelwall

attacks Burke's *Thoughts on a Regicide Peace* (1793) from which he quotes:

> Are these the institutions which Mr B. wishes to support? ... Are these ... the regular and orderly fabrics of the ancient legitimate 'government of states' whose plans and materials were 'drawn from the old Germanic or Gothic customary' and of which those famous architects, 'the civilians, the jurists and the publicists' have given us such flattering draughts, ground plots, and elevations? If they are, away with your idle jargon of venerable antiquity ... they are Bastilles of intellect, which must be destroyed. They are insulting mausoleums of buried rights.[43]

Burke recurs to the venerable Whig belief in an ancient Gothic consti-tution as a means of providing intellectual support for the status quo, a position Thelwall attacks. To use another of Thelwall's metaphors, Burke's political rhetoric of Gothic customs 'forged' mental 'fetters,' which imprisoned the citizen, depriving individuals of their rights. What Thelwall is striving toward is a concept of ideology as false conscious-ness. The uncritical internalization of the mythology of national origin – of ancient constitutions and chivalric codes – constitutes a mental Bastille or feudal remnant, one that imprisons us, concealing our true identity and our rights. This identification of deference to the past as a mausoleum, a 'dead hand' that palsies the living, is represented in *Caleb Williams* as the chivalric code that binds Falkland. Caleb may be in flight from Falkland, but Falkland is himself entombed within his own mental bastille. Moreover, the theme and mode of narration implies that Caleb, too, is ideologically immured. The feudal castle that blights the present is thus not an object out there, but a state of mind that immaterially fet-ters its victims, burying them, and their rights, alive. Caleb's own lack of ideological freedom is symbolized by his obsessive desire to get into Falkland's ancient, iron chest, the physical symbol of Falkland's mental state. Caleb ought to endeavour to free himself from such a structure, not get into it.[44] □

Miles refers to Burke's use of the legal term 'mortmain', which we examined in the first section of this chapter. He takes Burke's image to its Gothic conclusion, arguing that the 'dead hand' that Burke invokes 'palsies the living', entombing them in a Bastille of their own making. For Miles, the 'mental fetters' in the end are shared between Falkland and Caleb. At both the thematic and narratological levels, Caleb's ambi-tion to look into Falkland's iron chest is testament to his own mental imprisonment. Here, the Gothic feudal castle of Walpole's, Radcliffe's and Reeve's romances has been displaced by a psychological feudal castle that is every bit as oppressive.

William Godwin's condemnation of what the subtitle of *Caleb Williams* calls 'Things as they are' is a strong response to Burke's

*Reflections on the Revolution in France.* The novel critiques Burke's use of Gothic imagery and chivalry and entailed inheritance in a manner similar to Mary Wollstonecraft's (who later became Godwin's wife) attack on Burke in *A Vindication of the Rights of Men.* As Edmund Burke feared, the Revolution in France created politicians of theologians, 'caballers' of literary writers and intriguers of philosophers.

However, Burke could not have anticipated that it was his own letter, *Reflections on the Revolution in France*, which would precipitate the Gothic engagement with the Revolution in France. The 'literature of terror' proliferated exponentially, owing to the political debate over the rights and wrongs of the French Revolution. As E. J. Clery argues in *The Rise of Supernatural Fiction: 1762–1800* (1995), 'the creeping democratisation of the republic of letters represented by the success of the popular novel was not unrelated to the threat of political democracy in the eyes of the British anti-Jacobins'.[45]

In its turn, the Gothic romance provided a new source of domestic anxiety in Britain. As we will explore in the following chapter, the Gothic genre's revolutionary displays of feudal castles, corrupt Catholicism, class mobility and angry mobs prompted its British critics to praise with renewed vigour Britain's Protestant and patriotic values. Chapter Four argues that in turn, this retrenchment influenced the subsequent portrayals of religion and nationalism in Gothic novels in Britain.

# CHAPTER FOUR

# 'The sanctuary is prophaned': Religion, Nationalism and the Gothic

> Partial features of the vast edifice she was approaching, appeared now and then between the trees; the tall west window of the cathedral with the spires that overtopped it; the narrow pointed roofs of the cloisters; angles of the insurmountable walls, which fenced the garden from the precipices below, and the dark portal leading into the chief court, each of these, seen at intervals beneath the bloom of cypress and spreading cedar, seemed as if menacing the unhappy Ellena with hints of future suffering.
>
> (Ann Radcliffe, *The Italian* (1797), ed. Robert Miles, London: Penguin, 2000, p. 77)

The Gothic genre's preoccupation with monasteries, convents, evil nuns, proud monks and the Inquisition has been noted and explored.[1] Critics have compared the labyrinthine nature of the cloisters and ruined monasteries to the element of mystery in which the Gothic's protagonists are shrouded, and the decaying ruins of abbeys and convents to the crumbling edifices of power portrayed in the novels.

Among the most prominent examples of this generic preoccupation is Matthew Lewis's *The Monk*, where the narrative of incest, rape, murder and religious punishment begins and concludes in the claustrophobic atmosphere of the Catholic Church. In the opening scene of the novel, set in the Church of the Capuchins in Madrid, the narrator adopts a deliberately directive tone with his readers as early as the second sentence:

■ Scarcely had the Abbey-Bell tolled for five minutes, and already was the Church of the Capuchins thronged with Auditors. Do not encourage the idea that the Crowd was assembled either from motives of piety or thirst of information. But very few were influenced by those reasons; and in a city where superstition reigns with such despotic sway as in Madrid, to seek for true devotion would be a fruitless attempt. The Audience now assembled in the Capuchin Church was collected by various causes, but all of them were foreign to the ostensible motive. The women came to show themselves, the Men to see the Women: Some were attracted by curiosity to hear an Orator so celebrated; Some came because they had no better means of employing their time till the play began; Some, from being assured that it would be impossible to find places in the Church; and one half of Madrid was brought thither by expecting to meet the other half.[2] □

The emphasis in this opening scene is upon spectacle, oscillating between seeing and being observed. The narrator warns his reader that 'to seek for true devotion' is fruitless; for the reader too, then, everything is laid upon display, and we are told that the superficiality of the scene does not conceal anything else. Discussing this scene, Robert Miles has argued in an essay entitled 'Europhobia: the Catholic other in Horace Walpole and Charles Maturin' (2002) that:

■ The Church is a site of magnificence rather than austerity, of display rather than of worship, and of sexual rather than religious pursuits. It is presided over by a power-mad monk, rather than an enlightened clergy; the society that clusters around him is disfigured by the extremes of class; and given the absence of a deeper understanding, by irreligion on the part of the rich, and superstition on the part of the poor. In short, it is a society that is worldly where it ought to be religious, and religious where it ought to be worldly.[3] □

Miles's comments here are borne out by the ensuing introduction of three of the novel's protagonists; the aristocratic Don Lorenzo and the impoverished Leonella with her niece Antonia. Wishing to create an impression upon the attractive but unbelievably naïve Antonia, Don Lorenzo tells Leonella and Antonia what he has heard of the eponymous monk's history:

■ 'He [Ambrosio] is now thirty years old, every hour of which period has been passed in study, total seclusion from the world, and mortification of the flesh. Till these last three weeks, when He was chosen superior of the society to which He belongs, He had never been on the outside of the Abbey-walls: Even now He never quits them except on Thursdays, when He delivers a discourse in this Cathedral which all Madrid assembles to hear. His knowledge is said to be the most profound, his eloquence the most persuasive. In the whole course of his life He has never been known to transgress a single rule of his order; The smallest stain is not to be

discovered upon his character; and He is reported to be so strict an observer of Chastity, that He knows not in what consists the difference of Man and Woman. The common People therefore esteem him to be a Saint.'
'Does that make a Saint?' enquired Antonia; 'Bless me! Then am I one.'[4] □

In his character summary, Lorenzo relies upon rumour and speculation, using such phrases as 'he has never been known' and 'He is reported'. His narration of Ambrosio's life is more indicative of the worldly spheres of gossip and rumour in which he moves as an aristocratic character, than of any spiritual devotion. By contrast, returning to Miles's point about lower-class characters, Antonia's incredulity in the light of Lorenzo's whispered hearsay immediately establishes her as a naïve and superstitious character with a laughably literal, superstitious interpretation of sainthood. The import of Don Lorenzo's report on Ambrosio is significant, however. Even at this early stage in the novel, a satirical stab is thrust at the equation of Catholic sainthood with sexual ignorance and infallibility.

*The Monk*'s critique of religion fostering ignorance is further strengthened by the parallel narrative of Agnes and Raymond's sexual transgression. Raymond's seduction of his beloved Agnes (within the boundaries of the convent garden) leads to her immurement in the convent's vaults. Agnes is left to die with her illegitimate child by the proud and unforgiving Prioress of St Clare, who only considers the reputation of her convent, and not the wellbeing of its inmates:

■ While she perused the letter, the Domina's countenance grew inflamed with passion. What! Such a crime committed in her Convent, and made known to Ambrosio, to the Idol of Madrid, to the Man whom she was most anxious to impress with the opinion of the strictness and regularity of her House! Words were inadequate to express her fury. She was silent, and darted upon the prostrate Nun looks of menace and malignity.[5] □

The stern brand of Catholicism that *The Monk* portrays is also to be found in some of Ann Radcliffe's fiction. Her second novel, *A Sicilian Romance*, depicts a debauched and unfeeling monastic order where the heroine Julia attempts to seek shelter, and both *The Mysteries of Udolpho* and *The Italian* contain criminal characters who seek protection from their crimes under the robes of various Catholic orders.

More famously in *The Italian*, the heroine Ellena di Rosalba is imprisoned in the convent of San Stefano and eloquently challenges another harsh and vindictive Abbess who acts as her gaoler.

■ 'The sanctuary is prophaned,' said Ellena, mildly, but with dignity, 'it is become a prison. It is only when the Superior ceases to respect the precepts of that holy religion, the precepts which teach her justice and benevolence, that she herself is no longer respected.'[6] ☐

The heroine Ellena's challenge to the Prioress focuses upon the latter's abrogation of the Christian duties of justice and benevolence. It is perhaps the most outspoken critique of any Radcliffean heroine, and it is a critique which is resumed when the hero Vivaldi is arrested and imprisoned by the Roman Inquisition.

Charles Maturin's Gothic novel *Melmoth the Wanderer* (1820) both unites and strengthens the critique of Catholicism which is present in Lewis and Radcliffe. Like Agnes in Lewis's *The Monk*, Monçada, one of the characters in *Melmoth*, is forced by his parents to take monastic orders in order to atone for their sins. His testimony alone expresses one of the most virulent condemnations of the superstitions and pride of Catholicism to be found in the Gothic genre. In a scene which takes its cue from the opening scene of *The Monk*, Monçada recounts with horror to Melmoth his protracted battle to extricate himself from the monastery where he has been placed, and the public fascination which his well-publicized case attracts:

■ 'This house was the first in Madrid, and the singular circumstance of the son of one of the highest families in Spain having entered it in early youth, – having protested against his vows in a few months, – having been accused of being in a compact with the infernal spirit a few weeks after, – the hope of a scene of exorcism, – the doubt of the success of my appeal, – the probable interference of the Inquisition, – the *possible* festival of an auto da fe, – had set the imagination of all Madrid on fire; and never did an audience long more for the drawing up of the curtain at a popular opera, than the religious and irreligious of Madrid did for the development of the scene which was acting at the convent of the Ex-Jesuits.'

'In Catholic countries, Sir, religion is the national drama; the priests are the principal performers, the populace the audience; and whether the piece concludes with a 'Don Giovanni' plunging in flames or the beatification of a saint, the applause and the enjoyment is the same.'[7] ☐

This scene from *Melmoth the Wanderer* develops the theatrical theme that haunts the portrayal of Catholicism in the opening of Lewis's *The Monk*, but here metaphors are replaced with concrete assertions, 'religion *is the* national drama; the priests *are* the principal performers'. Every possible source of terror in Catholicism is exploited here, with allusions to the Inquisition and autos-da-fé (the burning of a heretic, literally an 'act of faith'). This passage also specifically refers to the national drama of religion in 'Catholic countries'. Maturin's identification of countries with religions is important here, as *Melmoth the Wanderer* as well as many other examples of the genre are set very specifically in a Southern Catholic Europe (*The Monk* and *Melmoth the Wanderer* in Spain, and *The Italian*, of course, in Italy). These, and many other Gothic tableaux, exhibit Catholicism as a stern and unforgiving religion which can become despotic in the hands of tyranny.

In *The Popular Novel in England* (1932), J. M. S Tompkins notes the Gothic novel's Catholic depictions, initially dismissing the recurrence of the trope rather offhandedly, by noting, 'Even the Gothic Romances, which are full of unattached hermits in a state of contrition, make little more than a romantic background out of the organized Church, except where, to fill the role of villain, it becomes a tyranny.'[8] Further on in her account, however, she introduces a clearer distinction between the Protestant British reading audience and the Gothic's poorly informed depictions of Catholicism:

■ A ... wilful bias, this time in the direction of melodrama, is obvious when the story approaches a convent. The dealings of the literary men of Protestant England in the eighteenth century with the institutions of the Roman Catholic Church are a little disingenuous. They are very conscious of the picturesque attractions of convents, vows of celibacy, confession and penance; they are seduced by the emotional possibilities of the situations that can be based on these usages; but they seldom fail to make it quite clear that they regard the usages as superstitious and irrational, and, if they did, there was not wanting a critic to blame this 'attempt to gloss over the follies of popery, or to represent its absurdities as sacred.'[9] Thus Mrs. Radcliffe, having introduced a monk's tomb as a picturesque property in *The Romance of the Forest*, is careful to express through the mouth of Louis La Motte her real opinion of monasticism. 'Peace be to his soul,' soliloquizes the young man; 'but did he think a life of mere negative virtue deserves an eternal reward? Mistaken man! Reason, had you trusted its dictates, would have informed you, that the active virtues, the adherence to the golden rule, "Do as you would be done unto", could alone deserve the favour of a Deity, whose glory is benevolence.' [From *Theodosius and Constantia* [1711] by Joseph Addison (1672–1719) to *Death of Arabert, Monk of La Trappe* (1771) by [Edward] Jerningham [1727–1812]] the conflict of love and vows was a recognized source of pathos, and Mrs. Radcliffe seized on it in *A Sicilian Romance* when she made the nun Cornelia die at the high altar in her lover's presence, in 'a fine devotional glow.'[10] Mrs. Radcliffe's convent is one of those odd affairs, imagined by Gothic romancists, where monks and nuns in adjacent buildings are shepherded by an abbott. ... Ignorance enhanced the charm of this material. There were no convents in England, and though a certain number of English girls attended French convent-schools, where there were also to be found poor Englishwomen living cheaply as parlour-boarders, such information as they could supply did not seriously affect the readiness of the novel-reading public to believe that any extravagance could happen in such a setting;[11] moreover, to set against authentic accounts, such as [*Fray Gerundo de Campazos* (1758–68; translated 1772) by the Spanish Jesuit José Francisco de Isla (1706–81)], there were the secret violences divulged by Baculard d'Arnaud [François-Thomas-Marie de Baculard d'Arnaud (1718–1805), French author of many plays and novels] and Jean Gaspard Dubois-Fontenelle [(1737–1812) author of several significant fictions with an anti-clerical emphasis]. Out of two pictures, both hailing from Catholic countries, the Protestant public were bound to choose the more lurid, thus providing themselves not only with emotional excitement, but with a thrill of that warm complacency which always stole through a British bosom when meditating Continental tyrannies.[12] □

Tompkins's rendition of the British Protestant's appetite for Catholic superstition appears to follow the Marquis de Sade's assertion (discussed in Chapter Three) that for novelists who were aware of 'all the miseries with which the wicked can afflict humanity' it was 'necessary to call Hell to one's aid in order to draw up a title to our interest'.[13] She treats the Gothic's relentless fabrication of Catholic misdemeanour as an aesthetically sensationalist choice which was infinitely more satisfying to its Protestant readership than the realist memoirs of those who had experienced convent or monastic life.

In his 1960 study *Love and Death in the American Novel*, Leslie Fiedler also raises the issue of the anti-Catholic bias of the early Gothic romances. Similarly to Tompkins, he also ascribes this phenomenon to aesthetic sensationalism:

■ [The Gothic novelists'] attitude toward Catholicism is a case in point. Like most other classic forms of the novel, the gothic romance is Protestant in its ethos; indeed, it is the most blatantly anti-Catholic of all, projecting in its fables a consistent image of the Church as the Enemy; we have already noticed how standard and expected were the character of the depraved monk, the suborned Inquisitor, the malicious abbess. Yet the gothic imagination feeds on what its principles abhor, the ritual and glitter, the politics and pageantry of the Roman Church. The ideal of celibacy and its abuses particularly intrigue the more prurient gothic fictionists, as do the mysteries of the confessional, where for ages – into the ear of God knows what lustful priest – was whispered 'this secret sin, this untold tale', which they had made the subject of their art.[14] □

Fiedler locates the enduring Gothic fascination with Catholicism in the 'ritual and glitter' of the Catholic church, citing as one possible reason the enduring Protestant curiosity about Catholic celibacy and politics. In many respects he is right; the Prologue to Ann Radcliffe's *The Italian* performs precisely these roles with an English tourist being lured into the Catholic convent *Santa Maria del Pianto* by 'the magnificence of its portico'. It is the aesthetics of the building, then, that stimulates the curiosity of British Protestant readers and tourists alike, much as Fiedler argues. However, when in *The Italian* the unnamed English tourist discovers that this convent shelters an assassin, his appreciation of the aesthetic aspects of the convent dissipates swiftly:

■ When the party had viewed the different shrines and whatever had been judged worthy of observation, and were returning through an obscure aisle towards the portico, they perceived the person, who had appeared upon the steps, passing towards a confessional on the left, and, as he entered it, one of the party pointed him out to the friar, and enquired who he was; the friar turning to look after him, did not immediately reply, but, on the question being repeated, he inclined his head, as in a kind of obeisance, and calmly replied, 'He is an assassin.'

'An assassin!' exclaimed one of the Englishmen; 'an assassin and at liberty!'

An Italian gentleman, who was of the party, smiled at the astonishment of his friend.

'He has sought sanctuary here,' replied the friar; 'within these walls he may not be molested.'

'Do your altars, then, protect the murderer?' said the Englishman.

'He could find shelter nowhere else,' answered the friar meekly.

'This is astonishing!' said the Englishman; 'of what avail are your laws, if the most atrocious criminal may thus find shelter from them?'[15] □

It is true that this extract begins by demonstrating what Fiedler identifies as a certain type of Protestant pruriency for Catholic ornamentation and ritual, but this aesthetic appreciation is supplanted almost immediately by the Englishman's concern over the entanglement of the Catholic Church with Italian legal matters. The passage moves on to a pressing concern about the jurisdiction of the Catholic religion that maps quite specifically onto issues surrounding the French Revolution. Both Tompkins and Fiedler fail to account for this concern with political issues when they dismiss the Gothic novelists' engagement with Catholicism as a mere aesthetic issue. Yes, the Catholic settings do provide 'thrills' for the predominantly Protestant readership, but as we shall see in the remainder of this chapter, these settings function in more complex ways than this.

Despite evidence of the Gothic novel's obsession with Catholicism, then, there has been a tendency in earlier critical accounts to ascribe the recurrent religious motifs to sensationalist value alone. As we have seen with the opening of *The Italian*, such explanations can only partially account for the genre's religiously-fuelled plots, which almost always appear to devalue Catholicism in the face of Protestantism. Only recently Chris Baldick and Robert Mighall have noted in the history of twentieth-century Gothic criticism 'an embarrassed silence upon the matter of early Gothic fiction's anti-Catholicism'.[16] They trace this back to the two formative strands of twentieth-century Gothic criticism, one from the Surrealist André Breton (1896–1966), who celebrated Walpole's *Castle of Otranto* as a precursor of Surrealism, and the Gothic genre in general for its foregrounding of dream and fantasy.[17] The second critical influence, which grew in opposition to Breton's argument, comes from arguably the most well-read scholar of the Gothic, Montague Summers (1880–1948). As Baldick and Mighall explain, however, Summers's 1938 work *The Gothic Quest*, through his own stance resolutely opposed to Breton, offers an equally biased agenda:

■ With the arrival of a new Freudian agenda for Gothic criticism in the writings of Breton and his followers, however, the fears and phobias of Gothic fiction quickly became internalised as a primal psychomania, while the most enduring and formative ideological conflict of modern European history disappeared into the footnotes.

At the same time, the leading Gothicist in England, styling himself the Reverend Doctor Alphonsus Joseph-Mary Augustus Montague Summers, had, as a zealous Catholic, his own curious reasons for distracting attention away from the aggressive Protestantism of early Gothic writings. Convinced that the Gothic novels represented a nostalgically romantic 'revival' of the supernatural beliefs of the great Age of Faith, Summers insisted, against the anti-Catholic surrealists, that 'there is no true romanticism apart from Catholic influence and feeling' (Summers, 1938, 390). Had he ever attempted a study of William Blake [1757–1827], or had his history of Gothic fiction ever got as far as Maturin, Summers would have had extraordinary difficulties in maintaining such a position; and indeed his *Gothic Quest* goes through some remarkable contortions in denying the obvious.[18] □

This historicizing of Gothic criticism is useful in its identification of certain critical trends that have sprung from these two early sources. One, the psychologically-driven account that comes from Breton, is still a prevalent investigative tool in the Gothic (which will be discussed in Chapter Five). The second trend, from Montague Summers's own investment in Catholicism, has certainly led to a curious silence upon the genre's anti-Catholicism until recent decades. Baldick and Mighall's agenda in this particular essay is to reaffirm the anti-Catholic bias in early Gothic fiction and reassess the reasons for such critical silence. In order to do this they return to one of the Gothic's most famous contemporary critics, Sir Walter Scott. In Sir Walter Scott's 'Introduction' to a volume on Ann Radcliffe for *Ballantyne's Novelist's Library*, he specifically connects Radcliffe's choice of geographical location in Southern Europe with her exploration of Catholic superstition:

■ She has uniformly (except in her first effort) [Radcliffe's first novel, *The Castles of Athlin and Dunbayne*, published in 1789, was set in Scotland] selected for her place of action the South of Europe, where the human passions, like the weeds of the climate, are supposed to attain portentous growth under the fostering sun; which abounds with ruined monuments of antiquity, as well as the more massive remnants of the middle ages; and where feudal tyranny and Catholic superstition still continue to exercise their sway over the slave and bigot, and to indulge to the haughty lord, or more haughty priest, that sort of despotic power, the exercise of which seldom fails to deprave the heart, and disorder the judgment. These circumstances are skilfully selected, to give probability to events which could not, without great violation of truth, be represented as having taken place in England.[19] □

With acute perception, Scott identifies the attraction of the foreign Catholic locations of Radcliffe's fiction, linking the despotic power indulged by Catholicism with the corruption of the heart and judgement. And of course, as he argues, this could not be further from England. Tying Scott's argument in with the predominantly middle-class Protestant readership of Radcliffe's fiction, Baldick and Mighall argue that:

■ For Scott, the exotic distance employed by Radcliffe serves the interests of *probability* rather than fantasy; and far from being indifferent to setting, she 'skilfully selected' these locales in the interests of a supposed socio-political truth. This 'truth' is a culturally conditioned one, premised on chauvinism and sectarianism, but is nonetheless endorsed by those who consumed or commentated on its representations. Scott understands the motivations of the early Gothic and, unlike modern commentators, is prepared to accept the accuracy of its historical representations, which accorded with the political needs and standards of the time. There is nothing of 'nostalgia' or 'escapism' in his formulation: Italy, Spain and Southern France were chosen because, to the Protestant mind, they were firmly associated with the twin yoke of feudal politics and papal deception, from which they had still to emancipate themselves. Put simply, Gothic novels were set in the Catholic south because, 'without great violation of truth', Gothic (that is, 'medieval') practices were believed still to prevail there. Such representations drew upon and reinforced the cultural identity of the middle-class Protestant readership, which could thrill to the scenes of political and religious persecution safe in the knowledge that they themselves had awoken from such historical nightmares.[20] □

Whilst Baldick and Mighall are right to identify a middle-class Protestant readership, their essay does not account for the reasons for the class and religious make-up of the Gothic's readership. Nor are they right, I think, in their argument that this presumed Protestant readership is 'safe in the knowledge that they themselves had awoken from such historical nightmares'. Robert Miles convincingly demonstrates in his 'Introduction' (2000) to *The Italian*, for example, the climate of political paranoia that existed in Britain in the late 1790s, when *The Italian* was composed. Here he argues that '*The Italian* is a tale of "forged plots, spies, informers, and false witnesses", in a way quite unlike any of Radcliffe's previous romances.'[21] The reason for this, so Miles argues, is the British government's own paranoiac attempt to suppress Jacobinism in Britain in the 1790s, which led to the 'treason trials' of the London Corresponding Society.[22] Miles demonstrates that in *The Italian* Vivaldi's imprisonment and psychological torture by the Inquisition, in particular, can be read metonymically for the authoritarian persecution of Jacobinism in Britain.

The recently renewed commitment to historical context that has characterized a number of studies on the Gothic within the past decade has produced some surprising and revealing links between the rise of the Gothic, the rise of the novel and national debates on patriotism and Protestantism in the eighteenth century. After a brief contextualization of some of these historical factors, the following section of this chapter will discuss some of these studies and the new emphases that they have revealed in the field of Gothic criticism.

## Protestantism, nationalism and the Gothic

The contemporary concerns over the effects of 'Gothic romances' on a young and vulnerable female readership detailed in Chapter One of this Guide exhibit an anxiety at the heart of the 'secure' and Protestant British nation about the invasion of Catholic sentiment and tyranny from the continent.[23] In order to understand this anxiety, we need to return to the year of the 'Glorious Revolution', 1688, and the accession of a Protestant monarch to Britain's throne. The period of the so-called 'Glorious Revolution' saw parliament finally able to wrench the whip-hand of effective government from the monarchy. The spectre of a Catholic monarch (James II) gaining the throne by simple succession was finally exorcised. In guaranteeing a Protestant succession, although it probably did not know at the time, parliament also severed a series of long-standing paradigms such as the divine right of kings, historic right and continuity of rule, and religious toleration and co-habitation in

Britain.[24] As the historian Linda Colley has argued in *Britons* (1992), these severances irrevocably linked Protestantism with the emerging commercial and civic values of Britain. The idea of Britain was itself in the melting pot at this time, and the events of the late seventeenth century moulded the fundamental form of a newly resurgent 'British' nationalism, given a final imprimatur by the Union of the Scottish and English parliaments in 1707 following a period of intense debate. By 1707, then, the English parliament had locked the backdoor to the challenge of Catholic monarchy and, by guaranteeing an emerging 'British' patriotism across the archipelago, had initiated the lock-down of easy access to Britain by French arms.

The debates on literature in the eighteenth century are closely connected to this history, and nowhere is this more prominent than in the debates on 'novel' versus 'romance'. As Angela Keane argues in *Women Writers and the English Nation in the 1790s* (2000):

■ The novel's apologists argued that the distance between the truths of their new fictional form and the fancies of romance reflected a historical and ideological split between an age of enlightenment and real and imagined eras of popular subordination, credulity and arbitrary rule. Novels stood to Protestant, Whiggish progressivism as romance stood to regressive, Catholic feudalism. The epistemic uncertainty of the late eighteenth century disturbed the confidence of the progressive novelists' claims to truth in representation. Diminishing confidence in the 'Enlightenment project' and rapid changes in the bases of political authority in Britain in the later part of the eighteenth century produced a new, if ambivalent fascination with pre-modern epistemology and its cultural and political signs, not least its national signs. Anxiety about English national identity, which was produced by British imperial growth, and new domestic political alliances (Whig and Tory, land and trade, Catholic and Protestant, Scottish and English) was reflected in the 'Little Englandism' which surfaced from the 1770s until the end of the century. This was expressed not just in the political associations and protests of radical patriots but in the literary domain. The production of genealogies of a vernacular English literary tradition, the lionisation of the English bards (Shakespeare, Spenser and Milton) and the unprecedented interest in regional folklore and customary culture demonstrated a consolidated effort on the part of the writing classes to construct an essential Englishness that, in its cultural traditions, mirrored the nation's customary constitution.[25] □

Keane's illuminating explanation draws attention to the perceived need for a specifically English tradition of writing in order to consolidate the nation's interests and civic duties.[26]

Before moving on, we might wish to consider here Horace Walpole's construction of a specifically English literary lineage in his apologia for the trick that he played upon his readership in the first Preface to *The Castle of Otranto*. At the conclusion of the second 'Preface', having disowned the French Enlightenment writer Voltaire (1694–1778), Walpole acknowledges his debt to Shakespeare:

■ The result of all I have said is to shelter my own daring under the cannon of the brightest genius this country, at least, has produced. I might have pleaded, that having created a new species of romance, I was at liberty to lay down what rules I thought fit for the conduct of it: but I should be more proud of having imitated, however faintly, weakly, and at a distance, so masterly a pattern, than to enjoy the entire merit of invention, unless I could have marked my work with genius as well as originality.[27] □

Walpole's invocation of Shakespeare as his literary inspiration is framed here in interestingly defensive terms, using deliberately militaristic images such as 'shelter' and 'cannon' in relation to the 'brightest genius of this country', Shakespeare. It is as if Shakespeare needs to be defended from the encroachment of Voltaire and other French influences. E. J. Clery's essay 'The Genesis of Gothic Fiction' sheds vital historical light onto this type of imagery, explaining that it is due in part to the direct mapping of the literary wars (with Voltaire critiquing Shakespeare) onto the nationalistic concerns in England:

■ Shakespeare had a very specific value for the romance revival in Britain. Historically, he was situated on the cusp between Gothic and enlightened times. His plays were believed to combine the benefits of Protestantism and Renaissance learning with ready access to the resources of popular folklore and Popish superstition, so conducive to the imagination. Even his language was regarded as striking a perfect balance between ancient and modern. ... Ideologically, Shakespeare also played an important part in the nationalist myth surrounding the reign of Elizabeth [1533–1603]. It was no accident that the cult of the Immortal Bard intensified during the period of the Seven Years' War, 1756–63, when France's living national poet Voltaire chose to launch an attack on the English dramatic tradition. Walpole's second preface, partly addressed to Voltaire, was a notable contribution to the war of words and a ringing defence of one aspect of Shakespeare's practice that remained controversial even in Britain: the inclusion of comic scenes in the tragedies. Walpole adopted this practice in *Otranto*, and it was to remain a feature of Gothic romance through to Ann Radcliffe, 'Monk' Lewis and beyond.[28] □

By appealing to Shakespeare as his literary muse, then, Walpole also *defends* Shakespeare from French attack (through the medium of Voltaire). This is a cunning ruse, because at the very end of his second

Preface, Walpole thus deflects attention away from his claim to 'having created a new species of romance'. Earlier in the same Preface, Walpole explains that *The Castle of Otranto* 'was an attempt to blend the two kinds of romance, the ancient and the modern. In the former all was imagination and improbability: in the latter, nature is always intended to be, and sometimes has been, copied with success.'[29]

But what, then, are we to make of Walpole's self-acknowledged attempts to fuse the ancient and modern genres of 'romance' in *The Castle of Otranto*? His practice gave birth to a new type of writing in Britain, with Radcliffe in particular embracing the term 'Romance' explicitly and wholeheartedly; it appears in two of her novels' titles (*A Sicilian Romance* and *The Romance of the Forest*), and in the subtitles of all her other works. In *Women Writers and the English Nation in the 1790s* Angela Keane explains the distinctions between the two versions of 'Gothic romance' that are drawn upon in the eighteenth century; one from an English tradition and the other from an Italian tradition associated with aristocracy and individualism:

> ■ For over two decades the aesthetic and political significance of the work of the English and Italian romancers had been exhaustively debated, and a cultural space had been cleared for new contributions to the canon in the form of the modern romance. That blend of the marvellous with the probable, of pre-modern wonder with modern rationality was defined most authoritatively and enthusiastically in the preface to Walpole's second edition of *The Castle of Otranto*. In a definition that echoes the old romance–novel distinction, Walpole suggests that ancient and modern romance are distinguishable as the fictions of two historical moments, divided by the revolutionary settlement of 1689.[30] □

Keane's argument for the use of Romance after 1689, and for the Gothic romance in particular, is that it embraces the values of the Protestant middle-class readership that it was aimed towards. Romances in the eighteenth century, and particularly in the Gothic tradition, retain the moral trappings of ancient romances, with moral messages encoded around tales of personal valour and sensibility (hence Vivaldi rescuing Ellena from the convent of San Stefano in *The Italian* and St Aubert warning his daughter Emily in *The Mysteries of Udolpho* of the dangers of excessive sensibility). However, these heroes and heroines are no longer of royal origin, although they may be aristocratic. As Keane argues, the purpose of this shifting definition of the Romance is to encode the values of the emerging Protestant identity: 'Fiction, including Radcliffe's, had a crucial role to play in this redefinition of heroic enterprise, for the puritan values of commercial productivity needed to be packaged with the pleasures of measured consumption.'[31]

In *Contesting the Gothic: Fiction, Genre and Cultural Conflict, 1764–1832* (1999), James Watt also detects in the Gothic a similar gesture of patriotism. Going back to earlier Gothic works such as Clara Reeve's *The Old English Baron*, Watt coins the term 'Loyalist Gothic Romance' in order to describe a particular strain of Gothic novel that emerged in the late 1770s and early 1780s, and lasted until the early 1800s. Watt claims that:

■ Reeve's work was the forerunner of what I term the 'Loyalist Gothic' romance, a critically neglected yet significant line of works which were particularly prominent in the 1790s and early 1800s. From around the time of the British defeat in America ... the category of Gothic was widely redefined so as to denote a proud heritage of military victory. In the context of this increasingly powerful loyalist discourse, I argue that the majority of works after *Otranto* which called themselves 'Gothic', along with numerous other 'historical' romances, served an unambiguous moral and patriotic agenda. These little-known works rely upon an English medieval setting, and locate their action in and around a real castle, identified primarily as the symbol of a stratified yet harmonious society. Loyalist Gothic romances refer to real historical figures from the pantheon of British patriotism, and depict the defeat of dubiously effeminate or foreign villains.[32] □

Watt cites here the equally important factor of the American Revolution for earlier Gothic novels and the impact of the British defeat upon the fiction of the time. For Watt, the category of 'Loyalist Gothic' describes a type of Gothic romance which promotes military valour and patriotism in its heroes, and devalues the villains as effeminate and/or foreign. His argument here in relation to Reeve is very compelling, but his subsequent categorization of the later Radcliffe as 'conservative' is, I think, misleading. The recent biographical work on Radcliffe executed by Rictor Norton in *Mistress of Udolpho* (1999) has revealed her strong dissenting heritage, and as this chapter later reveals, the counter-argument for her novels entertaining the values of toleration and dissent is more persuasive.[33]

Adopting a more theoretical approach to the issues of nationalism and Protestantism raised in Walpole's two Prefaces, Robert Miles's essay 'Abjection, Nationalism and the Gothic' (2001) also addresses the patriotic Protestant project of the Romance in the eighteenth century.[34] But in contrast to James Watt, he finds that the examples that he examines vex the categories of the patriotic Englishman against the foreign 'other'. Miles uses the example of Walpole's two Prefaces in *The Castle of Otranto* to demonstrate how the Gothic's haunting obsession with issues of religion and nationalism can be fruitfully read against Julia Kristeva's theory of abjection from *Powers of Horror: An Essay on Abjection* (1982).[35] Miles begins by arguing that the ultimate ambition of any nationalist ideology is to create a unified myth of national origin by erasing any counter-narratives of defiance and conflict.[36]

Clearly, however, Walpole's two Prefaces, taken together, draw attention to their own internal contradictions, the first Preface purporting that the story is translated from the Italian, the second that it is an attempt to 'fuse' two types of romance, or, in other words, to erase contradictions. In order to excavate these contradictions, Miles focuses upon Kristeva's location of the abject's ambivalence in its noun/verb ambiguity: 'while an individual subject may suffer the deadly grip of the abject, the work of art realizes the abject as "verb", as actions which work to place a "prohibition, a rule, or a law" in a new, or different, "corrupting" context, one tending towards the relaxation of the abject's social hold'.[37] Framing Walpole's Prefaces within these terms, Miles is able to argue that:

■ Walpole focuses on abject material, on that which must be expelled from the national body to allow its hygienic imagining (the abject as noun); but he also places the abject in a different light through the confusion of boundaries (the abject as verb). Thus he begins his preface with the culturally oxymoronic figure of the British Catholic, William Marshall, Esq. The abject nature of this figure is slowly revealed through association as Marshall unravels the genealogy of his 'discovered' text. Insofar as it appears to be the contemporary record of twelfth-century events, it is pre-Reformational, and therefore (possibly) historically neutral. However, Marshall speculates that it is in fact the work of a Counter-Reformational priest who has disguised it as an earlier text in order to strike a blow against Protestantism. Given that the Reformation and its legacy is a pillar of the British constitution, the priest's forgery is an attack on the law. William Marshall comments, apparently with approval, on the forgery's ability to stir up controversy even to the 'present hour'; on its power to bring confusion upon the law. William Marshall first appears to us an upright British subject, as a gentleman from an ancient family in the North of England, one with a venerable 'library'. The more we read, the more this figure becomes contaminated with the abject values of the sneaky priest intent upon bringing down, directly or indirectly, the British constitution. By the end of the preface, 'William Marshall' is revealed in his full abjection, as a 'British Catholic', as an abject Other who seeks to steal our 'Thing', our enjoyment, utilizing the most underhand means possible.

Walpole's second preface obliquely, yet tellingly, glosses his imposture as Marshall. Famously, Walpole defends his hoax in aesthetic terms: it was an 'attempt to blend the two kinds of romance'. The appeal to the precedent of Shakespeare, and the aside to the controversy with

Voltaire, firmly situates his experiment within an emerging nationalist ideology. Nor are his terms entirely innocent, for by 'modern' romance we should understand the controversial luxury item then fuelling the book trade, and by 'ancient' romance, a species of 'writing' associated with legendary folk culture.[38] In other words, Walpole's *Otranto* is itself an embodiment of the contradictory fusion of 'originality' ... with folk art, of high masquerading as low.[39] □

Here Miles fruitfully reads the vexed portrayal of religion (with the Catholic figures) alongside issues of literary legitimacy in order to argue that 'Walpole wishes to render transparent the "false consciousness" of his own, much protested, nationalist Whig ideology.'[40] In addition to using Kristeva's theoretical arguments on abjection, where she argues that the abject destroys boundaries, Miles also refers to Slavoj Zizek's arguments from his long essay 'Enjoy your Nation as Yourself!' (1993) where Zizek argues that we organize our sense of national identity around our shared enjoyment of a 'Thing' that remains unidentifiable.[41] Its very unidentifiability highlights, as do Walpole's Prefaces, the myth-making structures that lie at the heart of the eighteenth-century construction of a Protestant, nationalist identity. 'Abjection, Nationalism and the Gothic' very usefully deconstructs the binary formations on which this identity is secured in the eighteenth century. It demonstrates how the Gothic novel, in its debates over Romance, Catholicism and forgeries, pinpoints the contradictions in this nationalist construction.

At this point, then, our critical account is moving away somewhat from Chris Baldick and Robert Mighall's identification of the staunch anti-Catholicism of these early Gothic novels. Whilst it is difficult to ignore the seeming anti-Catholic impulses lying behind Lewis's *The Monk* and Maturin's *Melmoth the Wanderer*, we need to exercise care that we do not brand all Gothic novels as straightforwardly anti-Catholic. The Gothic's challenge to generic boundaries between novel and romance, its close attention to issues of legitimacy and legality all testify to a complex questioning of boundaries. And this questioning inevitably disturbs the demarcations between Protestantism and Catholicism within the Gothic. One other emergent critical trend remains to be explored, and this accounts for the negative portrayal of Catholicism in a rather different way.

## Religious toleration?

The informed and persuasive accounts of the Protestant British readership expelling or abjecting their fears of invasion and revolution onto a

Catholic 'other' continent demonstrate an increased attention in Gothic criticism to the historical and religious contexts from which the Gothic was born. And certainly these contexts appear to suggest a deeply embedded anti-Catholicism which was closely linked to nationalistic issues in Britain. The laughing, drunken monks that Julia de Mazzini discovers in Radcliffe's *A Sicilian Romance* thematically share much with Matthew Lewis's depiction of the greedy, lustful monk Ambrosio who breaks the bonds of civilized behaviour to satisfy his lustful appetite. If we continue to dwell upon these instances of depravity within the Catholic Church (and there are, indeed, many to dwell upon) we will find much to consider.

However, it is possible to detect occasionally more ambivalent portrayals of the Catholic Church, particularly in the fiction of Ann Radcliffe. What do we make, for example, of the fact that Radcliffe's *The Italian* occasionally focalizes its portrayal of the Roman Inquisition through the Inquisitors themselves? At one point the narrative says of the Inquisition tribunal's response to an appeal from Vivaldi: 'The tribunal acknowledged the justness of this injunction, and exculpated [Vivaldi] from any harm that should be the consequence of the summons.'[42] We cannot really account for such a qualified portrayal of the Inquisition through the theory of abjection, because the Inquisition does not consistently appear as the horrific Catholic 'Other' in *The Italian*.[43]

One of the most recent critical interventions on the subject of the Gothic and religion in fact moves away from the anti-Catholic accounts of the Gothic that we have examined so far in this chapter. Mark Canuel's *Religion, Toleration and British Writing, 1790–1830* (2002) makes a persuasive case for the Gothic novel's intervention in the eighteenth-century debates in Britain on religious toleration:

■ The rise in popularity of Gothic novels during the latter half of the eighteenth century, it turns out, coincided rather conspicuously with the increasingly heated discussion of the importance of established religion to Britain's self-constitution. And while the Gothic has often been understood as the archetypal paranoid genre in its attempt to establish uniformity (of manners, of custom, of ideology), I believe that the Gothic novel generally ... leads us towards an altogether different account of the genre and the social organization that it envisions. Monasticism, the images of which are pervasive enough in Gothic novels to look like one of the most conspicuous features of the genre, arose as a subject of concern not because monasticism could be separated from British customs (in order to separate Britain from Catholic countries, or fan the flames of anti-Catholic sentiment at home): not, in short, because monasticism was the representative of a certain (Catholic) set of *beliefs*. Rather, it was a subject of concern because it represented a mode of *governing* the beliefs

of political subjects, visible in Britain itself, which the Gothic novel participated in dismantling and modifying. In their fictional renderings of
monasticism, writers from Walpole to Radcliffe and beyond depicted the
political mechanisms of confessional regimes of power that continually
demanded, and attempted to enforce, a uniformity of belief amongst
members of the national community. The innovative response taken by
the Gothic novel was to expose what it deemed to be a terrifying logic of
confessional government and then to assume – precisely as a remedy to
the anxieties about Catholicism it generated – a more tolerant relation to
religious belief. With their plots as well as their elaborate prefaces,
Gothics used the imagery of monastic terror in order to distinguish a confessional rule by belief from their own alliance with a more expansive
secular rule *over* belief: a practice of government that exposed religion
itself to new techniques of observation, analysis, and manipulation.[44] □

This is an important intervention in the debate on the Gothic and
religion as it suggests an alternative explanation of the Gothic genre's
anti-Catholicism which is based upon the fear of 'confessional
government' rather than monasticism in itself. Canuel proceeds to
analyse the Gothic's portrayal of the Church as representative of the
more secularized function of ecclesiastical government. He argues that
the Gothic novel:

■ continually casts the church in an analogously complex and fluctuat-
ing role – wavering between an acquiescence to, and a control of, the
conformity exacted by private affective associations within familial and
religious groups. ... The place of church authority in the Gothic emerges
most distinctly in its alternating roles in relation to these alliances: the
ecclesiastical institution is, on the one hand, the model for an oppressive
conformity demanded by the family unit with which the church then com-
peted for allegiance. On the other hand, the Gothic accompanies this
gesture by imagining ecclesiastical government as if it could oppose –
indeed, as if it could serve as an *antidote* for – the terror inspired by
mutually reinforcing and competing religious authorities.[45] □

Canuel's analysis here presents a more fluid representation of the
Church and its authority in the Gothic. He sees the Gothic challenging
the current oppressive institutionalism of the Church and imagining an
alternative Church. This could account for the two models of convent
invoked, for example, in Ann Radcliffe's *The Italian*. The first, oppressive
and monologic, demands compliance from the heroine Ellena; the
second welcomes and protects her from her pursuant Schedoni.

In *Horror Fiction and the Protestant Tradition* (1988), Victor Sage first
tested the hypothesis that 'the rise and currency of literary Gothic is
strongly related to the growth of the campaign for Catholic

Emancipation from the 1770s onward until the first stage ends temporarily with the Emancipation Act of 1829'.[46] This argument is compelling as these dates do indeed mirror the first flourish of the Gothic genre. Mark Canuel also makes this point in his argument that the Gothic reflects a more ambivalent portrayal of religious institutions than its seeming anti-Catholicism might suggest:

■ If the Parliamentary debates of the late eighteenth and early nineteenth centuries mobilized the plots and images of the Gothic novel, the Gothic novel itself in still more obvious ways betrayed an unusual fascination with scenarios of religious – and particularly Catholic – subversion and oppression. With monastic settings populated by savage monks and nuns bringing violence upon over-credulous victims, the novels of Radcliffe and Lewis attracted an enthusiastic readership long after 1800; shortened 'blue-book' versions of these novels attempted to reproduce the shocking effects for an even wider audience. Writers with an enduring reputation such as William Godwin and Charles Maturin invoked the conventions of monastic settings, and countless anonymous productions with titles such as *The Midnight Assassin, Amalgo and Claude; or Monastic Murder*, and *The Abbott of Montserrat, or the Pool of Blood* appeared in the early 1800s as variations on familiar Gothic themes. ... [T]he immense popularity of the Gothic genre – just like the Gothicism of parliamentary debates and popular journalism – could be interpreted as a highly politicized mode of exposing and excluding certain modes of unenlightened or irrational beliefs. But, from another point of view, it would be possible to see that even early instances of the Gothic novel deploy monastic settings and devices as a more complex way of exploring the relationship between beliefs and social groups more generally.

Horace Walpole's *Castle of Otranto* (1764) and Clara Reeve's *The Old English Baron* (1778; previously published as 'The Champion of Virtue' in 1777) present their figures of ecclesiastical authority – Father Jerome in Walpole and Father Oswald in Reeve – as oddly poised between a condition of powerlessness and power, hostile competitors with the authority of the family yet ultimately the guarantors of secular order. In *Otranto*, the 'subterranean passage' between the castle and the church conveys some of this ambiguity surrounding the place of ecclesiastical government, for the entire novel shows the church to be either a mutable, infinitely corruptible mirror-image of patriarchal power or a foundation for legitimate authority. The 'sacred' offices of Jerome, that is, are at first threatened by the 'profane' power of the state embodied in the tyrannical figure of Manfred. As Manfred's power exercised in pursuit of an heir manifests itself in the most extreme forms of brutality, the church's role eventually becomes defined as a protection against feudal brutality. The novel procures a resolution to the problem of ecclesiastical power in a way that is typically Gothic: for the church eventually proves its long-established relation to legitimate succession as Jerome reveals his protection of and devotion to Theodore, the rightful heir of Alfonso. By supporting parental authority, however, the church also sets a limit upon it, protecting legitimate succession by supervising it and limiting its excesses. Similarly, *The Old English Baron*'s Father Oswald acts not only as a confessor, but also as an agent of detection who brings the violence of private relations under public scrutiny; the church does not merely support claims to heredity but superintends them and serves as a 'witness' to the rightful heir Edmund Twyford's claims to legitimacy. The lofty references to the 'conduct' of 'Providence' or the all-seeing 'eye of heaven' is thus consonant with the rational, meticulous guidance of the church. The novels, in short, eventually implicate the ecclesiastical institution within a disintegration of the family – a disintegration that continually clears the way for the reintegration or reconstruction of new domestic arrangements under the auspices of secular government.[47] ☐

Canuel's exploration of these ecclesiastical figures and their functions as guarantors of justice emphasizes the multiplicity of roles that church figures perform in the Gothic. These figures can be rational and enlightened, and their protection of the individual's rights distinguishes them from their more famously negative counterparts in later Gothic fiction. Canuel also explores the Prefaces of Walpole's and Reeve's novels in order to stress (rightly, I think) that these novels are equally concerned with 'the terror of religious uniformity' and that this terror is present in the very directive nature of these Prefaces. He then proceeds to analyse this argument particularly with regard to the fiction of Ann Radcliffe, and strengthens his analysis through an examination of *A Sicilian Romance* and *The Italian*. In relation to the latter, he argues that:

■ Monasticism's centrality in the novel is owing not only to its tendency to double the tyranny of the family, but to its even more conspicuous technology for securing the uniformity exacted within familial privacy: it most clearly embodies a social model that – as I have been arguing – seeks to elicit a uniform consciousness from the members of a group. For Ellena, the deep level of psychological conformity within the monastic institution in fact serves as both an initial source of comfort and eventual source of terror. The 'sanctuary' she finds in the convent is 'especially adapted to the present state of her spirits' (57); when she is kidnapped and brought to the monastery, the songs she hears are in 'perfect unison with her feelings' (65). The notion of the institution as a correspondence between minds, however, is ultimately less comforting when considered from the vantage point of a nun she observes, 'characterised by a gloomy malignity, which seemed ready to inflict upon others some portion of the unhappiness she herself suffered.'[48] ☐

Canuel reads the villainous monk Schedoni as emblematic of monasticism's 'tendency to double the tyranny of the family', as well as the Abbess at the monastery of San Stefano, who places the rank of the Vivaldi family above her concerns for the individual and unprotected Ellena. Whilst this chapter has demonstrated that monastic institutions are more often than not portrayed in the Gothic as a source of terror (which, as we have explored, has been critically equated with aestheticism, anti-Catholicism and anti-uniformity), it is important to acknowledge that some portrayals of monastic spaces are substantially less condemnatory. In particular, in Radcliffe's *The Mysteries of Udolpho*, Emily St Aubert, after the death of her father, seeks refuge in a convent that is only described as benevolent and nurturing. Furthermore, as I have already suggested above, in Radcliffe's *The Italian*, the portrayal of San Stefano is significantly counter-pointed with Ellena's second conventual experience in Santa della Pietà. Ellena finds refuge here after Schedoni's fruitless attempt to murder her. Both Mark Canuel and Robert Miles rightly read this more benevolent model as symbolic of Radcliffe's politics of tolerance, with Miles arguing, 'Just as Vivaldi and Ellena represent a modern, enlightened sensibility, so, too, does the Superior of the Santa della Pietà. In the case of all three, prejudices are encountered, while tyrannies surrender to reason and tolerance.'[49] The narrative portrayal of the Abbess in particular is significant, stating that she 'encouraged in her convent every innocent and liberal pursuit, which might sweeten the austerities of confinement, and which were generally rendered instrumental to charity'.[50]

By way of concluding this discussion of the function of religion and nationalism within the Gothic, we can remain with this emergent critical discussion of toleration by comparing Radcliffe's physical description of the convent of Santa della Pietà with her earlier description of San Stefano quoted as an epigraph to this chapter:

■ The local circumstances of this convent were scarcely less agreeable than the harmony of its society was interesting. These extensive domains included olive-grounds, vineyards, and some corn-land; a considerable tract was devoted to the pleasures of the garden, whose groves supplied walnuts, almonds, oranges, and citrons in abundance, and almost every kind of fruit and flower, which this luxurious climate nurtured. These gardens hung upon the slope of a hill, about a mile within the shore, and afforded extensive views of the country round Naples, and of the gulf. But from the terraces, which extended along a semicircular range of rocks, the prospects were infinitely finer. They extended on the south to the isle of Capri, where the gulf expands into the sea; in the west, appeared the island of Ischia, distinguished by the white pinnacles of the lofty mountain Epomeo; and near it Prosida, with its many-coloured cliffs, rose out of the waves.[51] □

Whereas, in the opening description of San Stefano, the limitations of the place are repeatedly underlined with the 'narrow pointed roofs', 'angles' and 'fenced' garden, in the description of Santa della Pietà, Radcliffe emphasizes abundance and extensiveness, with the structure of the convent working in harmony with nature. Nature supports the convent's environs, with the gardens being 'hung upon' a hill and the terraces extending 'along a semicircular range of rocks'. Natural structures therefore support the cultural edifice of the convent in this section, and this, I think, epitomizes Radcliffe's ideal of a liberal society, where Nature and civilization co-exist peacefully in an environment of mutual support.

Of Radcliffe's fiction in general, Angela Keane argues that 'Liberty is figured in the relief of the imaginary landscapes, in the privileged cultural artefacts and even in the narrative movement of Radcliffe's fictions, which all come to us as picturesque experience refracted through the consciousness of her liberal protagonists.'[52] Radcliffe's portrayal of 'liberal protagonists' is, of course, very different from the duty-driven Catholic caricatures that Matthew Lewis portrays in *The Monk* but Lewis's satirical stab at a caricatured Catholicism in the end achieves a similar outcome, to critique a brand of Catholicism which demands unthinking conformity of its devotees.

The range of arguments on religion and nationalism within the Gothic novel bears testimony to a strong critical tradition that closely analyses the birth of the genre in relation to its late eighteenth-century contexts. As this chapter recalls, issues of class and nationalism are strongly linked to the Gothic obsession with religion. In his 'Introduction' to the *Cambridge Companion to Gothic Ficion* (2002), Jerrold E. Hogle eloquently summarizes the complex relationships between religion, nationalism and class:

■ the early Gothic ... for Walpole and his immediate successors sees its characters and readers as torn between the enticing call of aristocratic wealth and sensuous Catholic splendour, beckoning toward the Middle Ages and the Renaissance, on the one hand, and a desire to overthrow these past orders of authority in favour of a quasi-equality associated with the rising middle-class ideology of the self as self-made, on the other – but an ideology haunted by the Protestant bourgeois desire to *attain* the power of the older orders that the middle class wants to dethrone. Such a paradoxical state of longing in much of the post-Renaissance western psyche fears retribution from all the extremes it tries to encompass, especially from remnants of those very old heights of dominance which the middle class now strives to grasp and displace at the same time.[53] □

Hogle's excellent explanation retains the national and religious concerns that we have explored in this chapter. He stresses the importance of the rising Protestant middle class in eighteenth-century Britain, the consumers of Gothic fiction, whose emergent bourgeois identity itself reveals class and religious contradictions in their impulses. Whilst Hogle's critique here is largely historicist in emphasis, his use of the phrases 'post-Renaissance western psyche' and 'a state of longing' point us towards another significant (and often, as in Hogle's and Miles's case, inter-related) strand of Gothic criticism. This important and widely-embraced critical strand deploys a rich variety of psychoanalytic perspectives in order to explore the Gothic's vocabulary of loss, desire and death.

# CHAPTER FIVE

# 'This narrative resembles a delirious dream': Psychoanalytical Readings of the Gothic

> Shall I even confess to you, what was the origin of this romance? I waked one morning in the beginning of last June, from a dream, of which, all that I could recover was, that I had thought myself in an ancient castle (a very natural dream for a head filled like mine with Gothic story), and that on the uppermost banister of a great staircase I saw a gigantic hand in armour. In the evening I sat down, and began to write, without knowing in the least what I intended to say or relate. The work grew on my hands, and I grew fond of it ...
>
> (Horace Walpole, letter to William Cole, 9 March 1765)

As Horace Walpole testifies, since its beginnings the Gothic novel has been associated with dreams and fantasy. Gothic novels have always drawn on the unreality of their narrative components. Not only does Walpole confess to having dreamed up his 'Gothic story', but he also locates the origins of his dream in 'a head filled like mine with Gothic story'. Walpole changed his subtitle for *The Castle of Otranto* from 'A Story' to 'A Gothic Story' in his second edition: why? He changed it because the word 'Gothic' in the phrase 'Gothic story' has an ambiguous value, because it suggests something that could colonize the waking and the sleeping mind. The chain of influence here is interesting. The 'Gothic stories' that Walpole devoured by day invaded his dreams by night. In turn, they dictated his unconscious creative process.[1]

In several well-publicized accounts, Gothic novelists claimed that the inspiration for their tale came to them through a dream. In a previous letter, Walpole had confided that '[*Otranto*] was so far from being sketched out with any design at all, that it was actually commenced one evening, from the very imperfect recollection of a dream with which I waked in the morning.'[2] Similarly, Mary Shelley's account of the nocturnal incubation of *Frankenstein* emphasized the passivity of her vision:

▪ I saw – with shut eyes, but acute mental vision – I saw the pale student of unhallowed arts kneeling beside the thing he had put together. I saw the hideous phantasm of a man stretched out, and then, on the working of some powerful engine, show signs of life and stir with an uneasy, half vital motion.[3] □

Shelley's repeated emphasis upon the verb 'saw' stresses the liminal position that she assigns herself in the process of this composition. The 'pale student' and the 'hideous phantasm of a man' appear, in this account, to have been produced entirely independently of her.[4]

In Chapter One I argued that the anonymous author of 'Terrorist Novel Writing' dismissed the emergent Gothic genre as 'the distorted ideas of lunatics'.[5] Early on, then, this kind of denunciation associated the Gothic novel with dreams and insanity. In contrast to this harsh eighteenth-century judgement, twentieth-century criticism has celebrated the Gothic's irrationality. By 1937, the Gothic was claimed by the French surrealist movement as a source of inspiration. One of surrealism's most famous practitioners, André Breton, wrote a manifesto which translates as 'Limits not Frontiers of Surrealism' (1937). There, quoting Walpole's account of the genesis of *Otranto*, Breton proudly stated that:

▪ The production of such a work, about which we have the good fortune to have information, approaches, indeed, nothing less than the *surrealist method* and adds once more to its complete justification. ... [Walpole's] account shows that the message obtained, the future model of so many others, highly significant in their cumulative effect, must be put to the credit of *dreams* and of the employment of *automatic writing.*[6] □

Here, Breton refers to the compulsion to write that Walpole describes experiencing after his dream. This, of course, pre-dates the surrealists' adoption of the technique that they named 'automatic writing'. But despite the retrospective nature of the Surrealists' claim for Walpole's technique, Devendra P. Varma fully supports Breton's embracing of the Gothic genre as Surrealist. With reference to *The Castle of Otranto* in particular, Varma recounts Walpole's urgent eight-day composition of the novel, and asks 'Now, if this was not "automatic writing" what else could it be?'[7] For Breton (and for Varma later), the Gothic genre is an unconscious expression of the turbulence of the time in which the novels are composed. Breton claims that its unrealistic mode embodies the 'expression of con-fused feelings awakened by nostalgia and terror. The pleasure principle has never avenged itself more obviously upon the principle of reality.'[8] In the latter sentence, Breton invokes Sigmund Freud's theory of the pleasure principle as being in opposition to reality. For these early twentieth-century admirers, the Gothic novel still occupies a borderland between pleasure and reality, between fantasy and realism.

It is entirely right to argue that the Gothic novel acknowledges and plays with its emergent reputation for irrationality, nightmares and insanity. In one of the earliest examples of the genre, Sophia Lee's *The Recess*, one of the heroines, called Ellinor, goes insane. In her insanity, she is able to shed light upon the true position of herself and her sister Matilda in society. 'Ah! How visionary seems on recollection our new situation! Seen without being known; adored without being esteemed; punished without being guilty; applauded without being meritorious, we were all an illusion.'[9] The perceptively described insanity of Ellinor acts as a method of questioning the rationality of the society which the heroines inhabit. The heroines, the subjects of the novel, become an 'illusion' in a society which does not recognize or value them. In Lee's novel, the two sisters exist as spectres on the margins of Elizabethan society that haunt and trouble the seemingly 'rational' characters with power.

*The Recess's* self-conscious interrogation of the arbitrary divisions forged by society between logic and illogic is taken up by later Gothic novels at the narratological level. Frequently in the fiction of Ann Radcliffe, for example, there are characters who draw attention to the lack of realism in the plot. In *The Mysteries of Udolpho*, Emily St Aubert reflects upon her change in circumstances after the death of her parents and her enforced journey with Montoni: 'to her, the late events and her present situation – in a foreign land – in a remote castle – surrounded by vice and violence – seemed more like the visions of a distempered imagination, than the circumstances of truth'.[10] Here, Radcliffe draws attention to the unreality of her narrative, with the heroine reflecting on the irrational nature of the landscape through which she travels. Likewise, in volume III of *The Italian*, a guide's convoluted tale of murder and betrayal prompts the monk Schedoni to exclaim that 'the narrative resembles a delirious dream, more than a reality' and that the story is nothing more 'than the vision of a distempered brain!'[11] Later, in *Melmoth the Wanderer*, the eponymous wanderer, destined to recite his narrative to unwilling ears, encounters a cold reception from the pious Don Aliaga: 'it is inconceivable to me how this person forces himself on my company, harasses me with tales that have no more application to me than the legend of the Cid'.[12] These examples bear witness to the Gothic's sustained engagement with the borders between imagination and reality, fantasy and the everyday.

In *The Literature of Terror*, David Punter is quick to acknowledge the Gothic's lack of investment in realism from the very beginning. He connects this process to Freud's insights on sublimation, arguing that like Horace Walpole, Ann Radcliffe and Matthew Lewis are not realist writers, and nor do they seek to be recognized as such:

■ [Radcliffe's and Lewis's] insistence on a poetic cogency of thematic oppositions at the very expense of narrative probability; the self-conscious references to the very processes of fictionalisation; the refusal to distinguish decisively between character trait and environmental pressure: all these produce a literary mode which is 'bracketed' from reality from the very outset, and which, although it bears an important relation, as it must, to wider societal concerns, mediates these concerns through a symbolic structure which was already coming to have its own conventions and acceptances. Distancing in time and place was coming to serve a double function: on the one hand, it lowered the pressure on the writers to compromise with developmental realism of character or situation, while on the other it allowed a depiction of social and psychological tendencies, of states of mind, in extreme and grotesque form. The process reminds one irresistibly of Freud's notion of sublimation, whereby unwillingness or incapacity directly to confront experiential contradiction finds expression in an apparently different, but in fact related, system of meanings in which the pain of contradiction is cancelled by the pleasure of fantasy. Freud points out that the reader's responses to literature cannot be dissociated from a recognition of the very unreality of the fictional world:

The unreality of the writer's imaginative world ... has very important consequences for the technique of his art; for many things which, if they were real, could give no enjoyment, can do so in the play of fantasy, and many excitements which, in themselves, are actually distressing, can become a source of pleasure for the hearers and spectators at the performance of a writer's work. (*Works*, IX, 144)[13] □

Punter goes on to argue that the Gothic genre's participation in a non-realist mode, its self-conscious allusions to untrustworthy narratives and characters, lead to a more demanding role for the reader. He contends that Radcliffe's *The Italian* in particular compels the reader to become more discerning:

■ When a narrator describes a character's face, we normally accept the description without question; when he or she describes a character's mental processes and emotional responses, we balance these against what we are told of external reality and make judgements on this basis; but when the narrator points out to us that the character's grasp on reality is at best shaky and at worst quite deluded, we are forced into a different order of response, and our interpretative role becomes both greater and more ambiguous. In *Udolpho* we certainly experience this dislocation, but largely within the circumscribed limits of the castle itself, and Radcliffe later formally dispels our doubts. But *The Italian* slides dizzily between distortion and the real, making us attribute different values and statuses to different elements in the story, and demanding that we separate out the various subtexts which Radcliffe has welded together. From familial collaborator and half-willing victim, the reader has suddenly turned into creative participant. In this developed form, the Gothic is revealed as not an escape from the real but a deconstruction and dismemberment of it, which we as readers can only put together by referring its materials to our own assumptions about the relations between world and mind and by entering actively into the self-conscious play of the text.[14] □

Punter's account offers a valuable insight into the mechanics of the reader's narrative participation in the Gothic. While insisting that the Gothic's use of fantasy is not an escapist measure, he uses an appropriately violent anatomical metaphor (dismemberment) to describe the Gothic's relationship to the real.[15]

Gothic fiction does not offer a finely-drawn demarcation between reality and its opposite; rather, the relationship between the two is often described in a suitably antagonistic way to make readers question their own assumptions about the relative values of each category. In Maturin's narratologically convoluted *Melmoth the Wanderer*, for example, the demarcation between sanity and insanity is tested constantly and found wanting. At one point, the unwilling novice Monçada, persecuted by other monks, reflects that 'It is better to be mad at once, than to believe that all the world is sworn to think and *make* you be so, in spite of your own consciousness of your sanity.'[16]

The borders between sanity and insanity, fantasy and reality have, of course, been fiercely contested by differing critical approaches to the Gothic. Whilst critics such as Markman Ellis, in *The History of Gothic Fiction*, reject the attractions of a psychoanalytic account of Gothic fiction, claiming (somewhat misleadingly) that 'critical accounts of Gothic fiction have been dominated by psychoanalytic theory', a wide variety of critics have used differing psychoanalytic theories and approaches to explore the Gothic.[17] These range from early allegorical surrealist critiques of the Gothic through Freud (as we saw earlier with Breton, Varma and surrealism), through to more sustained accounts of the genre in relation to different Freudian explanations. Whilst earlier twentieth-century critiques of the Gothic genre focused upon the Freudian motif of incest within an Oedipal plot, more recent Freudian analyses have examined his commentary on looking, gazing and the 'uncanny'.[18] During recent decades, post-Freudian psychoanalytic accounts have also become attractive, with critics using Jacques Lacan's account of language to illuminate the Gothic's disjointed narratives, Julia Kristeva's idea of abjection to discuss borders, and the French feminist psychoanalytic theories of Luce Irigaray (born 1932) and Hélène Cixous (born 1937) to discuss issues of sex and gender. The remainder of this chapter will try to provide a representative sample and appraisal of these approaches in relation to the first wave of Gothic novels. As we will see, particularly in more recent psychoanalytic explanations of the Gothic, history, context and psychoanalysis are often invoked simultaneously and provide mutually illuminating explanations of the genre.

## The eighteenth century, the 'uncanny' and *The Mysteries of Udolpho*

In a recent survey essay entitled 'Psychoanalysis and the Gothic' (2000), Michelle A. Massé begins her argument by discussing the mutual concerns shared by the Gothic novel and psychoanalysis:

■ The Gothic is ... a genre ... that is important to psychoanalytic critical inquiry not solely for its ongoing popularity and easily recognisable motifs, but for the affinities between its central concerns and those of psychoanalysis. Psychoanalysis examines how and why our most strongly held beliefs and perceptions are sometimes at odds with empirical evidence. We work incessantly to maintain a simulacrum of congruence between fantasy and reality, but the boundaries blur in the most routine of everyday events, such as 'slips of the tongue', day-dreams or simply dissonance between what other people mean as opposed to what we want to hear. Usually we quickly reconcile such breaches, but when it cannot be done readily, Freud tells us that this gap can call forth the uncanny, which is 'often and easily produced when the distinction between imagination and reality is effaced' (Freud, 1953–74, 244).[19] □

As with Punter's earlier analysis, Massé focuses upon the ever-important boundaries of reality and fantasy that both the Gothic and psychoanalysis challenge. She argues that the 'easily recognisable motifs' of the Gothic novel (which eighteenth-century critics lampooned so effectively, as we saw in Chapter One) work hand-in-hand with the dreams and violence portrayed, in a manner very similar to psychoanalysis. Here, Massé invokes Sigmund Freud's 1919 essay 'The Uncanny', which has justifiably assumed a great significance to psychoanalytic accounts of the Gothic. Its revolutionary blend of linguistic excavation and literary analysis, coupled with its exploration of everyday sources of fear that we experience, have made Freud's essay justifiably relevant to Gothic studies.

Freud begins his uneven and fascinating account of the 'uncanny' by examining the differing definitions of the German term for the uncanny, *das Unheimlich*, and its linguistic opposite, *das Heimlich*. At face value, the word *Heimlich*, as Freud discovers, connotes the homely and the native. As a word, it stands for that which is familiar, comforting and intimate. It offers a sense of familiarity that at first seems to be entirely at odds with *das Unheimlich*, which, by being a negation, signifies the unfamiliar and strange. However, as Freud's exploration of dictionary definitions of the terms reveals, the two opposing definitions coincide uncannily: 'What interests us most in this long extract is to find that among its different shades of meaning the word "*heimlich*" exhibits one which is identical with its opposite, "*unheimlich*". *Das Heimlich* also stands for what is hidden and concealed from others: "Concealed, kept from sight, so that others do not get to know of or about it, withheld from others." '[20] Its opposite, *das Unheimlich*, therefore functions to excavate what has been concealed, all that has been hidden or obscured. Freud states that 'the uncanny is that class of the frightening which leads back to what is known of old and long familiar'.[21] A childhood memory long-buried, for example, can be resurrected by an uncanny experience.

Freud proceeds to analyse this theory in relation to the short story 'The Sandman' by the German writer E. T. A. Hoffman (1776–1822). Freud contends that the main protagonist, Nathanael, has a long-standing phobia about eyes which stems from childhood. This phobia resurfaces in a possibly random everyday encounter with his professor at university. Nathanael interprets a random chain of events in his life through this reawakened childhood experience. His obsession with this childhood memory eventually leads to his insanity by the end of the tale.

Freud reads Hoffman's tale as uncanny because of the constant repetition of the eye motif throughout the story. He argues that Nathanael's mounting phobia surrounding eyes demonstrates a deep-seated castration anxiety, a fear that paternal threats to the young boy's sexuality will be realized.

As the contemporary theorist Hélène Cixous has indicated in a critique of Freud's 'The Uncanny,' Freud's over-riding focus upon the motif of the eyes in Hoffman's tale leads to him overlooking the strange event in the story of the doll Olympia coming to life.[22] Cixous rightly indicates that Freud's relentless analysis and accounting for the recurrence of the eye motif leads to him closing down debate about a strangely open-ended tale. She argues that the very vagueness which surrounds linguistic definitions of the 'uncanny' means that we cannot attempt to explain the concept. Cixous challenges our linguistic understanding of the uncanny by defining it as a phenomenon that 'infiltrates itself in between things, in the interstices, it asserts a *gap* where one would like to be assured of unity'.[23] In her more contemporary post-structuralist account, then, the 'uncanny' refuses definition, and this is precisely where its 'uncanny' nature lies.

Returning to the Gothic, Michelle Massé rightly argues that the Gothic explores the uncanny effects produced when our 'simulacrum of congruence between fantasy and reality' collapses.[24] This is strongly tied to Cixous's argument that the 'uncanny' as a concept troubles the borders of these two categories, fantasy and reality, building upon Freud's own linguistic exploration of the definitions of *Heimlich* and *Unheimlich*. It reinforces the idea that the 'uncanny' appears to challenge our definitive modes of thinking, to question our certainties regarding the boundaries between concepts such as rationality and insanity, reality and fantasy.

Many critics of the Gothic, following Freud's own lead with Hoffman, analyse 'The Uncanny' in relation to nineteenth-century Gothic fiction.[25] In *The Female Thermometer: Eighteenth-century Culture and the Invention of the Uncanny* (1995), however, Terry Castle (as her title suggests) traces the notion of the 'uncanny' back to the eighteenth century, and argues that it arises as a critique of enlightenment forms of knowledge:

■ But what if we lean on the 'enlightenment' metaphor? What if we give it (so to speak) a capital letter – and treat it as a mode of historical assertion? Might one argue, extrapolating from Freud, that the uncanny itself first 'comes to light' – becomes a part of human experience – in that period known as the Enlightenment? That the uncanny itself has a history, originates at a particular historical moment, for particular historical reasons, and that this history has everything to do with that curious ambivalence with which we now regard the eighteenth century? Obviously, as my subtitle suggests, I think we can. The assumption (tacitly Freudian) ... is not simply that the eighteenth century is 'uncanny' – though that may be true – but that the eighteenth century in a sense 'invented the uncanny': that the very psychic and cultural transformations that led to the subsequent glorification of the period as an age of reason or enlightenment – the aggressively rationalist imperatives of the epoch – also produced, like a kind of toxic side effect, a new human experience of strangeness, anxiety, bafflement, and intellectual impasse. The distinctively eighteenth-century impulse to systematize and regulate, to bureaucratize the world of knowledge by identifying what [the English philosopher John Locke (1632–1704)] called the 'horizon ... which sets the bounds between the enlightened and dark parts of things,' was itself responsible, in other words, for that 'estranging of the real' – and impinging uncanniness – which is so integral a part of modernity.[26] □

This recasting of Freud's theory of the 'uncanny' into the eighteenth century may initially appear anachronistic, and Castle is aware that this charge may be laid at her door. But as she makes clear here, the eighteenth-century investigative need to rationalize everything also, crucially, made possible the attempt to rationalize uncanny events that Freud's 1919 essay explores. In addition to this, Freud's main literary example comes from Hoffman, and as Castle rightly argues, 'that Hoffman's characteristic uncanniness was decisively bound up with the evolution of Enlightenment philosophical and technological innovation will be immediately apparent to anyone familiar with his stories'.[27]

While tying the notion of 'the uncanny' to the eighteenth century, Castle also argues persuasively that 'The crucial developmental process on which the Freudian uncanny depends is rationalization: the "surmounting" of infantile belief,' a process which, she asserts, is rooted in the eighteenth century.[28] The eighteenth-century Enlightenment's urge to rationalize and account for every human action and motivation, whilst displaying a good and optimistic faith in humankind, inevitably led to feelings of alienation within society, and this is what gives rise, for Castle, to the feeling of uncanniness that haunts us.

Castle brilliantly demonstrates her argument in a chapter entitled 'The Spectralization of the Other in *The Mysteries of Udolpho*'.[29] In what is certainly, to date, one of the best critical accounts of Radcliffe's fourth novel, she focuses upon the novel's tendency to make the unreal become real, and vice-versa. Using *The Hour of our Death* (trans. 1981), by the French historian Philippe Ariès (1914–1984), Castle explores what she calls 'the supernaturalization of the mind' in *Udolpho*.[30] By this she means the strange haunting of each character in the novel by absent friends or departed dead.

By way of an example, we can consider here the heroine Emily St Aubert's constant mourning and melancholia for both of her parents, or the servant Dorothée's mourning for the long-departed Marchioness at Château le Blanc. This pervasive mourning is distinctly at odds with the novel's rationalization of any potential ghosts at the end, and the father St Aubert's attempt to cultivate rational thinking in his daughter Emily.[31] In *The Mysteries of Udolpho*, the absent and the dead appear more alive in the minds of living characters such as Emily and Dorothée than the living characters who surround them, such as Valancourt, in Emily's case, and Emily herself, in Dorothée's case. For example, when Dorothée shows Emily around the apartments of her late aunt the Marchioness, the narrative clearly demonstrates how Dorothée fixates upon the departed Marchioness almost to the point of obsession:

■ 'Alas! there she is, ma'amselle,' said Dorothée, pointing to a portrait of a lady, 'there is her very self! Just as she looked when she came first to the château. You see, madam, she was all blooming like you, then – and so soon to be cut off!'

...

'Pray, ma'amselle, stand beside the picture, that I may look at you together,' said Dorothée, who, when the request was complied with, exclaimed again at the resemblance. Emily also, as she gazed upon it, thought that she had somewhere seen a person very like it, though she could not now recollect who this was.

In this closet were many memorials of the departed Marchioness; a robe and several articles of her dress were scattered upon the chairs, as if they had just been thrown off. On the floor, were a pair of black satin slippers, and, on the dressing-table, a pair of gloves and a long black veil, which, as Emily took it up to examine, she perceived was dropping to pieces with age.

'Ah!' said Dorothée, observing the veil, 'my lady's hand laid it there; it has never been moved since!'

Emily, shuddering, laid it down again. 'I well remember seeing her take it off,' continued Dorothée, 'it was on the night before her death, when she had returned from a little walk I had persuaded her to take in the gardens, and she seemed refreshed by it. I told her how much better she looked, and I remember what a languid smile she gave me; but, alas! she little thought, or I either, that she was to die, that night.'

Dorothée wept again, and then, taking up the veil, threw it suddenly over Emily, who shuddered to find it wrapped round her, descending even to her feet, and, as she endeavoured to throw it off, Dorothée intreated that she would keep it on for one moment. 'I thought,' added she, 'how like you would look to my dear mistress in that veil; – may your life, ma'amselle, be a happier one than hers!'[32] □

This is a scene that becomes almost farcical in its memorialization of the dead at the expense of the living. In her desperation to recall her former employer, Dorothée terrifies the young Emily by throwing the dead Marchioness's veil over her head. The narrative is careful to tell us that, from Emily's perspective, the veil 'was dropping to pieces with age', indicating that for Emily, the memorial that Dorothée has created for the Marchioness holds far less significance. It is only on the page previous to this passage that we have learned that the Marchioness's death occurred twenty years ago, but Dorothée insists that 'all the time between then and now seems as nothing'.[33] The museum that Dorothée has created for the dead Marchioness (none of her objects have been touched since her death) testifies to the pleasure which Dorothée seems to derive from mourning itself. Terry Castle explains this pervasive phenomenon in *The Mysteries of Udolpho* both through contextual linking to the cult of mourning during the Romantic era, and through Freud's theory of the pleasure principle:

■ Romantic mourning gave pleasure, one suspects, precisely because it entailed a magical sense of the continuity and stability of the 'I' that mourned. To 'see' the dead live again is to know that one too will live forever. Thus at times Radcliffe hints at a peculiar satisfaction to be

found in grief. The vision of life-in-death is so beautiful one wants to grieve forever. ...
That this supernaturalization of the mind should occur precisely when the traditional supernatural realm was elsewhere being explained away should not surprise us. According to the Freudian principle, what the mind rejects in one form may return to haunt it in another.[34] A predictable inversion has taken place in *The Mysteries of Udolpho*: what once was real (the supernatural) has become unreal; what once was unreal (the imagery of the mind) has become real. In the very process of reversal, however, the two realms are confused; the archaic language of the supernatural contaminates the new language of mental experience. Ghosts and spectres retain their ambiguous grip on the human imagination; they simply migrate into the space of the mind.
The Radcliffean model of mourning nonetheless presents certain problems. The constant denial of physical death results, paradoxically, in an indifference toward life itself. Common sense suggests as much: if one engages in the kind of obsessional reflection that Radcliffe seems to advocate – a thinking dominated by a preoccupation with the notion that the dead are not really dead (because, after all, one can still 'see' them) – the real distinction between life and death will ultimately become irrelevant.[35] □

Castle links *Udolpho*'s very rejection of the supernatural to the 'supernaturalization of the mind' that the novel exhibits throughout, explaining that it is precisely the eighteenth century's (and by extension here, the text's) rejection of real ghosts that paves the way for a more troubling haunting of the mind. Castle's argument, that the roots of the psychoanalytical phenomenon of the 'uncanny' can be traced to the Enlightenment and its attempt to silence its irrational counter-discourses, accords well with Massé's explanation of the 'congruence' that we attempt to maintain between fantasy and reality. The rupture of that congruence, so Massé and Castle argue alongside Freud, is what calls forth the 'uncanny'.

In an article entitled 'Social Relations of Gothic Fiction' (1981), David Punter also explores the rupture that Gothic novelists in the 1790s summoned:

■ the writers of the 1790s are concerned with connections between past and present: with, on the one hand, what the violence and crudity of past economic and social relations can reveal about these relations to the present, and with, on the other hand, the possibility that present 'civilization' can tell us something about the barbarity of the past, and especially about the extent to which it might still be inside us.[36] □

Punter's analysis of the exploration of the connections between the barbaric past and the 'civilized' present by the Gothic novelists of the 1790s also accords well with Castle's historical relocation of the rise of the 'uncanny'. If we recall, Freud describes the 'uncanny' as 'that class of the frightening which leads back to what is known of old and long familiar'.[37] The Gothic's exploitation of the irrational and the barbaric compels its contemporary readers not only to contemplate their collective pasts, but also to revisit them. This is exactly the same strategy that some critics of the Gothic assign to psychoanalysis, with Maggie Kilgour, for example, observing that 'psychoanalysis is itself a gothic, necromantic form, that resurrects our psychic pasts'.[38] If we compare this to David Punter's insight that Gothic writing focuses upon a 'deeper wound', 'a fracture, an imbalance, a "gap" in the social self which would not go away' we can see that critics have found much common ground between the discourses of the Gothic novel and of psychoanalysis.[39]

Critics of the Gothic disagree regarding the exact timing of the emergence of psychoanalysis. On the one hand, in *The Rise of the Gothic Novel*, Kilgour firmly maintains that psychoanalysis is 'a late gothic story which has emerged to help explain a twentieth-century experience of paradoxical detachment from and fear of others and the past'.[40] On the other hand, Massé argues that 'Psychoanalysis and the Gothic are cognate historical strands made up of the same human hopes and anxieties and then woven into particular patterns by the movements of sociocultural change.'[41] Robert Miles agrees with Massé and Terry Castle when, in *Ann Radcliffe: The Great Enchantress* (1995), he argues that 'as narratives, psychoanalysis and the Gothic are coeval. They begin to take shape around the end of the eighteenth century.'[42] Despite these critical differences, there is relatively little dissent regarding the congruence between what the Gothic and what psychoanalysis unearth. These critics share a determination to excavate and explore the Gothic novel's obsession with barbarity and irrationality. In the following sections of this chapter, we will examine how some psychoanalytic readings explore barbarity within the Gothic genre at the level of gender, sexuality, structural and, more recently, historicist concerns.

## Vision, psychoanalysis, the Gothic and gender

Many critics have rightly argued that the Gothic novel is, in essence, a genre predicated upon a violent form of voyeurism. Such voyeurism is immediately evident, for example, from the very opening page of Matthew Lewis's *The Monk*. Here, the reader is sternly told not to expect either piety or a desire for knowledge within the congregation of the Church of the Capuchins. Instead, 'The Women came to show themselves, the Men to see the Women.'[43] This opening gives us a strong clue as to how voyeurism and display work within *The Monk*. It hints that the characters themselves are strong participants in this process, but in addition, the emphatic narratological directions on the opening page of the novel suggest a strong reader-participation within the process of voyeurism. When the following description of the heroine Antonia's entrance to the Church is given from the perspective of the cavaliers Don Christoval and Don Lorenzo, we are forced to become complicit with their lingering appraisal of Antonia:

■ [Antonia] was silent, but made no further opposition to Don Lorenzo's efforts, who armed with the Aunt's sanction hastened to remove the Gauze. What a Seraph's head presented itself to his admiration! Yet it was rather bewitching than beautiful; It was not so lovely from regularity of features, as from sweetness and sensibility of Countenance. The several parts of her face considered separately, many of them were far from handsome; but when examined together, the whole was adorable. Her skin though fair was not entirely without freckles; Her eyes were not very large, nor their lashes particularly long. But then her lips were of the most rosy freshness; Her fair and undulating hair, confined by a simple ribband, poured itself below her waist in a profusion of ringlets; Her throat was full and beautiful in the extreme; Her hand and arm were formed with the most perfect symmetry; Her mild blue eyes seemed an heaven of sweetness, and the crystal in which they moved, sparkled with all the brilliance of Diamonds: She appeared to be scarcely fifteen; An arch smile, playing round her mouth, declared her to be possessed of liveliness, which excess of timidity at present represt.[44] □

As readers, we are forced to adopt the perspective of Don Lorenzo's appraisal of Antonia's features. With him, we linger over her beauty, her 'Seraph's head', 'the perfect symmetry' of various parts of her body, and 'the most rosy freshness' of her lips. This self-appointed connoisseur of female beauty, however, still finds much to criticize in Antonia's form, which was rather 'bewitching than beautiful'. This is, I think, the point where Lewis forces us to experience discomfort in our complicitous appraisal of Antonia. The dissonance of these negative qualifications from Don Lorenzo reminds us of our own voyeuristic position as readers, and our own complicity in (re)constructing this image of Antonia. The self-conscious references to the 'arch[ness]' of her smile which 'plays' around her mouth are reminiscent of that first statement on display and image-making in the novel, that 'The Women came to show themselves, the Men to see the women.' Don Lorenzo and the reader seem to (re)construct the naïve and innocent Antonia as the knowingly sexualized vision with the 'arch' smile. Robert Miles has commented upon Lewis's trenchant critique of the visual in *The Monk*, arguing that 'The Church is a site of magnificence rather than austerity, of display rather than of worship, and of sexual rather than religious pursuits.'[45] But this visual critique is enacted at the authorial, narratological, reading and straightforwardly representational positions in Gothic fiction.

In terms of readership, in *Love, Mystery and Misery* Coral Ann Howells argues that in Gothic novels:

■ As readers we are consistently placed in the position of literary voyeurs, always gazing at emotional excess without understanding the why of it: what we are given are the gestures of feeling rather than any insight into the complexity of feelings themselves. The springs of these emotions elude us, so that we can only look on with appalled fascination as floods of feeling rush through the characters distorting their physical features with alarming rapidity.[46] □

Howells's argument here emphasizes the passivity and helplessness of the reading process, where, like spectators at a play, we gaze at emotional excess without being able to understand it. In appalled and helpless fascination, when we read a Gothic novel which is replete with violent emotion and action, we can only continue to watch or read passively as the violence continues. In a sense, as readers, we also become victims as well as complicit literary voyeurs. This process is self-consciously represented within Gothic fiction. In Maturin's *Melmoth the Wanderer*, for example, Monçada comments that: 'The drama of terror has the irresistible power of converting its audience into its victims.'[47] Such a reflection is entirely applicable to the process of reading a Gothic novel, where, in the words of Anna Laetitia Aikin, 'We rather chuse to suffer the smart pang of a violent emotion than the uneasy craving for an unsatisfied desire.'[48]

In recent decades, psychoanalytic feminist criticism has questioned how to deal with the gendered implications of Anna Laetitia Aikin's 'paradox' of watching and suffering in Gothic fiction. In Gothic fiction, passive, helpless spectating is often the lot of the victim, and that victim is often female. But the paradox lies in the fact that the 'gaze' has frequently been coded as masculine in its objectification of female victims, and this poses a problem at the level both of female readership of Gothic fiction, and of the female spectators portrayed within Gothic fiction.

In *Gothic (Re)Visions: Writing Women as Readers* (1983), Susan Wolstenholme embarks upon the vital and complex investigation of the gendered visual coding of Gothic fiction. Beginning with the paradox that many women wrote Gothic fiction that was both violent and voyeuristic in its portrayal of female victims, Wolstenholme argues that:

■ The Gothic structure of looking and being-looked-at offers certain 'covers' for the coding of women within the text, because its plot often revolves around the issues of seeing and hiding. The main attraction and raison d'être of Gothic cathedrals resembles that of the Gothic structures of their literary counterparts: both contain secrets and mysteries within their innermost parts, with which they entice the spectator/reader. The Gothic architectural spectacle hides its theological mysteries under the cover of opulent display. Playing upon the notion of spectacle with which the cathedral issues its invitation to people, churches make use of literal veils and enclosures – for example, the veil that hides the tabernacle, or the tabernacle itself – as well as of sacramental symbols which both hide and make available the theological mysteries they represent. The sacramental outward sign becomes not only a cover; it also provides access to what it covers. Gothic novels also make use of visual patterns of veiling and hiding, both on a verbally explicit level and structurally, also as a way of simultaneously hiding and giving form. Like the uncanny, a 'Gothic moment' is a moment of (mis)recognition, where hiding from sight and revealing become indistinguishable from one another. Reflexively, it meditates on the problem of representation in terms especially appropriate for suggesting the double role of woman as writer. Its Gothic vision doubles the artist's vision of the text, at the same time suggesting what representation lacks. Sometimes a Gothic vision (in the sense of dream or hallucination) and artistic 'vision' (in the sense of the author's idea of what she is about) completely merge.[49] □

Wolstenholme explores the representation of veiling and hiding in relation to Ann Radcliffe's *The Italian,* and there she offers an important analysis of the motif of veiling within that novel. From the literal unveiling of the heroine Ellena di Rosalba at the beginning, to the gradual unveiling of Ellena's family, Wolstenholme argues that *The Italian's* dramatic visuality is in fact a 'textual theater' which restages scenes compulsively:

■ In its concern with reading, *The Italian* suggests motifs from Freud's 'The Uncanny'. Like Freud in 'The Uncanny', we find ourselves in *The Italian* to be repeatedly walking down the same street, in obsessive repetition of scenes, though the text seemed to have directed our steps elsewhere. Like 'The Uncanny', *The Italian* concerns woman and the theme of seeing and being seen; as in Freud's essay, 'veiling' becomes a double movement, synonymous with its opposite.

But unlike Freud, Radcliffe does not avert her gaze from the veiled woman. She places her on center stage in the opening scene after the prologue. Radcliffe herself is not a 'veilmaker'; she is an observer of veils that have already been made. And ironically – ironic because Radcliffe's medium is 'literature', though of the popular sort, and Freud's is 'science' – Freud is the writer who places greater faith in representation. Unlike Freud, Radcliffe suggests a radical mistrust of representation, particularly of the stage representation of which she makes such free use.[50] ☐

In her analysis here, Wolstenholme focuses upon the structures of representation within the novels that she addresses. This is a valuable approach, and as such makes a good argument for Radcliffe's mistrust of visual display in *The Italian*.

However, it is important to bear in mind that Wolstenholme's analysis rests upon Radcliffe's fifth published novel, the one that, following Matthew Lewis's *The Monk*, is held by critics to have responded to his visual indulgences in framing female victims. Robert Miles has called Radcliffe's third novel, *The Romance of the Forest*, more 'naturalistic' in its plot devices, and this is also applicable to the fourth novel, *The Mysteries of Udolpho*.[51] Both of these novels also present a much more explicitly victimized heroine. For example, in *The Romance of the Forest*, the heroine Adeline is initially focalized as an object of desire through the eyes of the ambivalent male character Monsieur La Motte: her habit 'was thrown open at the bosom, upon which part of her hair had fallen in disorder, while the light veil hastily thrown on, had, in her confusion, been suffered to fall back'.[52] Because this is seen through the eyes of La Motte, we must partake of his voyeurism as we are also compelled to do with Don Lorenzo's voyeurism in *The Monk*. Similarly, in Radcliffe's *The Mysteries of Udolpho*, Emily St Aubert's period of confinement in Montoni's eponymous castle renders her a female victim, forced by Montoni to wear pleasing clothes when he entertains in an attempt to make a match for Emily which will be financially advantageous to him. We are salaciously entertained with descriptions of her clothing and looks.

It is this type of victimization that Michelle A. Massé's *In the Name of Love* (1992) chooses to analyse through a similarly psychoanalytic focus upon the visual aspects of Gothic texts. Like Wolstenholme before her, Massé places significance upon the repetitions that occur within Gothic novels, but her analysis is more explicitly concerned with the victimization of the heroine:

■ I here want to consider the erased, retrospectively trivialized heroine's text and the trauma and repetition that give it shape. Repetition compulsion shapes individual texts, the genre's propagation of new texts, and the genre's relationship with culture. My argument is that repetition in the Gothic functions as it does for certain other traumas: the reactivation of trauma is an attempt to recognize, not relish, the incredible and unspeakable that nonetheless happened. If we situate the source of horror or trauma in the 'real' world of 'rightful' authority that frames early narratives such as Ann Radcliffe's *The Mysteries of Udolpho*, the structural and thematic repetition of the novel's body moves beyond the pleasure principle. The originating trauma that prompts such repetition is the prohibition of female autonomy in the Gothic, in the families that people it, and in the society that reads it. History, both individual and societal, is the nightmare from which the protagonist cannot awaken and whose inexorable logic must be followed.[53] □

Massé's argument here differs from Wolstenholme's earlier argument in her focus upon what these novels represent and reinforce, namely, that the young heroines depicted within Gothic fiction *are* victims confined by paternalistic structures of authority. Due to the relatively low rung of importance that they occupy in family and society, they are unable to act independently. This certainly holds true for all of Radcliffe's heroines, confined in castles by family, unable or unwilling to effect their own escapes. The same entrapment is even exercised on Charlotte Dacre's anti-heroine Victoria di Loredani in *Zofloya*, who is imprisoned unknowingly by her mother in an elderly aunt's home, and then is entrapped by marriage when she does eventually escape. Such examples of women's Gothic writing enable Massé to argue that:

■ The Gothic plot is thus not an 'escape' from the real world but a repetition and exploration of the traumatic denial of identity found there. Both the nightmare stasis of the protagonists and the all-enveloping power of the antagonists are extensions of social ideology and real-world experience. The silence, immobility, and enclosure of the heroines mark their internalization of repression as well as the power of the repressing force. Indeed, their frequently commented-on passivity, lack of differentiation, and lack of development through experience only emphasize this point. As Joanna Russ notes, 'The Heroine's suffering is the principal action of the story *because it is the only action she can perform*.'[54] □

Massé extends her analysis of the Gothic heroine's suffering to consider how the heroine exchanges passivity and masochism for a subtle form of sadism. In order to explore how this works in Gothic fiction, she uses Freud's essay 'A Child is Being Beaten' (1919).

'A Child is Being Beaten' considers the ramifications of looking, curiosity, and their more aggressive counterpart, the gaze. So far, this section has examined the position of voyeurs, and the position of the female victims who are objectified by voyeurism. In this essay, however, a third position is negotiated which problematizes the gazing subject/object opposition: that of a spectator who watches a powerful struggle being enacted between two others. Freud begins by examining gazing young females, but ultimately denies the existence of a female gaze by suggesting that instead the girl, in negotiating an ungendered position for herself as spectator, masochistically identifies with the boy she is watching. She identifies with the beater in the dyad, instead of seeing any similarities between herself and the person being beaten. The role of the spectator is thus ungendered in a sense, as the female spectator is not obliged to side with the other female. However, in her complicity with the male, it can be suggested that her gaze does not function autonomously, but is in fact controlled by the beater. The three stages of the beating fantasy according to Freud are as follows: (1) My father is beating a child; (2) My father is beating me; (3) A child is being beaten. Freud describes the first and third stages as sadistic, and the repressed second stage as masochistic. The first and third stages are sadistic because the child or woman is passively looking on a scene of someone being beaten by someone else, and not actively participating in the spectacle. Passivity signals protection and complicity with the beater as it is not the spectator who is being beaten this time.

The urges to look and to know, which Freud terms the scopophilic and epistemophilic instincts, are closely related to one another and to sadism. The spectator of the beating fantasy thus watches a dynamic of power being enacted, and may even replicate the beater/beaten dyad in his/her own relationships with people. In this way, s/he achieves a form of active agency by repeating the very cycle of which s/he is a victim. The triangular structure of beater/beaten/spectator, emphasized by Freud in stages (1) and (3) of the beating fantasy, enables the heroine to escape the masochism implicit in part (2) of the beating fantasy where 'My father is beating me.'

This essay by Freud has been used widely in order to explore the image of woman as victim *and* to subvert that image through the exploration of scopophilia. Laura Mulvey's important early essay upon this topic, 'Visual Pleasure and Narrative Cinema' (1975), argues that 'the look, pleasurable in form, can be threatening in content, and it is woman as representation/image that crystallizes this paradox'.[55]

'A Child is Being Beaten' can be useful in analyses of the Gothic in several ways. Massé uses it to demonstrate how in Gothic novels petty oppressions can be replicated at the level of the visual. One example of how Massé's critique works can be taken from Emily St Aubert's passive spectating of Montoni hurting her aunt in Radcliffe's *The Mysteries of Udolpho*. When Emily is brought to the Castle of Udolpho, she begins to witness a power struggle between her aunt and Montoni. This involves her aunt's fortune, which Montoni fully expects to be signed over to him after their marriage. Imprisoning Emily's aunt in a room in the castle, he threatens and mistreats her in order to get his way, and much of this protracted torture is silently witnessed by Emily, who hovers on the threshold:

■ Having, therefore, set down the lamp in the passage, she gently opened the door, within which all was dark, except from an inner apartment a partial light appeared; and she stept softly on. Before she reached it, the appearance of Madame Montoni, leaning on her dressing-table, weeping, and with a handkerchief held to her eyes, struck her, and she paused. Some person was seated in a chair by the fire, but who it was she could not distinguish. He spoke, now and then, in a low voice, that Madame Montoni, at those times, wept the more, who was too much occupied by her own distress, to observe Emily, while the latter, though anxious to know what occasioned this, and who was the person admitted at so late an hour to her aunt's dressing-room, *forbore to add to her own sufferings* [emphasis added] by surprising her, or to take advantage of her situation, by listening to a private discourse. She, therefore, stepped softly back, and, after some further difficulty, found the way back to her own chamber, where nearer interests, at length, excluded the surprise and concern she had felt, respecting Madame Montoni.[56] □

In this scene, Emily sets down her lamp in the passage, thereby surrendering the object which will simultaneously herald her presence and reveal to her the entire, unshaded picture of the events played before her eyes. Relegated to the realm of the spectator, Emily imagines pain by viewing her aunt's distress. Although she sympathizes with her aunt, she does not wish to place herself in a position of danger in order to protect her. After mutely regarding the ongoing torture, Emily eventually withdraws to her room to prevent adding to 'her own sufferings', where, it is stated, 'nearer interests' supplant the sufferings of her aunt. Her reaction is clearly self-preservative both in her refusal to intervene and in her ongoing spectating. It can be argued that in this spectatorial role, Emily learns vital lessons of self-preservation.

Massé argues that 'The role of spectator seems to promise protection. ... What the spectator learns at the pageant of horror may also prevent her from becoming a victim later.'[57] Such a critique sheds light upon the motivations of Radcliffe's heroine. The *'nearer interests'* that Emily withdraws to contemplate signify that the self-preservation mechanism has prevented her from becoming engulfed in the horrors that she has just witnessed. This mechanism also later fortifies Emily when she does indeed discover that her aunt has died, and that she must remain in Montoni's castle entirely unprotected. Referring to Freud's beating fantasy, Massé comments:

■ the formation and maintenance of often fragile ego boundaries may come to seem possible only within the constraints of the beating fantasy. The stability of the beating fantasy's drama of triangulation itself fosters credence in the strictures of authority thus created. Within the fantasy, the shifting identification of the spectator with the beaten or the beater marks a further risk: those who are beaten may, in their turn, replicate oppression. Few, because of their own experience, can subordinate their actual oppressors or the systems that validate them: instead, they re-enact their own gender reification by insisting upon hierarchies of class, race, and age. There is thus in such cases a basic conservative identification with the very system that assures their oppression: their limited status and power are asserted within such a system by damaging other women, children, and servants, for example.[58] □

Returning to my analysis of *The Mysteries of Udolpho*, we can see that upon her aunt's death, Emily's sole source of conversation and remaining female companionship rests with her servant Annette. But *The Mysteries of Udolpho* carefully persists in highlighting the class hierarchy that Emily insists upon. She invokes Montoni as a fellow figure of authority when she reproves her servant for her superstition:

> ■ 'I hope,' said Emily, 'you will not suffer Signor Montoni to hear of these weak fears; they would highly displease him.'
> 'What, you know then, ma'amselle, all about it!' rejoined Annette. 'No, no. I do know better than to do so; though, if the Signor can sleep sound, nobody else in the castle has any right to lie awake, I am sure.' Emily did not appear to notice this remark.[59] □

Whilst Annette, the maidservant, is courageous and truthful enough to enunciate her fear and disdain of Montoni, Emily clearly takes his side and reproduces his own scolding for superstitious nonsense. Whilst Emily assumes his position in this argument, we are privy to the knowledge that she is as much prone to these fears as Annette, if not more. In the final sentence of this exchange, however, the narrator uses humour against her heroine in order to highlight her faults. This humour subverts the authoritative complicity that Emily aspires to between herself and Montoni. Emily's deference to his wishes in front of her servant is ironized to indicate how misplaced it is. Having learned the lessons of self-preservation through watching passively, Emily now replicates these lessons in her dealings with her own subordinate, Annette.

Through its gentle mockery of Emily, *The Mysteries of Udolpho* suggests that watching and learning in battles of self-preservation is, in the end, a hollow victory. Indeed, one could go so far as to argue that Emily trades in the position of spectator simply in order to replicate the position of the oppressor. Such lessons of self-preservation in the Gothic genre seem to collude with the later psychoanalytic narrative of victim and oppressor that Freud records in 'A Child is Being Beaten'. Elisabeth

Bronfen, writing of the challenge and simultaneous support of the masculine gaze in the parodic strategy of female writing in *Over her Dead Body* (1992), forges an important connection between a parodic and an hysteric strategy:

> ■ The problem is that if the mastering gaze which separates subject from object of gaze is inherently masculine, can there be a feminine gaze? In response to this impasse hysterical writing installs conventions such as the masculinity of the gaze, the deadness of the feminine body, only to subvert and disturb the security of these stakes in cultural self-representation. Though such a critique is inscribed by complicity, such complicity may also be the most effective critique.[60] □

Bronfen's defence here seems applicable to what is portrayed in *The Mysteries of Udolpho*. Emily's position as a petty oppressor does not proceed uncensored, and the subordinate, Annette, is able to undermine her assumed position. Bronfen's argument also defends the wide range of critical psychoanalytical analyses of the Gothic that invoke Freud's beating fantasy as a model to analyse the complicity of the genre's victims.[61]

In *The Romantic Unconscious* (1989), David Punter warns against analysing characters' unconscious motives in Gothic fiction in a straightforwardly 'real' way. He reminds us that 'We have to be clear that if we do this we are in fact engaging in a further participation in the potentially unlimited flow of fictions ... which, in itself, may be a perfectly worthwhile activity, but is not to be confused with the analysis of real people.'[62] This warning can apply to the type of analysis of the character motivations of Emily St Aubert that we have examined above. It indicates the potential pitfalls of analysing one particular character through the lens of an essay by Freud as if that character were a 'real' person. Instead, as Punter warns, we must remain constantly alert to the 'bundle of codes, categories and markers out of which fictional persons are built'.[63]

With this in mind, I will now examine how the 'codes, categories and markers' in Gothic fiction can be approached through post-Freudian psychoanalytic theories in order to arrive at deeper structural signification.

## Loss, absence, faking and the Gothic

A good number of Gothic critics have used Freud's psychoanalytic insights in order to illuminate their readings of the genre. Many of these critics argue for the simultaneous emergence of the Gothic and psychoanalysis. A substantial number of critics, however, particularly in recent years, have turned to the trope of the absent mother in Gothic fiction, and have produced critiques of the Gothic which focus on loss and absence. In order to support their analyses, these critics have turned to French psychoanalysis, and particularly the theories of Jacques Lacan, Luce Irigaray, Julia Kristeva and Hélène Cixous.

We have already seen how Cixous rereads Freud's 'The Uncanny' in this chapter, and now we will examine briefly the position of Jacques Lacan's psychoanalysis in order to understand how loss and absence in Gothic fiction can be explored. The 'Introduction' to *The (M)other Tongue: Essays in Feminist Psychoanalytic Interpretation* (1985) helpfully clarifies Jacques Lacan's psychoanalytical approach and its distinctions. Referring to Lacan's foundational essays 'The Mirror Stage as Formative of the Function of the I', 'The Symbolic Order' and 'The Agency of the Letter in the Unconscious', Garner and her co-authors explain:[64]

■ Lacanians translate maternal loss into the more generalized concept of originary loss, of a lack in the subject, displaced and veiled by language but persisting as unconscious desire. Desire, Lacan's key concept, challenges the unity of the subject, and thus any fixed unitary sexual identity.

Whereas the self in object-relations theory is constituted as a unity through the process of differentiation, for Lacanians that self is a fiction, a creation of desire, organized around a fantasy of wholeness and integration, reflected in the mirror image. The mirror stage thus represents the moment when the subject is alienated, located within an order outside itself, and subject to that order. In Lacan's complex narrative of mirror relations, the child desires to be what the mother desires. But both mother and child are themselves already located within the Symbolic order of language and culture, in which the mother's desire is governed by the 'law of the Father'.[65] □

According to Lacan, desire is always deferred in the Symbolic Order, always beyond the subject's grasp owing to that initial separation between mother and child. Desire is remembered through the process of the mirror stage, where the fantasy of desire was fictionalized for the child as something attainable.

In her essay 'The Gothic Mirror' (1985), Claire Kahane reads Lacan's theory into the very narrative structure of Gothic fiction:

■ Within an imprisoning structure, a protagonist, typically a young woman whose mother has died, is compelled to seek out the center of a mystery, while vague and usually sexual threats to her person from some powerful male figure hover on the periphery of her consciousness. Following clues that pull her onward and inward – bloodstains, mysterious sounds – she penetrates the obscure recesses of a vast labyrinthian space and discovers a secret room sealed off by its association with death. In this dark, secret center of the Gothic structure, the boundaries of life and death seem confused. Who died? Has there been a murder? Or merely a disappearance? This is the conventional plot of the Gothic novel, first popularized by Ann Radcliffe in the late eighteenth century. ... Its confusions – its misleading clues, postponements of discovery, excessive digressions – are inscribed in the narrative structure itself.[66] □

Kahane's opening to her essay importantly highlights the process by which desire itself is constantly deferred in the reading process of a Gothic novel. Gothic fiction champions digressions into other stories. This is highlighted in particular throughout Radcliffe's novels. Later, Maturin's *Melmoth the Wanderer* perfects the art of digression in the maddening convolutions of its structure, and is structurally suggestive of the endless postponement of gratified desire.[67]

Kahane, however, also sees this deferral of desire located within the central absence of the novels, 'the spectral presence of a dead–undead mother, archaic and all-encompassing, a ghost signifying the problematics of femininity which the heroine must confront'.[68] As a trope, the figure of the absent mother haunts Gothic fiction pervasively, from Sophia Lee's fictionalization of the two orphaned sisters of the dead Mary, Queen of Scots, through Radcliffe's orphans to Charlotte Dacre's dramatization of the absent and remiss mother in *Zofloya*. In relation to Radcliffe in particular, in *Ann Radcliffe: The Great Enchantress*, Robert Miles argues that:

■ For Radcliffe's female characters, the absent maternal body is the ground of their being. Julia's obsessive interest in *A Sicilian Romance* in her miniature of her 'dead' mother figures the loss of the maternal body. The mother herself is characterised by 'sensibility', by a feeling heart and a receptive imagination. Julia on the threshold stands for those other Radcliffe heroines who find themselves at a window, staring out, caught in a 'neither/nor' of two unsatisfactory choices. ... There is the impulse to revolve inwards into the self, into 'maternal' sensibility, into reverie and dream. But without the beloved other (the prohibited suitor) this proves a regressive world, one stripped of desire and hence meaning. The former state of childish plenitude is no longer a possibility.

In this respect an analogy arises between Radcliffe's figure of the heroine on a threshold and Lacan's mirror stage. For both, to move 'forward' is to enter a state of 'desire', of endlessly deferred presence.[69] □

For Miles, then, Radcliffe's Gothic heroines hover on the threshold of adulthood, deprived of their own choice of suitor, denied their mothers.

He relates this state of indecision to Lacan's theory of the mirror stage, because the heroines exist in the neither–nor world, deprived of both choice and desire. He concludes that 'Radcliffe's heroine on a threshold looks both ways, inwards towards "maternal" sensibility with its delusive image of subjective wholeness ... and outwards towards a patriarchal order of repression and deferral.'[70]

The key distinction that Miles's Lacanian analysis highlights here is the distinction between the maternally driven mirror stage, and the paternalistically driven 'law of the Father'. Lacan's symbolic Father is the figure which breaks the relation between mother and child, between self and 'other-as-image-of-self'. The Father's law, like the tyrannical Gothic fathers, compels subjects to take up a place in its Symbolic Order, in a pre-existing order of language and culture. As Miles highlights in his analysis above, in Gothic fiction, this process can translate into the marriage choices that the heroine is forced to make, and the father figure's intervention in this.

Lacan's psychoanalysis, which has been used widely in Gothic criticism, has the drawback that it insists that this paternalistic Symbolic Order, the Law of the Father, is paramount and insurmountable. According to the strictures of such analysis, the Gothic heroine will always be subject to the desires of the Father, and will always be destined to renounce the absent mother figure in her life. Claire Kahane even reads this into the pastoral, happy-marriage endings of Radcliffe's fiction, arguing by way of example that the ending of Radcliffe's *Udolpho* places its heroine and its readers 'in an idealized nurturing space, the space provided for heroines by patriarchal narrative convention'.[71] This position is entirely persuasive: like the use of Freud's 'A Child is Being Beaten' such Lacanian approaches to Gothic fiction often only serve to reinforce the inevitability of the heroine's powerlessness in forging her own story.

Recently, other psychoanalytical analyses of the Gothic have begun to focus on French feminist psychoanalysis. They have thus been able to produce more positive accounts of the heroine's position within the novel. In particular, the writings of Cixous and Irigaray have become useful. Their formulation of a female poetics, based upon the child's pleasure in the mother's body (which has been repressed by Freud's and Lacan's accounts), is based on there being a kind of language specific to women. They call this *l'écriture féminine*. This language, for Cixous and Irigaray, is fluid. It does not respect the boundaries of patriarchal discourse.[72] Using Irigaray's theories in particular, Alison Milbanke has produced a more positive reading than Kahane of the ending of Radcliffe's *A Sicilian Romance*. For Milbanke, the heroine's (Julia's) rediscovery of her mother in a cave is symbolic of a rediscovery of the 'maternal'.[73]

As we shall also see in the following chapter, Anne Williams invokes
Julia Kristeva's use of 'narrative poetics' in *Art of Darkness: A Poetics of
Gothic* (1995) in order to debunk 'the Gothic myth' of the genre's patri-
archal lineage from Walpole onwards.[74] Wishing to reclaim the Gothic
genre's maternal roots, she uses Kristeva's theories of a maternal pre-
language to challenge the prevailing belief that Horace Walpole's *The
Castle of Otranto* is solely responsible for inaugurating the Gothic genre.
In her opening arguments, Williams draws attention to the ubiquitous
familial metaphors which resurface when we consider the origins of the
Gothic:

■ The lineage of Gothic, this literature itself so concerned with genealogy,
is far from easy to determine. Some works were born Gothic – as when
*The Castle of Otranto* sprang fully armed from Horace Walpole's dream-
ing brow in 1764. In calling his progeny 'A Gothic Story', he gave later
critics grounds for regarding him as progenitor of 'the Gothic tradition,'
and for later generating widespread critical anxieties about the differences between modes of fiction. But other works seem to have *achieved*
Gothic, to belong presently to the family although not born in the direct
line. ... The reader searching for 'Gothic' in a novel (as well as 'the novel'
in Gothic) realizes that Walpole's inspiration derives not only from a few
scenes in Smollett and Richardson, but also from a farrago of poetry,
drama, architecture, painting, landscape gardening, and antiquarian
enthusiasm for the medieval (or rather for eighteenth-century fantasies
of those 'Dark Ages').[75] □

Williams effectively draws attention to the erroneous assumptions
made about the Gothic's starting point, rightly indicating that the
genre's genealogy is grounded not only in the eighteenth-century
novel, but also in a range of other genres. Her reference to the latter category of 'antiquarian enthusiasm for the medieval' is especially significant. This eighteenth-century pursuit was widespread and its influence
on the Gothic genre has been underestimated.

In an important essay, 'The Gothic Ghost of the Counterfeit and the
Progress of Abjection' (2000), Jerrold E. Hogle uses Julia Kristeva's neo-
Freudian work *Powers of Horror* to good effect in order to argue that:
'From its beginnings in the eighteenth century, in the "Gothic revival"
in architecture or the "Gothic Story"... the modern "Gothic" as we
know it has been grounded in fakery.'[76] He proceeds to justify this claim
by citing Walpole's contrived 'Gothic' house at Strawberry Hill as an
example of fake antique Gothicism, as well as the fake 'editorship' of his
first edition of *The Castle of Otranto*. Hogle then rightly argues that 'Even
the principal hauntings in *Otranto* are by ghosts of representations, spectres
of counterfeits, rather than the shades of bodies.'[77] Hogle carefully
explains Kristeva's theory of abjection from *Powers of Horror* and how it

relates to the process of counterfeiting, or effectively concealing, that the Gothic enacts:

■ How is it that a mode based on a kind of fakery can both contain and arouse those half-conscious/half-unconscious feelings that are the objects of Freudian psychoanalysis, that influential set of schemata for which the neo-Gothic helped to provide a topography and which has therefore provided a revealing way to interpret Gothic texts? In particular, how do Gothic fiction's roots in counterfeitings of the past enable it to perform what its most sophisticated recent critics have found it to be playing out: a process of 'abjection', as defined in Julia Kristeva's neo-Freudian *Powers of Horror*, whereby the most multifarious, inconsistent and conflicted aspects of our beings in the West are 'thrown off' onto seemingly repulsive monsters or ghosts that both conceal and reveal this 'otherness' from our preferred selves as existing very much *within* ourselves? Noting that 'abjection' literally means 'throwing off' and 'being thrown under', *Powers of Horror* finds the quintessential state of primordial non-identity to be the condition of being half inside and half outside the mother at the moment of birth – of being half dead and half alive from the start and thus undecidably in motion between logically contradictory states, including life and death. And it is this betwixt-and-betweenness (which can take many other forms, including a person's emergence from a welter of different existential, class, racial and sexual or gendered conditions) that most of us in the West strive to 'throw away' from ourselves as repugnant, and 'throw under' a cultural norm as being outside it, in order to interpret ourselves and be interpreted as having a solid 'identity', a oneness to ourselves instead of an otherness from ourselves in ourselves. □ (Kristeva, 1982: 3–60)[78]

Kristeva's theory of abjection foregrounds the loss of all boundaries, or the dissolution of the individual, 'human' subject. She argues in *Powers of Horror* that, in our attempt to maintain the simulacrum of individuality, we 'abject' or throw off everything which is 'other' to us. In our attempts to justify this process, we render these beliefs as 'horrific' or 'abnormal'. In Chapter Four, we saw how Robert Miles uses Kristeva's theory of abjection in relation to the contemporary nationalistic, Protestant issues in the Gothic novel of the 1790s.[79] Here, Hogle focuses upon the structural fakery of the Gothic form in order to interrogate more closely the Gothic's engagement with the past:

■ Why, then, are spectres of what is already counterfeit particularly useful in our culture for these kind of abjective 'otherings', so useful that we cannot stop re-enacting such abjections ... ? What is it about the Gothic pattern of resymbolising the fake that lends itself to being a locus of abjection? Why, too, have the different kinds of abjection developed as they have in

Gothic fictions over time, along with transformations in how the counterfeit archaism is resignified in the construction of later Gothic texts? How and why has Gothic abjection *progressed* as it has as part of the historical, cultural and artistic development of the Gothic spectre of the falsified past? I want to propose the beginnings of some answers to these questions here, first by returning to the literary and ideological foundations of the 'Gothic' – epitomised by what I call 'the ghost of the counterfeit', the symbolic basis of it – and then by discussing how those foundations have been transformed over the last three centuries by drives that are basic to them from the very beginnings of the neo-Gothic mode. ... Walpolean Gothic fakery is not as simply different from its source in the Shakespearean spectre as it first appears to be. In fact, the neo-Gothic turns out to be referring, with its ghosts of various kinds, back to a Renaissance symbolisation of the self that was already 'counterfeit' in Shakespeare's day: hence the Gothic sign as the *ghost* of the counterfeit. Fictions arising from the 'Gothic revival' therefore oscillate between different discourses of self-definition in the eighteenth century by being later and more uprooted signifiers of the conflicts in modes of symbol-making and beliefs about 'self-fashioning' that arose in fifteenth- to sixteenth-century Europe. Once these ideological tugs of war reach the articulations of them in the eighteenth-century Gothic, they manifest the transitional quality of that era for rising middle-class readers, a betwixt-and-betweenness in which ageing and aristocratically based concepts of signification pull nostalgically backward while newer, more early-capitalist alternatives try to make cultural capital of the older ones so as to advance the power of the self through an 'enterprise' supposedly more 'free' than it was.

By allowing such an emphatic conflation of beliefs and interplays of feeling, where ideologies and their symbols pull in different directions at once, Gothic fiction, with its ghosts of counterfeits, becomes a site into which widely felt tensions arising from this state of culture can be transferred, sequestered, disguised, and yet played out. Indeed, such a cultural locus, since it employs symbols from earlier times largely emptied of older meanings, quite readily becomes a symbolic space into which the fears and horrors generated by early modern cultural changes can be 'thrown off' or 'thrown under' as though they exist more in the now obscure and distant past than in the threatening present.[80] □

Hogle argues that the acts of repeated fakery which lie at the (shaky) foundation of the Gothic genre enable the prevailing (middle-class) culture to 'play out' and 'throw off' the tensions of prevailing beliefs. The Gothic's engagement with the rise of antiquarianism in the eighteenth century (and with it the taste for *faux* medievalism), the return to the (already counterfeit) idea of Renaissance self-fashioning, its confused genealogy of sources (which Williams also highlights) are, for Hogle, all part of the process of continuous abjection, or throwing off, of the 'cultural quandaries' of the present.

Hogle's argument is sophisticated and compelling, and enhances David Punter's earlier thesis that Gothic novelists 'are concerned with connections between past and present: with … what the violence and crudity of past economic and social relations can reveal about these relations to the present'.[81] Hogle's revelatory insight, however, lies in his excavation of the process of counterfeiting of the past which is at the heart of the Gothic genre. How this counterfeiting process is abjected by the Gothic and its readership tells us much about our own complacent engagement with the past.

As a conclusion on the Gothic's relation to its past, I want to briefly invoke one final argument. In 'Violence, Trauma and the Ethical', David Punter and Elisabeth Bronfen argue in relation to the Gothic, history and psychoanalysis, that:

> ■ [the Gothic] recognises that in fact wherever one digs one will come across the bones of the dead – hence the functional prolixity of the Gothic – and that instead of such excavations providing a new historical security, a new sense of order and origin, they will merely produce an 'overhang', an increasingly unstable superstructure as the foundations are progressively exposed.[82] □

The archaeological metaphor used by Punter and Bronfen attests to the Gothic genre being not simply a tool of history, but a mode that reminds us just how insecure the entire notion of history is. For Hogle, Punter and Bronfen, the excavation of history seemingly enacted in the Gothic reveals the falsity of our comfortable assumptions about the past.

Gothic criticism's continued engagement with psychoanalysis has become increasingly sophisticated. Critiques have come a long way from the Surrealist analyses provided by Breton and Varma, and the early exploration of incest motifs by Praz and Railo. Recent symbioses of psychoanalysis and historicism in Gothic criticism demonstrate that the Gothic novel and the discipline of psychoanalysis can prove mutually illuminating in their excavation of the past.[83] The following final chapter of this study, on 'Gender and the Gothic', demonstrates in places the continuing relevance of psychoanalytic criticism to many critical explorations of the function of gender and sexuality in the Gothic. In fact, this final chapter demonstrates that the differing approaches examined in the previous five chapters converge and diverge in the much-contested issues surrounding 'Gender and the Gothic'.

# CHAPTER SIX

# 'It is not ours to make election for ourselves': Gender and the Gothic

Heaven knows! we have more authors now than ever: if a father writes, the son is straightaway attacked with the *cacoethes scribendi*, and thinks to become – a greater man than his father! – As for the female part of the community, I verily believe that every third woman in these happy united kingdoms, considers herself a genius – nay, I have heard, and readily believe it, that there are many thick-headed female dames of fortune who sacrifice hundreds to establish – the reign of dullness and folly!

(Sarah Green, 'Literary Retrospection', the Preface to *Romance Readers and Romance Writers: A Satirical Novel* in three volumes, London: T. Hookham, 1810, p. xiii)

## Female authorship and 'Female Gothic'

The epigraph to this chapter comes from the pen of a relatively unknown female author who both wrote Gothic novels and satirized them, closely following the literary market's appetite for Gothic fiction. Sarah Green's preface to her satirical work *Romance Readers and Romance Writers* (1810) mocks a culture apparently plagued by the *cacoethes scribendi* – the stubborn disease of writing – and mischievously implies that producing Gothic Romance is a both costly and presumptuous exercise: presumptuous, because women authors lacked 'genius'; costly, because women often had to pay for the publication of their Romances. While the accusation of vanity publishing may have been true in the case of a few individuals, her generalization belies the extent to which female authors of Romance dominated the literary marketplace in the

1790s. Thomas Talfourd (1785–1854), for example, in his *Life and Writings of Mrs Radcliffe* (1826), acknowledged that:

■ The pecuniary advantages, which [Mrs Radcliffe] derived from her works ... were considerable, according to the fashion of the times. For 'The Mysteries of Udolpho' she received from Messrs. Robinson £500.; a sum then so unusually large for a work of fiction, that Mr. Cadell, who had great experience in such matters, on hearing the statement, offered a wager of £10. that it was untrue. By the Italian, although considerably shorter, she acquired about the sum of £800.[1] □

For Talfourd, the 'fashion of the times' dictated considerable 'pecuniary advantages' for authors. Mrs Radcliffe's reputation as the principal beneficiary of the publishing appetite for Gothic Romances was secure, although she was by no means alone in being paid large sums of money for her Gothic works. In *Women's Gothic* (2000), E. J. Clery lists 'more than fifty women writers from the 1790s to the 1820s writing in what we now call the Gothic genre'.[2] The six writers that she chooses to focus upon, Clara Reeve, Sophia Lee, Ann Radcliffe, Joanna Baillie (1762–1851), Charlotte Dacre and Mary Shelley, were all 'successful professional writers, ambitious and innovative, openly courting the public with sensational material'.[3] But these six authors are representative of a far larger body of women writers; they are not exceptions.

The presence of these women in the pantheon of Gothic fiction goes some way towards explaining the periodical press's discomfort with the literary marketplace. Women were not simply consumers of Gothic fiction, but also the producers of it. This tension, where women were seen to produce a literary economy which could be run independently of male intervention, inevitably led to a critical backlash against their works.[4] After Radcliffe, women's Gothic writing was accused of being imitative and derivative, as articles such as 'Terrorist Novel Writing', examined in Chapter One, suggest.

However, the fact that women's Gothic writing was imitative suggests that Gothic fiction written by women became a genre that was easily recognizable. Its overwhelming success also testifies to an identifiable categorization where young women, borrowing books from a circulating library, could easily discover exactly what they wanted.[5] This argument is reflected by the twentieth century's critical approach to this type of writing.

The term 'Female Gothic' was first used by Ellen Moers. It has since gained widespread critical currency. In *Literary Women* (1976), Moers explained her definition of 'Female Gothic' very briefly: 'What I mean by Female Gothic is easily defined: the work that women writers have done in the literary mode that, since the eighteenth century, we have called the Gothic.'[6] Moers's succinct definition of 'Female Gothic' belies the complexity that underscores the current use of the term. Indeed, the initial simplicity of her association of 'Female Gothic' with the author's gender is eroded in the following stages of her argument:

■ At the time when literary Gothic was born, religious fears were on the wane, giving way to that vague paranoia of the modern spirit for which Gothic mechanisms seem to have provided welcome therapy.[7] Walter Scott compared reading Mrs. Radcliffe to taking drugs, dangerous when habitual 'but of most blessed power in those moments of pain and of languor, when the whole head is sore, and the whole heart sick. If those who rail indiscriminately at this species of composition, were to consider the quantity of actual pleasure which it produces, and the much greater proportion of real sorrow and distress which it alleviates, their philanthropy ought to moderate their critical pride, or religious intolerance.' A grateful public rewarded Mrs. Radcliffe by making her the most popular and best-paid English novelist of the eighteenth century. Her pre-eminence among the 'Terrorists,' as they were called, was hardly challenged in her own day, and modern readers of *Udolpho* and *The Italian* continue to hail her as mistress of the pure Gothic form.

As early as the 1790s, Ann Radcliffe firmly set the Gothic in one of the ways it would go ever after: a novel in which the central figure is a young woman who is simultaneously persecuted victim and courageous heroine.[8] □

In Moers's argument, the definition of 'Female Gothic' shifts rapidly from being straightforwardly defined through the gender of the author to an exploration of the aesthetics of the form. Radcliffe's publishing success secures her reputation as 'mistress of the pure Gothic form', but for Moers, Radcliffe's reputation rests upon her enterprising use of a 'young woman' in all of her novels. For Moers, this is the theme that launched the 'Female Gothic' genre. Besides Moers's hesitation in categorizing 'Female Gothic' through gender or aesthetics, there is a more immediate problem in her identification of Radcliffe as the pioneer of this form. Moers does not acknowledge previous women writers, such as Sophia Lee, who as early as 1785 produced a narrative with two young women at its centre entitled *The Recess*.[9]

Ellen Moers's own ambivalent use of the term 'Female Gothic' has since been explored and challenged in a range of articles and works. One of the first challenges to the assumptions of 'Female Gothic' was issued by Jacqueline Howard in her 1993 monograph *Reading Gothic Fiction: A Bakhtinian Approach*. There, Howard provided an excellent survey of feminist criticism of the Gothic and investigated how the term

'Female Gothic' had gained such currency, arguing that, 'While the term "women's writing" has obvious advantages, application of the epithets "male" and "female" to writing is more problematic. ... While the fact of certain biological distinctions between the sexes is indisputable, that these have any necessary psychological consequences is unclear.'[10] In addition, Howard takes issue with Moers's specific championing of Mary Shelley's *Frankenstein* as typical of the 'Female Gothic' genre because the text concerned a 'birth myth' which was linked to Shelley's own maternity. Howard rightly argues that 'With this psychological orientation ... Moers ultimately moves beyond the discussion of Gothic texts as belonging to distinct historical moments. Instead she constructs an overarching framework in which "Female Gothic" ... can be read as psycho-biographical expressions of women's sexual feelings, particularly fear, guilt, depression, and anxiety.'[11] Moers's ahistorical construction of 'Female Gothic' from Radcliffe through to the American novelist and short-story writer Carson McCullers (1917–67) is indeed problematic in its focus upon the biological imperative of women's writing. None the less, its significant work in revising the predominantly male canon of literature has sparked intense debate in relation to Gothic fiction in particular, and the continuing lively discussion of the term 'Female Gothic' sustains a strong focus upon women's Gothic writing.

During the past decade, two journals, *Women's Writing* and *Gothic Studies*, have devoted special issues to a range of essays which explore 'Female Gothic'.[12] In 1994, the first issue of the journal *Women's Writing*, guest-edited by Robert Miles, was devoted to 'Female Gothic'. In one of the most significant essays of this collection, 'Ann Radcliffe and D. A. F. de Sade: Thoughts on Heroinism', E. J. Clery also questions the assumptions of Moers's unproblematized use of this term by correcting Moers's selective use of literary history:

■ Moers's coinage has since played a part in reviving the reputation of Ann Radcliffe and, to a lesser extent, other female writers of the Gothic. But it has also encouraged certain assumptions about their writings. The notion of the intrinsic 'femaleness' of Gothic fiction by women has too often been taken for granted, giving rise to constructions of a generalised female psyche or lessons in women's history offered up as a 'natural' cause of literary fantasy. 'Female Gothic', used as a common-sense category, has tended to prevent even the formulation of basic questions about the genre; for instance, the question, Why a heroine?

Feminist criticism tends to view the heroine as the vehicle of the author's naturally feminine perspective, and as a source of identification for a largely female readership. Maybe this is why Moers states that as 'early as the 1790s, Ann Radcliffe firmly set the Gothic in one of the ways it would go ever after: a novel in which the central figure is a young woman who is simultaneously persecuted victim and courageous heroine.' But it is a half-truth only: yes, Radcliffe was considered a founding figure in her time, but for her atmospheric landscape description and device of the 'explained supernatural', not for the heroine-centred narrative. ... The story of a young woman, unprotected by family or fortune and submitted to a variety of dangers, was the most popular and enduring fiction of the eighteenth century. It was reiterated by both male and female authors with infinite variations and consumed by both male and female readers with a seemingly unappeasable appetite.[13] □

Clery rightly argues that the heroine-centred novel is ubiquitous in the eighteenth century, and that it attracted a mixed readership. She is sceptical of thematic studies that have been executed along the demarcations of gender by feminist critics.[14] Like Howard, Clery argues that 'this has the effect of restricting the meaning of feminocentric fictions to what one might call the author's "gender intentionality", a cultural outlook determined by biological sex'.[15] Instead, Clery calls for an analysis of this exchange of ideas on the function of the heroine between male and female authors during the eighteenth century, citing, amongst others, Jean-Jacques Rousseau, Ann Radcliffe and D. A. F. de Sade (the Marquis de Sade). Clery's attention here to context and literary influence is important. To argue for a continuous 'Female Gothic' tradition, as Ellen Moers does – from Ann Radcliffe to the present day – is over-simplified in its neglect of different literary discourses and different contexts.

Clery's suspicion of the universalizing category of 'Female Gothic' is shared by a number of critics. In the same collection of essays on 'Female Gothic', Robert Miles also warns against regarding this 'as a self-evident literary classification'.[16] More recently, Andrew Smith and Diana Wallace have also described 'Female Gothic' as 'possibly, too essentialising' in a critical 'Introduction' to their fresh collection of essays on 'Female Gothic' for the journal *Gothic Studies* in 2004.[17]

The collective critical suspicion of what 'Female Gothic' might mean may initially appear to be confusing for those readers who are new to Gothic fiction and criticism. However, the inability to reduce 'Female Gothic' to one single essentialist definition is indicative of the multiplicity of possibilities in exploring gender in the Gothic. The problems raised by the coinage of the term 'Female Gothic' provide three gender-based issues to explore in relation to Gothic fiction. The first, female authorship, has already been discussed following Moers's own opening definition of what constitutes 'Female Gothic'. The exploration of this term will now segue into the next strand of the chapter, concerning representations of reading and gender relations within Gothic fiction. This will then lead to an exploration of the critiques of marriage and the legal process, as well as explorations of the hero/heroine plots in Gothic fiction, in order to decide whether the female-centred plots constitute 'Female Gothic'. In the final section of this chapter, we will move on to discuss wider representations of gender and sexuality within the genre, broadening the discussion out to explore criticism of how Gothic writing challenges contemporary assumptions about men and women.

## Feminized narratives for female readerships?

In the provocatively titled essay 'Can You Forgive Her? The Gothic Heroine and Her Critics' (2000), Kate Ferguson Ellis discusses the cultural implications of early gender portrayals offered by the likes of Horace Walpole, Ann Radcliffe and Matthew Lewis. For Ellis, these authors present male villains such as Manfred, Montoni and Ambrosio in opposition to persecuted heroines such as Hippolita, Emily St Aubert and Antonia. Ellis argues that:

■ The early versions of the 'men on the rampage' Gothic expressed a similar protest against the feminisation of culture as their wandering 'outsider' villain-heroes saw it. But its misogyny and nihilism were contained within a religious discourse which, however crumbling, linked the Gothic villain to Satan's rebellion and revenge against 'the happy pair' as they enjoyed 'pleasures not for him ordain'd'. At the same time, the Gothic heroine was working from the inside, as it were, as a participant in the debate about women as daughters, wives, mothers, rational beings, writers and readers in an emerging domestic formation, the 'affective nuclear family', working to destabilise the patriarchal underpinnings of this formation, albeit with the aim of reforming it.[18] □

Ellis identifies here the Gothic's representation of concerns surrounding women as authors and readers in the late eighteenth century. She compares the Gothic villain to Milton's Satan from *Paradise Lost*, doomed to disrupt pleasures in which he cannot participate. For Ellis, the Gothic heroine, by contrast, works to 'destabilise' the patriarchal foundations underpinning the eighteenth century's critiques of women as writers, readers, family members and 'rational beings'. An example of this might be taken from Walpole's *The Castle of Otranto*. When Hippolita, the wronged wife of Manfred, hollowly protests that, 'It is not ours to make election for ourselves; heaven, our fathers, and our husbands, must decide for us,' her fatalism is immediately challenged by the younger heroines Matilda and Isabella. These heroines defy Manfred's marriage ambitions for them, thus 'destabilising', in Ellis's words, the eighteenth century's critique of women as 'rational beings'.[19] However, despite the attractions offered by Ellis's neat gendered parcelling of the male villain's reinforcement, and the heroine's disruption, of patriarchal order, more needs to be said about the 'feminisation of culture' that she alludes to in the eighteenth century, and whether this does in fact lead to the gender-caricatured demarcations in Gothic fiction that she suggests.

As we saw in Chapter One, Jane Austen's *Northanger Abbey* reproduced concerns about romance-reading and romance-writing that were particularly prevalent throughout the 1790s. Like Austen's focus in *Northanger Abbey* upon Catherine Morland's over-zealous consumption of Gothic novels, these concerns were often targeted at women as both the audience and the producers of 'romance'. In the anonymously penned 'Terrorist Novel Writing' of 1797, for example, the writer began by saying that he never 'complain[ed] of fashion, when it is confined to externals'. But he then proceeded to inveigh against the 'dresses and decorations of a modern novel', thereby metonymically linking fashion clothing with fashionable reading.[20] The link established here was by no means new; the consumption of Gothic fiction was swiftly associated with the rise of consumerism and its attendant concerns in eighteenth-century Britain. In *The Rise of Supernatural Fiction* (1995) E. J. Clery insightfully explains this association:

■ The issue of novel-reading (a representative by-product of consumerism at large) reduced the scope of the problem, and offered a language with which to 'narrate' it. Concern about the spread of leisure and luxury to the lower orders would be conveyed by a story about the corruption of a milliner or a lady's maid by reading fiction, as if the problem could only become discursively visible when charged with the sexual theme.

This discursive technique is supported by a considerable genealogy. The linking of female sexuality with the eighteenth-century consumer revolution is, in effect, a variant of the long-standing link between women and luxury, which John Sekora has traced to classical Rome.[21] In Augustan England, civic humanism – the prevailing political discourse of the time, which described economics in terms inspired by the classical republican tradition – rearticulated this link in the context of capitalism. The civic humanist mapping of gender in the realm of the economic is not entirely congruent with the private/feminine vs public/masculine configuration that was to be a central feature of bourgeois hegemony in the following century. The latter ordering underlies the separation of the domestic sphere from the workplace and *polis* [the public, political sphere]; gender categories here coincide with the discrete realms of activity of the two sexes. Civic humanism, while identifying 'private' with 'feminine', reveals its allegiance to aristocratic interests and values by classifying commerce, as a private and hence 'feminine' activity.[22] □

Clery's argument, that the 'feminization' of commerce is linked to the 'feminization' of romance in the eighteenth century, provides a good contextualization of this debate. It also offers a useful insight into the reasons for the frequent publication of such articles as 'Terrorist Novel Writing' which complain about the pernicious effects of romance-reading on females.[23] More significantly, however, Clery's attention to the discourse of civic humanism, and its attendant troubling of the straightforward gender demarcations of the eighteenth century, has implications for any gendered assumptions we may make (and which, I think, Ellis makes) regarding the readership/consumption of, and representations within, Gothic fiction.

In an essay entitled 'The Wanton Muse: Politics and Gender in Gothic Theory after 1760' (1992), Harriet Guest also grounds her analysis of Gothic theory and criticism in relation to eighteenth-century concerns about commerce. Guest draws upon early theories of the Gothic by Thomas Warton (1728–90), Richard Hurd and Clara Reeve (amongst others) in order to explore the complexities of the gendering of Gothic in relation to consumerism. She argues that the tensions between a 'fantastic political reality of public and masculine purity' and its correspondent discourses of an effeminized and elegant commercial luxury produce a Gothic that 'is characterized in terms of extravagant fictions imbued with the luxuriant and voluptuous materialism of the feminized Orient'.[24]

Clery and Guest's vital contextual work demonstrates the complexity of discourses surrounding the gendering of the Gothic, and proves that we cannot accept in any straightforward way the gender bias of eighteenth-century concerns over female consumption of the Gothic. Indeed, as Clery indicates, there is no evidence from eighteenth-century circulating libraries to support the satirical articles' complaints that women are the sole readers of Gothic fiction.[25] Nor is the eighteenth-century equation of Gothic with female readerships borne out entirely in the fictional representations of reading practices during this time. In *Northanger Abbey*, for example, Henry Tilney, Catherine Morland's suitor, also confesses to being a reader of Gothic fiction, and, while walking with Catherine and his sister Eleanor Tilney, he admits to enjoying Ann Radcliffe in particular. Catherine opens the discussion upon reading:

■ 'But you never read novels, I dare say?'
'Why not?'
'Because they are not clever enough for you – gentlemen read better books.'
'The person, be it gentleman or lady, who has not pleasure in a good novel, must be intolerably stupid. I have read all Mrs. Radcliffe's works, and most of them with great pleasure. The Mysteries of Udolpho, when I

had once begun it, I could not lay down again; – I remember finishing it in two days – my hair standing on end the whole time.'

'Yes,' added Miss Tilney, 'and I remember that you undertook to read it aloud to me, and that when I was called away for only five minutes to answer a note, instead of waiting for me, you took the volume into the Hermitage-walk, and I was obliged to stay till you had finished it.'

'Thank you, Eleanor; – a most honourable testimony. You see, Miss Morland, the injustice of your suspicions. Here was I, in my eagerness to get on, refusing to wait only five minutes for my sister; breaking the promise I had made of reading it aloud, and keeping her in suspense at a most interesting part, by running away with the volume, which, you are to observe, was her own, particularly her own. I am proud when I reflect on it, and I think it must establish me in your good opinion.'

'I am very glad to hear it indeed, and now I shall never be ashamed of liking Udolpho myself. But I really thought before, young men despised novels amazingly.'

'It is *amazingly*; it may well suggest *amazement* if they do – for they read nearly as many as women. I myself have read hundreds and hundreds. Do not imagine that you can cope with me in particulars, and engage in the never-ceasing inquiry of "Have you read this?" and "Have you read that?" I shall soon leave you as far behind me as – what shall I say? – I want an appropriate simile; – as far as your friend Emily herself left poor Valancourt when she went with her aunt into Italy. Consider how many years I have had the start of you. I had entered on my studies at Oxford, while you were a good little girl working your sampler at home!'[26] □

Questions and assumptions about women's place in the emergent Romantic literary economy are explored to great effect in Austen's satire of the Gothic, *Northanger Abbey*. Here, the debate about readerships of romance is brought to the very heart of the novel with Henry, Catherine and Eleanor's discussion about reading fiction. The public masculine sphere of Oxford is conjured only to suggest that whilst studying there, Henry reads fiction just as frequently as Catherine does while she works with her sampler in the feminine domestic sphere. Henry's appeal to the plot of *The Mysteries of Udolpho* serves him well as a simile for his greater consumption of Gothic fiction. Crucially, he compares himself with Emily St Aubert (leaving Valancourt behind), and Catherine with Valancourt. This tongue-in-cheek gender inversion suggests that heroine-centred plots are not exclusively for female readerships, and that no straightforward gender identification should be made within Gothic fiction.

Later in *Northanger Abbey*, Catherine is chastised severely for her imaginative reconstruction of a Gothic plot in present-day England. Catherine has nourished herself almost exclusively upon the Gothic fiction of Ann Radcliffe, Regina Maria Roche and others, and her visit to the

Tilney family at the eponymous Northanger Abbey becomes embedded within her fictional experience. Excited at staying in such a Gothic locale, she begins to imagine a dark, Gothic mystery at the heart of the family:

■ Her passion for ancient edifices was next in degree to her passion for Henry Tilney – and castles and abbies made usually the charm of those reveries which his image did not fill. To see and explore either the ramparts and keep of the one, or the cloisters of the other, had been for many weeks a darling wish, though to be more than the visitor of an hour, had seemed too nearly impossible for desire. And yet this was to happen. With all the chances against her of house, hall, place, park, court, and cottage, Northanger turned up an abbey, and she was to be its inhabitant. Its long, damp, passages, its narrow cells and ruined chapel, were to be within her daily reach, and she could not entirely subdue the hope of some traditional legends, some awful memorials of an injured and ill-fated nun.[27] □

Despite Catherine's clichéd anticipations of her residence, her imaginative abilities are none the less enterprising and revealing. She later bases her emergent hypothesis of Mrs Tilney's wrongful death upon the Gothic plots that she has consumed from the pens of Radcliffe, Roche and others. Like the heroine Adeline in Radcliffe's third novel *The Romance of the Forest*, Catherine believes she has discovered a manuscript of some importance in Northanger Abbey; unlike Radcliffe's Adeline, however, Catherine's 'manuscript' turns out to be 'An inventory of linen, in coarse and modern characters'.[28] Catherine's continued hyperbolic assumptions about the marriage of General and Mrs Tilney derive from her uncritical consumption of Gothic Romance. She must refine the distinctions that she draws between Romance and reality: 'Charming as were all Mrs. Radcliffe's works, and charming even as were the works of all her imitators, it was not in them perhaps that human nature, at least in the midland counties of England, was to be looked for.'[29]

At face value, then, we can read *Northanger Abbey* as a critical exploration of women's relationship to, and consumption of, Gothic fiction. However, as Clery argues in *The Rise of Supernatural Fiction*, 'Catherine's Gothic imaginings about General Tilney and his late wife are partially borne out, for it emerges that Mrs Tilney had been imprisoned by her marriage, that unhappiness had contributed to her death and that the General, in accordance with the laws of England and the customs of the time, does wield near-absolute power "as an irrational tyrant" in the family.'[30]

The concerns evinced in the late eighteenth and early nineteenth centuries about the inevitable corruption of young women who read

Gothic fiction are, in many ways, misleading. In *Northanger Abbey* Catherine Morland in fact *does* uncover a tale of an unhappy marriage which has been contracted for material rather than spiritual interests. Her Gothic re-creation of Mrs Tilney's demise is not as misleading as we are led to expect in the novel. One could go so far as to argue that Catherine herself in fact becomes an author, re-creating a fictionalized version of the relationship between General and Mrs Tilney. Her 'passive' consumption of Gothic fiction is not as straightforward as we may imagine; instead, Austen represents Catherine as an active (if somewhat over-ardent) 'author' of a Gothic plot.

## Women and the law in Gothic fiction

Feminist critics have recently begun to focus upon the relationship between the law and the Gothic to great effect. The centrality of property law to the eighteenth century and the Gothic in particular has been noted. In *The Contested Castle* (1989), for example, Kate Ferguson Ellis argues that what she terms the 'feminine Gothic' revolves around the following Radcliffean motif: 'In the feminine Gothic the heroine exposes the villain's usurpation and thus reclaims an enclosed space that should have been a refuge from evil but has become the very opposite, a prison.'[31] Ellis's term here, 'feminine Gothic', is as much open to debate as 'Female Gothic'. None the less, the transformation of the gender debate from the biologically driven term 'Female Gothic' to the more culturally driven agenda of 'Feminine Gothic' enables debates on the Gothic and gender to focus upon the prevalence, for example, of legal motifs within Gothic fiction. Her exploration of 'usurpation' in relation to a piece of property, or the 'contested castle', is an insight that has been extended recently in a variety of explorations of women and the law in the Gothic.

Critics such as E. J. Clery, Wolfram Schmidgen and Sue Chaplin have explored the resonance of Gothic discourse in the most famous document on the laws of England in the eighteenth century, namely the *Commentaries on the Laws of England* (1765–9) by Sir William Blackstone (1723–80).[32] In this important legal work, Blackstone suggestively compares the law of England to an ancient Gothic castle:

■ We inherit an old Gothic castle, erected in the days of chivalry, but fitted up for a modern inhabitant. The moated ramparts, the embattled towers, and the trophied halls, are magnificent and venerable, but useless. The inferior apartments, now converted into rooms of convenience, are cheerful and commodious, though their approaches are winding and difficult.[33] □

Thus Blackstone draws attention to the feudal establishment of England's laws as well as the current day (the eighteenth century), suggesting that ancient legal traditions can still serve for the eighteenth century. In *Eighteenth-Century Fiction and the Law of Property* (2002), Wolfram Schmidgen comments on this metaphor:

■ Because it unites a certain aesthetic with the national myth of the English constitution and its liberties, and because it represents landed property – the central concern of the *Commentaries* – the metaphor of the Gothic castle can be complexly intertwined with the common law. That complexity is only increased by Blackstone's allusion to the popular notion of English constitutional rights as an inheritance. 'We inherit an old Gothic castle' – with this phrase Blackstone ties together the themes of property, common law, and the English constitution in a single image. ...

Here, indeed, lies the basic appeal of the Gothic metaphor: the common law, just like the ancient castle, grows by accretion. It is a structure that cannot be reduced to a simple plan because it evolves out of centuries of legal practice.[34] □

Whilst insisting upon the weighty tradition of the law, Blackstone's castle for Schmidgen 'accomplishes the concrete coalescence of past and present. Through the castle the past tangibly intrudes on the present and structures the latter's practices.'[35] One of the more questionable ways in which this coalescence of past and present is manifest is through eighteenth-century laws on property. Women's rights to property and legal representation remained suspended upon their marriage, and they were expected to consolidate and incorporate their 'very being or legal existence' with their husband's.

This smooth assumption concerning women's property rights did not go unchallenged during the eighteenth century, of course. Famously, in her posthumously published unfinished Gothic novella *The Wrongs of Woman: or, Maria* (1798), Mary Wollstonecraft's wronged heroine Maria claims that 'Marriage had bastilled me for life.'[36] Wollstonecraft links marriage with the very icon of tyranny in the late eighteenth century, the Bastille in Paris, which was stormed in 1789. Critics have also rightly viewed Ann Radcliffe's Gothic fiction as a sustained exploration of the relationship between women and property law, arguing, for example, that Emily St Aubert's struggle to hold on to her inherited property in *The Mysteries of Udolpho*, against Montoni's wishes, is the central motif of that novel. In *The Rise of Supernatural Fiction*, Clery forges a strong connection between the property thematic in Radcliffe's fiction and the supernatural:

■ Ann Radcliffe, by regularly endowing her female characters with inherited fortunes, foregrounds the ideological inconsistencies of the property laws relating to women of her time. In *Udolpho* Montoni forwards his claims under English common law to the estates of his wife: on marriage he has acquired a freehold interest, for life. After Mme Montoni dies without submitting to these claims, when Emily informs Montoni that she is 'not so ignorant ... of the laws on this subject, as to be misled by the assertion of any person', she refers to the 'natural justice' of equity which enabled her aunt to settle her estate on her next of kin without her husband's consent. The two different realities conflicting here are on a technical level these two perspectives in law.

The central Gothic indeterminacy illusion/reality enables legal metaphor to be represented as a lived experience. The 'civil death' required by common law is actualised in Mme Montoni's death. Elsewhere, married women reduced to 'ghosts' or the 'living dead' by law exist as supposed ghosts, notably in the story of Emily's other aunt, the Countess de Villefort, who died of poison administered by her adulterous husband and is rumoured to haunt Château-de-Blanc. In *A Sicilian Romance* the Marchioness of Mazzini is imprisoned, rumoured dead, for fifteen years in the south wing of the castle by order of her dissipated husband. When her daughters Julia and Emilia ask their governess whether a spirit could really be responsible for the mysterious noises and flashing lights, she responds 'such beings *may* exist'; certainly they may, for as the marchioness explains after her release, 'the marquis, you know, has not only power to imprison, but also the right of life and death in his own domain.' The law itself engenders the supernatural; women are the ghosts in its machine.

Radcliffe employs the libertarian language of natural justice against the oppressive usages of custom, not because she was a radical, but because this was the shape that terror took for the projected reader, middle class and female: the point at which fantasy and reality met and mingled. Her writings, at least at the height of suspense, encourage reflection on the illusory nature of the law's 'phantom objectivity', its interested, man-made nature, through a literal-minded representation of the law as haunted house. The metaphysical paraphernalia of an 'objectivist' system of justice is portrayed with objectivity in the terrifying phantasmagoria of Gothic fiction. 'Justice' is estranged from itself, retranslated into an unequal, repressive relation between people. Before the narrative reverts to a tidy dénouement there is a moment of illumination in which the unthinkable is felt to be real.[37] □

Clery's emphasis on readership here is significant, for whilst we have argued that the readership of Gothic fiction is not exclusively female, certainly a large number of middle-class females read and enjoyed Gothic fiction. Radcliffe's representation of the law as a 'haunted house', as Clery argues, is symptomatic of women's displaced rights within property law. The experience of Austen's heroine Catherine Morland is a case in point: it seems to be her reading of *The Mysteries of Udolpho* that enables her to view in General Tilney (with some justice) 'the air and attitude of a Montoni!'[38] The explicit link that she forges between the General and Montoni is indicative of the terror she feels in discovering that his behaviour is not far removed from that of Montoni; he has mistreated and neglected his former wife, and he then expels Catherine from his home unprotected when he discovers that she is without fortune.

In *Ann Radcliffe: The Great Enchantress*, Robert Miles discusses the issues of property in *The Mysteries of Udolpho*. He connects the seemingly benevolent and villainous actions of St Aubert (Emily's father) and Montoni through both characters' deliberate withholding of information from Emily. Miles argues rightly that the only way in which Emily can discover the true facts of her situation is by looking transgressively into forbidden things (the manuscript that her father forbids her to look upon, the waxen figure that is a reproduction of the former owner of Udolpho, Signora Laurentini). Miles comments:

■ Within Udolpho's Gothic society 'lifting the veil' reveals to Emily (through the mirror image of Laurentini's 'body') that her status is that of property, either to be bartered away – as Montoni attempts to do – or discarded, put out of sight, once her entitlements have fallen within the net of male acquisitiveness. In both cases, the ambiguity of 'witness' continues to resonate: as someone gaining an illicit glimpse of male power behind the arras, Emily is a transgressive spectator; at the same time she 'witnesses' acts that transgress against her – and Laurentini's – natural rights.[39] □

These 'natural rights' are, of course, the properties that Signora Laurentini and Emily have rightfully inherited, but which have been denied them. Reverting to the issues of spectatorship (which, as we saw in Chapter Five, Michelle A. Massé also explores in relation to Freud's essays upon spectating), Miles rightly argues here that Emily bears witness to Montoni's usurpation of her natural rights in *Udolpho*. There is little doubt that women's Gothic writing in the late eighteenth century in particular is intimately concerned with issues such as the law and its relation to women, and the usurpation of women's property rights by men.[40] This is not only evident throughout the fiction of Ann Radcliffe, but also provides the narratological motivation in Mary Wollstonecraft's *The Wrongs of Woman: or, Maria* and Regina Maria Roche's novels *The Children of the Abbey* (1796) and *Clermont*.

In *Law, Sensibility and the Sublime in Eighteenth-Century Fiction: Speaking of Dread* (2004), Sue Chaplin takes the legal exploration of Gothic fiction even further, and extends her analysis to a consideration of 'legal subjectivity' in eighteenth-century women's writing. Chaplin returns to William Blackstone's Gothic legal metaphor to argue that Radcliffe 'posits the paternal law, the Gothic castle of Blackstone's legal imagination, not as a source of transcendentally sublime power, but as a materialisation of dread'.[41] Chaplin takes one of Radcliffe's strongest heroines, Ellena from *The Italian*, in order to emphasize the inter-related significance of property and propriety:

■ Radcliffe's treatment of the law and its relation to subjectivity is ... complex. ...[42] Ellena at the beginning of the novel lives with her unmarried, property-owning aunt. Ellena is this woman's sole support; she works for a living as a dressmaker. Ellena's autonomy guarantees her a degree of proper legal subjectivity; she is unappropriated by either a husband or a father and she is economically active in her own right. That which guarantees her independence, however, at the same time undermines her propriety as a female subject. She may be termed an improper legal subject, one of those women whose independent, 'masculine' legal identity conflicts with feminine propriety such that she cannot achieve a stable, unequivocal subjectivity before patriarchal law. Ellena cannot be slotted into the aristocratic patriarchal family structure and it is this impropriety that stands as an insurmountable obstacle to her marriage to Vivaldi in the eyes of his family. Vivaldi cannot be allowed to jeopardise his family's position by means of marriage to a woman whose legal and economic status transgresses so completely patriarchal notions of property and propriety.[43] □

Chaplin then goes on to argue that Vivaldi's disenfranchisement in the choice of his marriage partner renders him as much a victim of eighteenth-century law as Ellena. Vivaldi is not free to choose; legally the state subjects him to parental consent. Chaplin argues that the Marriage Act of 1753 'undermined the significance of free contractual consent in respect of both men and women. It was no longer the consent even of the male participant, as a rational and free legal agent, that legitimated marriage after 1753: it was state power.'[44] Thus, for Chaplin, Vivaldi becomes a 'feminised subject, posited as the property of his aristocratic family who perceive of his filial duty purely in terms of "passive obedience" '.[45]

Chaplin's discussion of *The Italian* in relation to marriage law provides new and illuminating legal contexts for the work, and attests to Radcliffe's informed engagement with eighteenth-century jurisprudence. Significantly, her account moves beyond exploring the position of female characters in relation to the law, to a wider exploration of the exclusion of both men and women. Chaplin's intervention in this debate proves that the significance of Radcliffe's engagement with eighteenth-century property law, and its relation to marriage laws, is difficult to exaggerate.

As we have seen so far in this chapter, the debates over the constitution of 'Female Gothic' have not produced a single, essentializing definition of this term. If anything, they have undermined its currency. However, what the struggle over the category *does* achieve is a strong and continued focus upon the Gothic's appeal to both male and female authors, and the genre's consequent engagement with contemporary eighteenth-century narratives of female propriety, women and the law, and women's reading habits. The methods by which the Gothic subverts these so-called authoritative discourses has been called 'Female Gothic', and yet the Gothic consistently vexes and evades such categorization by proving, as Chaplin demonstrates above, that men are also disenfranchised by eighteenth-century law, and as Jane Austen demonstrated, that men also enjoyed reading Gothic fiction.

Nor, as several studies of 'Female Gothic' have argued, are the female characters portrayed in women's Gothic fiction consistently victims. Chaplin's qualification, that men can be portrayed as victims as much as women, is entirely correct, and timely. Jacqueline Howard rightly warns that the category 'Female Gothic' 'tends to suggest that women's writing is homogeneous and to universalize women as victims', and in the following section, we shall consider the debate which surrounds this.

## Are Gothic heroines victims?

In her 1995 monograph *Art of Darkness: A Poetics of Gothic* Anne Williams uses a theoretical model derived from psychoanalysis in order to explain her distinctions between the terms 'Male Gothic' and 'Female Gothic':

■ This overview of Male and Female Gothic conventions leads to the conclusion that their differences arise from the male's and female's different cultural positions: it is all in the 'I'. In English the first-person pronoun and the word for the organ of sight sound the same – an accident, but one that conveniently serves to repress speculation that all I's/eyes might *not* be the same. The existence of Male and Female Gothic narratives, however, demonstrates that they are not. Male Gothic is a dark mirror reflecting patriarchy's nightmare, recalling a perilous, violent and early separation from the mother/mater denigrated as 'female'. 'Female Gothic' creates a Looking-Glass World where ancient assumptions about the 'male' and the 'female', the 'Line of Good' and the 'Line of Evil', are suspended or so transformed as to reveal an entirely different world, exposing the perils lurking in the father's corridor of power.[46] □

Using a psychoanalytically-based account, then, Williams concludes that Male Gothic conventions, of which she takes Lewis's *The Monk* as representative, have as their narrative foundation a premature wrench from the mother, presumably reflected in Ambrosio's early separation from his mother, Elvira. By contrast, the 'Female Gothic' is constructed around the Lacanian Law of the Father, exposing the perils and difficulties to women of the Symbolic realm.

Following Moers's categorization, Williams argues for 'Female Gothic' as a continuing tradition over several centuries. As we have seen, this is a potential problem for critics such as Jacqueline Howard and E. J. Clery as it insists anachronistically upon a lineage of consistent themes within women's writing. Potentially more problematic, however, is Williams's psychoanalytic argument that because women are nurtured outside of Freud's Oedipal crisis (where father and son fight for dominance), they do not participate within the Gothic's triangulation of violence, desire and agency because they are biologically different. The main departure in her argument is the claim that, rather than 'Female Gothic' acting as a critique of victimization, it acknowledges and celebrates passivity and dependence. Confronting feminist critiques that focus upon the victimization and suffering of the heroine, Williams argues:

■ These objections all take it for granted that passivity and dependence on others are invariably bad things, a sign of weakness. But perhaps they seem so only to a culture assuming that independence and conquest are the supreme signs of accomplishment. If the Female Gothic plot in fact presents an alternative to the Oedipal crisis in the formation of the speaking subject, then it portrays a subject with different desires, who sees the world with a different eye/I. Since the 'female' gaze has *not* been created through conflict, division, and abrupt separation, she has a different relation to her own mother and to that cultural (m)other repressed in her access to the Symbolic. She also may have a different experience of 'Mother' Nature. Therefore ... the self nurtured outside the conflict of fathers and sons is much better prepared to see a world free of spectres (though not necessarily free of wonders).[47] □

The theoretical terms of Williams's argument are in part derived from Julia Kristeva's revision of Lacan's psychoanalytic theories, where Kristeva places primacy instead on the semiotic, the maternal space which linguistically *precedes* Lacan's Symbolic realm. Hence the subtitle of Williams's book, *A Poetics of Gothic*, which is seemingly inspired by

Kristeva's *Revolution in Poetic Language* (1974; trans. 1984).[48] By thus invoking Kristeva, Williams is able to negotiate a more positive psycho-analytical account of 'female' Gothic fiction.

Williams qualifies her theoretical account of the differences in 'Male' and 'Female' Gothic by conceding that although she has referred to the subject as a 'she', 'there is nothing essentially or biologically "female" about it; rather, it is nurtured within the "female" position in a patriarchal culture'.[49] Whilst this argument does not universalize the Gothic hero-ine's passivity and dependence as victimization, it none the less implies a universalized position of passivity and weakness in a patriarchal culture.

In *Gothic Feminism: The Professionalization of Gender from Charlotte Smith to the Brontës* (1998), Diane Long Hoeveler maintains the focus on victim feminism. She takes a slightly different approach from that of Williams by arguing that Gothic feminism enables its heroines to *masquerade* as victims in order to survive the patriarchally nightmarish spaces through which they travel:

■ The female gothic constitutes what I would call a rival female-created fantasy – gothic feminism – a version of 'victim feminism', an ideology of female power through pretended and staged weakness. Such an ideology positions women as innocent victims who deserve to be rewarded with the ancestral estate because they were unjustly persecuted by the cor-rupt patriarch. If the heroines manage, inadvertently of course, to cause the deaths of these patriarchs, so much the better. Montoni and Schedoni, the hapless villains of *The Mysteries of Udolpho* and *The Italian*, respectively, both appear to self-destruct through their own mis-guided arrogance and egoism, but we know better. The gothic feminist always manages to dispose of her enemies without dirtying her dainty little hands. The position that Radcliffe and her followers advocated throughout the female gothic was one of 'wise passiveness' or what we might more accurately recognize as a form of passive-aggression.

In its convergence of psychological and socio-political issues, the female gothic – from its inception during the Industrial and French Revolutions through [to] 1853 – stands as a distinctive artistic form spawned in reaction to the radical economic, social, and religious dislocations that occurred with the onset of industrialization and the triumph of a capitalist economy. Women now had the opportunity to express themselves in widely disseminated and cheaply printed novels and dramas that became immensely popular with the new reading audience – largely middle-class women enclosed in the newly created and idealized bourgeois home. These women responded to their sudden change in status with an ambivalence that found its expression in one of the dominant ideologies of the female gothic: the fantasy that the weak have power through carefully cultivating the appearance of their very powerlessness.[50] □

Whilst this argument modifies the woman/victim equation by placing the emphasis upon the performativity of this position, it does not account for the complexity of gender representations within Gothic fiction, nor for the representations of sex within the genre. This type of critical approach explores passivity and dependence within the cultural female position, but remains uneasy in addressing its opposite, the violent and passionate females represented within women's Gothic writing. One particularly complex area of ambivalence in the Gothic remains to be explored: that of sexuality, and its relationship with gender issues in the Gothic novel. This will provide the final challenge to gendered assumptions of the Gothic in the following section.

## Daring to express sex, violence and desire within the Gothic

The focus outlined above upon gender and cultural representations within Gothic fiction has been challenged, most recently by Adriana Craciun. In *Fatal Women of Romanticism* (2003), Craciun examines a number of Romantic women writers who use their writing to challenge the stereotype of women as non-violent. Craciun argues that 'Violence, both rhetorical and physical, presents the greatest challenge to ... gender-complementary feminist poetics, in part because it seems so clearly attributable to men and masculine interests.'[51] In *Fatal Women* Craciun contends that the work of Charlotte Dacre, for one, must be considered in relation to the '(ostensibly male) tradition of pornographic and sensationalist literature, a tradition in which she consciously situated her works, in order to appreciate the full significance of her fatal women figures and her focus on corporeal pleasure and destruction'.[52] She speculates that were the readers of Dacre's fiction not to know the author's identity, they would assume that the author was male because of the fictional focus upon sexual passion and murder. The content of Dacre's works, Craciun rightly argues, has more in common with the fiction of Jean-Jacques Rousseau, the Marquis de Sade and Matthew Lewis, than with any ostensibly 'female' tradition.

Charlotte Dacre's Gothic fiction firmly refuses to portray its female protagonists as victims. Dacre's pen name, Rosa Matilda, is clearly indebted to Matthew Lewis's she-devil and anti-heroine Rosario/Matilda from *The Monk*. Her 1806 novel *Zofloya, or the Moor*, in particular, shares thematic resonances with Lewis's earlier work, with the anti-heroine Victoria di Loredani being tempted to act upon her passions by a Moorish Satan, the eponymous Zofloya.[53] Victoria di Loredani, having married her lover Berenza, then begins to desire his brother Henriquez, who is betrothed to another younger woman, Lilla. Her insatiable passion for Henriquez reaches its apogee through a series of dreams that she experiences where Henriquez's servant, Zofloya, helps her to prevent Henriquez's marriage to Lilla in exchange for a more diabolical marriage pact:

■ [Victoria] now saw herself in a church brilliantly illuminated, when, horrible to her eyes, approaching the altar near which she stood, appeared Lilla, led by Henriquez and attired as a bride! In the instant that their hands were about to be joined, the Moor she had beheld in her preceding dream appeared to start between them, and beckoned her towards him; involuntarily she drew near him, and touched his hand, when Berenza stood at her side, and seizing her arm, endeavoured to pull her away. 'Wilt thou be mine?' in a hurried voice whispered the Moor in her ear, 'and none then shall oppose thee.' But Victoria hesitated, and cast her eyes upon Henriquez: the Moor stepped back, and again the hand of Henriquez became joined with Lilla's. 'Wilt thou be mine?' exclaimed the Moor in a loud voice, 'and the marriage shall *not be*!' – 'Oh, yes! yes!' eagerly cried Victoria, overcome by intense horror at the thoughts of their union. – In an instant *she* occupied the place of Lilla; and Lilla, no longer the blooming maid, but a pallid spectre, fled shriek-ing through the aisles of the church, while Berenza, suddenly wounded by an invisible hand, sunk covered with blood at the foot of the altar! Exultation filled the bosom of Victoria; she attempted to take the hand of Henriquez; but casting her eyes upon him, she beheld him changed to a frightful skeleton, and in terror awoke! □

The fervour with which Victoria accepts Zofloya's offer undercuts the nar-rative's allusion to her 'intense horror' at 'thoughts of their union'. She effectively signs a demonic pact within her dream which is reminiscent of the one that Ambrosio signs with Rosario/Matilda in Lewis's *The Monk*. If anything, though, Dacre pushes further than Lewis with her demonic pact. Victoria's 'exultation' when she dreams of Lilla transformed into a 'spectre' and her husband bleeding to death indicate that this heroine's passions have entirely obliterated any residual moral scruples.

Almost all of the contemporary reviews of the novel commented negatively upon the thematic similarities to Lewis's plot. Whilst Lewis's command of language may have 'elevated' his fiction, Dacre remained unpardoned owing to her lavish indulgence of the supernatural and her 'disgusting depravity of morals'. The periodical *Monthly Literary Recreations* typified the attitudes thus:

■ Indeed we may safely affirm, that there has seldom appeared a romance so void of merit, so destitute of delicacy, displaying such dis-gusting depravity of morals, as the present. It is a humble, very humble, imitation of the Monk, possessing in an eminent degree all the defects of that wild performance, but entirely destitute of all its beauties. The Monk, at least, has language to recommend it. The supernatural agent introduced is not unnecessary to the story; in order to tempt Ambrosio, he has great difficulties to encounter. As a contrast to the wicked, some virtuous, interesting characters are brought upon the scene – and, though we may reprobate the tendency of the work, we cannot help being attracted by its perusal. Here the language in general is bombastical; new words are introduced, such, for example as *enhorred* and *furor*, the latter of which is certainly used in the language of medicine, but in a sense which delicacy will not permit us to explain. Here the sentences are often constructed in an affected, artificial manner, as to render the sense obscure. Here the greatest number of characters are so depraved, as to excite no other sentiment but disgust; and there are, in the great number of characters introduced, but three that can be called good, and they are brought forward only for a short time, and then fall victims to the machinations of the guilty.[54] ☐

*Zofloya* is framed by a hollow moralizing narrative voice which does little to contain or comment upon the sensational tale of passion, jealousy and murder that the enclosed pages contain. *The General Review of British and Foreign Literature* was unconvinced by this moral framing device:

■ The author acquaints us that an historian who would wish his lessons to sink deep into the heart, in order to render mankind virtuous and more happy, must not simply detail a series of events, but must ascertain causes, follow effects, draw deductions from incidents, and ever revert to the actuating principle of his narrative. Though this introductory declaration is not remarkable for its perspicuity, we think we understand it sufficiently to apply it to the work so prefaced; and from this work we gather that ladies, who marry very young, ought to take care not to fall in love with accomplished seducers; that in case such ladies should run away with their seducers, it will be particularly incumbent on their daughters not to turn out as bad as their mamas; and more especially, if the devil should appear to them in the shape of a very handsome black man, they must not listen to him – for he will lead them from one crime to another, telling them the most horrible lies, and at length, when the crimes and the consequences have arrived at the utmost pitch, he will push them headlong from a rock, or finish their sublunary existence by some equally dreadful catastrophe.

We are well aware that the sublimest efforts of the imagination may be travestied and made ludicrous by a mere verbal effort, denoting very little ingenuity in the writer who may descend to such a performance. Far be it from us to court the smile which might be thus excited. By our present remark we mean to assert that *Zofloya* has no pretension to rank as a moral work.[55] ☐

These reviews concentrated upon what they viewed as the 'depraved' nature of the narrative, and its unconvincing moral strand. By comparing it to *The Monk*, the reviewers also drew attention to the sex of its author by alluding to her pen's comparative lack of 'chastity'. As Craciun charts, *The Annual Review*'s reception of *Zofloya* 'was distressed by this dissonance between the sexual content of Dacre's novel and Dacre's sex'. It remarked that '[t]here is a voluptuousness of language and allusion, pervading these volumes, which we should have hoped, that the delicacy of a female pen would have refused to trace'.[56] Women's writing at this time was seemingly contingent upon a strong moral control, and any female writer who transgressed these moral boundaries in order to explore female passion was upbraided severely in the periodical press.

Dacre's portrayal of a heroine who is unrepentantly violent, jealous and sexually active leads Craciun to argue against the criticism of 'Female Gothic' or 'Feminine Gothic' enunciated through the work of Kate Ferguson Ellis, Diane Long Hoeveler and Anne Williams that we have examined in the previous sections of this chapter:[57]

■ Dacre's revision of *The Monk* in *Zofloya* challenges delineations along gender lines in such works. ... These works elaborate a 'female Gothic' that centers on a reactive and entrapped heroine, and distinguish this from a male Gothic such as Lewis's, which focuses on a rebellious hero (masculine because exiled from the domestic sphere, according to Ellis ...). Dacre's heroine Victoria is exiled, seeks to master her world and those in it, and is decidedly sadistic, tormenting and murdering for the pleasure of exerting her will; she is thus neither within the female or male Gothic traditions but somewhere in between. While such 'negative' female characters do exist in women's literature of the period, they are typically secondary characters, dark doubles of the central heroine whose destructiveness must be expelled from the text before the heroine can reach her desired goal (examples include Maria de Vallerno in Radcliffe's *A Sicilian Romance*, Laurentini in her *The Mysteries of Udolpho*, and most famously, Bertha in *Jane Eyre* [1847]).[58] □

Craciun proceeds to argue that the 'desired goal' of marriage towards which the more conventional Gothic heroines aspire is demonstrated to be a sham in *Zofloya*. In a manner that is similar to the way that the legal discourses work to demonstrate the perils of courtship and marriage within the Gothic, the discourses of heterosexuality and marriage are similarly challenged by Dacre. Craciun states that 'Dacre also deliberately describes Victoria's eventual submission to Zofloya's will as a marriage, and his attempts to convince her to depend on him are expressed in the language of romantic courtship.'[59] However, this rhetoric of marriage and courtship demonstrates all the more incisively that 'The story of Victoria's downfall is thus also the story of the loss of social identity, mobility, and independence that a woman suffers in marrying her lover, who then becomes her legal master after having acted the part of her devoted and enthralled servant.'[60] Charlotte Dacre viscerally demonstrates that the heterosexual pact, offered to the Gothic heroine through the promise of love and marriage, is an unfulfilling exchange for agency and self-determination. Nor does marriage, in Dacre's fictional world, lead to sexual fulfilment. The Gothic genre's treatment of violence, murder and incest is linked symbiotically with issues of sexuality and gender within the fiction. The works of Charlotte Dacre prove this, and provoke us to ask some simple questions about 'female' authorship. As E. J. Clery remarks in *Women's Gothic*:

> ■ Any reader of today whose picture of Regency women's writing is based on Jane Austen will read *Zofloya; or, the Moor* (1806) in a state of wondering disbelief. How is it possible that Austen and Dacre existed in the same universe? How could a woman publish a work which features as its heroine a murderous nymphomaniac who gives her body and soul to the devil disguised as a black servant, and sign her name to it?[61] □

Clery's straightforward questioning regarding female authorship provokes us to revise any assumptions that we make about women's writing containing a certain set of 'female' thematics. Dacre dedicated her first novel, *Confessions of the Nun of St Omer*, to Matthew Lewis. Whilst in this dedication she denied any attempt to imitate his 'style or subject', this first 'Dedication' is none the less significant. While many other writers (such as Radcliffe in *The Italian*) were at pains to dissociate themselves from the opprobrium that *The Monk* attracted in the periodical press, Dacre was proud to acknowledge that she participated in the same tradition as its author. This surely indicates that we cannot presume any straightforward 'Female Gothic' as a continuous and coherent category.

Naturally, these issues of authorial sex and gendered portrayals in fiction do not apply uniquely to women writers' work. Just as women's Gothic writing is capable of portraying violent and sexually acquisitive female characters, so men's Gothic writing can follow the Radcliffean tradition of a persecuted heroine. The fiction of Francis Lathom is a case in point. Catherine Morland and Isabella Thorpe in *Northanger Abbey* group him alongside Radcliffe, Roche and Sleath on their Gothic reading list. Furthermore, in *The Literature of Terror*, David Punter describes his early fiction as 'thoroughly Radcliffean in most of the important ways: settings, the class stereotyping of character, the emphasis on sensibility are all out of the world of *Udolpho*'.[62]

Much has been done to demonstrate that the Gothic themes of paranoia and persecution are not the unique territory of the heroine. This is a point which is implicitly acknowledged in many of the critical positions that we have examined above, but the most significant enunciation of this argument in relation to Gothic heroes comes from Eve

Kosofsky Sedgwick. In *Between Men: English Literature and Male Homosocial Desire* (1985), Sedgwick views the Gothic novel as 'an important locus for the working-out of some of the terms by which nineteenth- and twentieth-century European culture has used homophobia to divide and manipulate the male-homosocial spectrum'.[63] Referring to Ellen Moers's *Literary Women* and Sandra Gilbert and Susan Gubar's *The Madwoman in the Attic* (1979), Sedgwick states that:

■ The ties of the Gothic novel to an emergent female authorship and readership have been a constant for two centuries, and there has been a history of useful critical attempts to look to the Gothic for explorations of the position of women in relation to the changing shapes of patriarchal domination. A less obvious point has to do with the reputation for 'decadence': the Gothic was the first novelistic form in England to have close, relatively visible links to male homosexuality, at a time when styles of homosexuality, and even its visibility and distinctness, were markers of division and tension between classes as much as between genders.[64] □

Sedgwick's argument is two-fold: the first link that the Gothic has to homosexuality is through authorship. She draws on the varying homosexual reputations of Horace Walpole, Matthew Lewis and William Beckford in order to argue that the Gothic genre's reputation for 'decadence' was partially indebted to these authors.[65]

From the Gothic's emergent reputation, Sedgwick proceeds to make a significant argument that 'The Gothic novel crystallized for English audiences the terms of a dialectic between male homosexuality and homophobia, in which homophobia appeared thematically in paranoid plots.'[66] Building in part upon David Punter's analysis in his chapter 'The Dialectic of Persecution' on Godwin, James Hogg (1770–1835) and Maturin, in *The Literature of Terror*, Sedgwick explores a 'large subgroup' of fiction within the 'classic' early Gothic novels: namely, William Godwin's *Caleb Williams*, Mary Shelley's *Frankenstein*, James Hogg's *The Private Memoirs and Confessions of a Justified Sinner* (1824), and, she speculates, 'probably *Melmoth*, possibly *The Italian*'.[67] Each of these novels, Sedgwick contends, 'is about one or more males who not only is persecuted by, but considers himself transparent to and often under the compulsion of another male'.[68] They emerge as Gothic novels strongly concerned with paranoia. Despite the fact that none of these novelists themselves were recognizably homophobic, these novels embody 'strongly homophobic mechanisms' through their paranoiac plot structures.[69] This argument is entirely compelling; *Caleb Williams*, *Frankenstein*, *Melmoth the Wanderer* and *The Private Memoirs and Confessions of a Justified Sinner* are intimately concerned with relationships of terror, persecution and obsession between men.[70] In the latter two, the persecutors take the form of a demonic tempter, but all four demonstrate strong homosocial bonds between men. Indeed, in relation to *Caleb Williams*, Punter has argued that the eponymous hero's feelings 'clearly partake of rejected love: through all his vicissitudes he bears with him a still, small acceptance of Falkland's tremendous worth, which, of course, renders his feelings all the more bitter'.[71]

In *Gothic Writing, 1750–1820: A Genealogy*, Robert Miles enunciates the question that the paradoxes surrounding the Gothic's sexual and gender thematics and authorship demand: 'given the permissiveness and increased care of the child around the end of the eighteenth century, and the stress on happiness in marriage, why were Gothic novels – reflective of the highly repressive patriarchal patterns of the seventeenth century rather than present reality – so popular?'[72] Referring to Michel Foucault's arguments concerning the regulation of sexuality in the eighteenth century through marriage, in *The History of Sexuality* (1976–84), Miles contends in relation to the late eighteenth century:

■ As sexuality detached itself from the deployment of alliance, with its juridical and religious backing, a new discursive field is created and problematized. This problematizing gave rise to the deployment of sexuality which overlapped, interpenetrated and contradicted its threatened predecessor, the deployment of alliance. During this prolonged moment of uncertainty, tension and ambivalence, Gothic writing begins to take familiar shape, spun from the discourses the moment itself engendered. ... At its simplest, the plot of Gothic romance is a threat to primogeniture [the rule on tradition of inheritance by the firstborn child], the arranged marriage gone wrong through the advent of a desire that proves literally unruly.[73] □

As Miles goes on to argue, 'unnatural sexuality', whether it be Manfred's desire for his future daughter-in-law Isabella in *Otranto*, Caleb Williams's obsession with Falkland, or Walton's increased warmth towards Victor Frankenstein, came to characterize anything which resisted the institutionalized discourses of marriage and procreation in the eighteenth century.[74]

It is little wonder, then, that the Gothic novel, with its self-consciously artificial structure, freights these 'unnatural sexualities' inside its 'unnatural' structures. For Diane Long Hoeveler, it is specifically 'gothic feminism' that critiques the institutionalized eighteenth-century discourses of marriage and sexuality and thus 'mak[es] the world a safe place for feminized men and masculinized women'.[75] But the works of William Godwin, Matthew Lewis, Francis Lathom, James Hogg and Charles Maturin (to cite a few examples) testify to a richness and reciprocity of ideas with women writers of the period that defy expectations of gender and sexuality. As always, the Gothic remains defiantly resistant and surprising.

# Conclusion

> Whatever [the author's] views were, or whatever effects the execution of them might have, his work can only be laid before the public at present as a matter of entertainment. Even as such, some apology for it is necessary. Miracles, visions, necromancy, dreams, and other preternatural events, are exploded now even from romances. That was not the case when our author wrote ...
>
> (Horace Walpole, Preface to the first edition of<br>*The Castle of Otranto*, 1764)

From this first, hesitant excursion into the realms of Gothic romance, the terrain of Gothic literature, film, fashion, music and criticism has continued to proliferate and yet offers much ground to chart and explore. This Guide has begun by offering a variety of critical approaches to the first seven decades of the Gothic romance. It testifies to a vibrancy and plenitude of criticism on the Gothic, from 1760 to the present.

There is yet much excavation to do on the Gothic, even during the period that this Guide covers. The Gothic 'horrors' on the list that Isabella Thorpe compiled for Catherine Morland (cited in Chapter One), for example, have recently been exhumed and are returning to print, along with many other Gothic novels and novellas of the 1790s and 1800s that fell from publishing grace after their heyday.[1] These publishing efforts will offer many further opportunities for scholars of the Gothic during the period that this Guide covers. Furthermore, although some excellent criticism is now emerging on Gothic drama and poetry, of the Gothic's generic mutations during the Romantic era, much remains to explore.[2]

Horace Walpole's apologia for *The Castle of Otranto* (above) falsely claimed that 'Miracles, visions, necromancy, dreams, and other preternatural events, are exploded now even from romances.' While the eighteenth-century writer may have felt the need to excuse his supernatural apparatus to his 'enlightened' eighteenth-century readers, such subterfuge has been deemed disposable from the nineteenth century onward. Classic nineteenth-century Gothic texts such as James Hogg's *The Private Memoirs and Confessions of a Justified Sinner*, Sheridan LeFanu's

*Carmilla* (1872) and Bram Stoker's *Dracula* (1897) celebrate the irrational, and defy explanation. This tradition continues to this day, with Walpole's 'exploded' 'miracles, visions, necromancy, dreams, and other preternatural events' reoccupying the genres of film, drama, poetry, music and art with a defiant vengeance.

To attend a conference on Gothic topics is to attend a truly interdisciplinary event, with scholars drawn from many different faculties. This testifies to the richness of the Gothic. In the wake of relentless criticism and endless satire, explored in Chapter One of this Guide, the Gothic romance seemed threatened with extinction in the 1820s. But predictions of its demise were premature. As Avril Horner and Sue Zlosnik have argued recently in *Gothic and the Comic Turn* (2004), the Gothic genre has always acknowledged and celebrated its comedic counterpart.[3] The Gothic's ability to reinvent itself rests in part on this celebration and acknowledgement of its partly comedic nature. Another equally significant reason for its continued survival as a fertile terrain for academic study is its ability to confront and articulate contemporary fears. As we have seen in this Guide, the Gothic romance during the Romantic era explored the fears provoked by the French Revolution, questions of nationhood and religion in Britain, and the pressing issues of gender in an age which saw an unprecedented number of women writers following Ann Radcliffe's example, and taking up their pens. These authors used the Gothic to explore both unconscious and politically pressing fears. To the present day, writers, directors and artists who exploit Gothic tropes share the same types of concern. There remains much to be excavated from the Gothic romances of the past, and much to be discovered in the Gothic's continued displacements and transformations.

# Notes

INTRODUCTION

1 E. J. Clery, 'The Genesis of "Gothic" Fiction', in *The Cambridge Companion to Gothic Fiction*, ed. Jerrold E. Hogle (Cambridge: Cambridge University Press, 2002), p. 21.

2 Robin Sowerby, 'The Goths in History and Pre-Gothic Gothic', in *Companion to the Gothic*, ed. David Punter (Oxford: Blackwell, 2000), pp. 15–16.

3 Richard Hurd, *Letters on Chivalry and Romance* (London, 1762), pp. 1–5.

4 For further reading on this poetry, see chapters 1 and 2 of David Punter's *The Literature of Terror: A History of Gothic Fictions from 1765 to the Present Day*, 2 vols (Harlow: Longman, 1996), pp. 1–53.

5 Anne Williams, *Art of Darkness: A Poetics of Gothic* (Chicago and London: Chicago University Press, 1995) p. 1; Robert Miles, *Gothic Writing 1750–1820: A Genealogy* (1993; 2nd edn, Manchester: Manchester University Press, 2002).

6 Michael Gamer, *Romanticism and the Gothic: Genre, Reception and Canon Formation* (Cambridge: Cambridge University Press, 2000), p. 4.

7 Readers may be surprised to discover that Mary Shelley's 1818 *Frankenstein* is not explored in this *Guide*. This is because this novel, which has attracted a huge range of critical interpretations in itself, already has a single guide devoted to it in this series. Cf. *Mary Shelley: Frankenstein*, ed. Berthold Schoene-Harwood (Basingstoke: Palgrave Macmillan, 2000).

8 J. M. S. Tompkins, *The Popular Novel in England: 1770–1800* (1932; London: Methuen, 1969), p. v.

9 Devendra P. Varma, *The Gothic Flame* (1957; New York: Russell and Russell, 1966), p. 1.


CHAPTER ONE

1 As E. J. Clery charts in her excellent 'Introduction' to the Oxford World's Classics edition, Walpole was the third son of the Whig statesman Sir Robert Walpole, who is generally defined as Britain's first prime minister (Horace Walpole, *The Castle of Otranto* (1764), ed. and introd. E. J. Clery (Oxford: Oxford University Press, 1996), p. vii). See also R. W. Ketton-Cremer, *Horace Walpole: A Biography* (London, 1940).

2 Robert Miles, 'Europhobia: the Catholic Other in Horace Walpole and Charles Maturin', in *European Gothic*, ed. Avril Horner (Manchester: Manchester University Press, 2002), p. 93.

3 *Monthly Review* (January 1765), pp. 77–9.

4 E. J. Clery, 'The Genesis of Gothic Fiction', in *The Cambridge Companion to Gothic Fiction*, ed. Jerrold E. Hogle (Cambridge: Cambridge University Press, 2002), p. 21.

5 Horace Walpole, Preface to the second edition of *The Castle of Otranto* (1764), ed. E. J. Clery (Oxford: Oxford University Press, 1996), pp. 9–10.

6 Richardson and Smollett were best-selling authors of popular novels.

7 Clery here references Samuel Johnson's essay from *The Rambler*, no. 4 (1750), reprinted in E. J. Clery and Robert Miles (eds), *Gothic Documents* (Manchester: Manchester University Press, p. 175). Reprinted in E. J. Clery, 'The Genesis of Gothic Fiction', in *The Cambridge Companion to Gothic Fiction*, ed. Jerrold E. Hogle (Cambridge: Cambridge University Press, 2002), p. 23.

8 *Monthly Review* (May 1765), p. 394.

9 *The Yale Edition of Walpole's Correspondence*, vol. 31 (1961), ed. W. S. Lewis, (New Haven: Yale University Press, 1937–1983), p. 221.

10 In her interesting feminist study *Art of Darkness* (1995), Anne Williams specifically takes issue with the claim that Walpole invented 'Gothic Story', arguing that 'Walpole's claim to be the Gothic creator *ex nihilo* is as dubious as Manfred's to the throne of Otranto.' Williams, *Art of Darkness* (Chicago and London: University of Chicago Press, 1995), pp. 9–10. See also pp. 11–14 for further exploration of her argument.

11 Clara Reeve, Preface to *The Old English Baron: A Gothic Story* (1778) (Oxford: Oxford University Press, 1967), pp. 1–2.

12 Clara Reeve, *The Progress of Romance, through times, countries and manners with remarks upon the good and bad effects of it, on them respectively, in a course of evening conversations* (2 vols) (Colchester and London, 1785), vol. I, p. xi.

13 Reeve (1785), vol. I, p. 6.

14 Reeve (1785), vol. I, p. 8.

15 Reeve (1785), vol. I, p. 13.

16 Reeve (1785), vol. I, p. 13.

17 Reeve (1785), vol. I, p. 21.

18 Reeve (1785), vol. I, p. 24.

19 Robert Miles, 'The 1790s: the Effulgence of Gothic', in *The Cambridge Companion to Gothic Fiction*, ed. Jerrold E. Hogle (Cambridge: Cambridge University Press, 2002), p. 60.

20 James Raven, 'The Novel Comes of Age', in Garside, Raven, Schöwlering, eds, *The English Novel 1770–1799: A Bibliographical Survey of Prose Fiction Published in the British Isles* (Oxford: Oxford University Press, 2000), vol. I, p. 27. This volume is an excellent source for research into early Gothic titles, and demonstrates the richness and diversity of Gothic fiction during the period covered.

21 Samuel Taylor Coleridge, review of *The Monk* (1796) in *Critical Review*, 19 (February 1797), pp. 194–200.

22 Coleridge (1797), p. 199.

23 Coleridge (1797), p. 200.

24 T. J. Mathias, *The Pursuits of Literature*, Preface to the Fourth Dialogue (July 1797), 13th edn (London: T. Becket, 1805), pp. 204–8.

25 T. J. Mathias, *The Pursuits of Literature*, Dialogue the Fourth (1797), ll. 543–6, p. 336.

26 T. J. Mathias, *The Pursuits of Literature*, Dialogue the First (1794), ll. 91–4, p. 56.

27 Mathias (1794), p. 56.

28 Fred Botting, *Gothic* (London: Routledge, 1996), p. 80.

29 For further exploration of these contexts, see also Michael Gamer's chapter 'Gothic and its Contexts', in *Romanticism and the Gothic: Genre, Reception and Canon Formation* (Cambridge: Cambridge University Press, 2000), pp. 79–89. In this section, Gamer explores in great depth the outraged reception of Lewis's *The Monk* and how Coleridge's 'obscenity' response was transformed swiftly into a charge of pornography.

30 Interestingly, however, in another footnote Mathias exempted the foremost Gothic novelist of the 1790s, Ann Radcliffe, from this category, adding: 'Not so the mighty magician of THE MYSTERIES OF UDOLPHO, bred and nourished by the Florentine Muses in their sacred solitary caverns, amid the paler shrines of Gothic superstition, and in all the dreariness of inchantment [sic].' Mathias, *The Pursuits of Literature*, First Dialogue, p. 56.

31 [Anon.], 'The Terrorist System of Novel Writing', *Monthly Magazine*, 4:21 (August 1797), pp. 102–4.

32 'The Terrorist System of Novel Writing', however, is more equivocal than it appears at first glance. The allusions to *habeas corpus*, the potentiality of violence that we have imitated 'if not in our fields', and the fact that this is written by 'A Jacobin Novelist' suggest that the Gothic tropes could be equally reminiscent of certain events in Britain. Like Jane Austen's later parody of the Gothic novel, this article also harbours some doubt as to just how unrealistic the Gothic genre is.

33 [Anon.], 'Terrorist Novel Writing', *Spirit of the Public Journals for 1797*, vol. 1 (London, 1798), pp. 223–5. Reprinted in Clery and Miles (eds), *Gothic Documents* (Manchester: Manchester University Press, 2000), pp. 183–4.

34 Eugenia C. DeLamotte, *Perils of the Night: A Feminist Study of Nineteenth-Century Gothic* (Oxford and New York: Oxford University Press, 1990). See also David Richter's 'Gothic Fantasia: the Monsters and the Myths – A Review Article', *The Eighteenth Century: Theory and Interpretation*, 28:2 (Spring 1987), pp. 149–70.

35 Editor, *Spirit of the Public Journals for 1797*, vol. 1, p. 223.

36 Editor, *Spirit of the Public Journals for 1797*, vol. 1, p. 223. Here, the editor refers to the novel *Paul et Virginie* by the French novelist and naturalist Bernardin de Saint-Pierre (1737–1814), first published in France in 1788, and translated into English in the same year, with various other translations issued between 1789 and 1800, including Helen Maria Williams's translation *Paul and Virginia* in 1795.

37 See note 30 of this chapter for further information on this.

38 Anon., Review of *Austenburn Castle* in the *Critical Review*, 16 (February 1796).

39 Sir Walter Scott, 'Ann Radcliffe', from the *Lives of the Novelists* from the *Miscellaneous Prose Works*(1827); ed. Ioan Williams, in *On Novelists and Fiction* (London: Routledge, 1968), p. 110.

40 Sir Walter Scott, 'Introductory' chapter to *Waverley, Or, 'tis sixty years since*, (Edinburgh: Constable, 1814), pp. 1–3.

41 Scott's references to Rosicrucianism and Illuminati in relation to the German romance tradition bring to mind in particular to *The Ghost-seer* by the German novelist, poet and dramatist Friedrich Schiller (1759–1805), first published in Britain in 1795. Schiller's paranoid and chilling tale of an unnamed Protestant prince who becomes obsessed by an Armenian monk bears many allusions to these belief systems.

42 Scott's historical specificity in *Waverley* gained him the questionable critical reputation as the first historical novelist. Although it may be argued that Scott was the first novelist to use the Historical Romance genre repeatedly and with considerable success, Sophia Lee's historical romance *The Recess, or a tale of other times*, set during the reign of Elizabeth I, is a significant precedent, and the Scottish historical fiction of Jane Porter (1776–1850) is contemporaneous with Scott.

43 Jane Austen, *Northanger Abbey* (1818), ed. and introd. Marilyn Butler (London: Penguin, 1995), p. 172.

44 Austen began writing *Northanger Abbey* in the late 1790s under the title of *Susan*. As we shall explore further in Chapter Six, there are some aspects of Catherine's Gothic imagination, particularly the legal aspects, that are suggestive of the Gothic romance's relevance for females in the 1790s and 1800s.

45 Jane Austen, *Northanger Abbey* (1818), ed. Claire Grogan (Ontario: Broadview Press, 1998), pp. 61–2.

46 Michael Sadleir, 'The Northanger Novels: a Footnote to Jane Austen', *English Association Pamphlet*, 68 (November 1927).

47 Sadleir (1927), p. 9.

48 Sadleir (1927), p. 10.

49 Guide Author's note: '[t]he fascination of the abomination' is a phrase from *Heart of Darkness* (1902; Harmondsworth: Penguin, 1995), p. 20: Joseph Conrad(1857–1924). Napier's note: 'Robert L. Platzner urges this view. See Platzner and R.D. Hume, " 'Gothic versus Romantic': A Rejoinder"', *PMLA* lxxxvi (1971), 266–7.

50 Elizabeth R. Napier, *The Failure of Gothic: Problems of Disjunction in an Eighteenth-Century Literary Form* (Oxford: Clarendon Press, 1987), p. 29.

51 David Punter, 'Review' of Elizabeth Napier's *The Failure of Gothic*, in *The Times Higher Education Supplement*, 20 March 1987, p. 26.

52 Coral Ann Howells, *Love, Mystery and Misery: Feeling in Gothic Fiction* (London: Athlone Press, 1978), p. 16. The affinity between the Gothic of the Romantic era and the contemporary stage is also pursued in a number of other works, notably E. J. Clery's *Women's Gothic* (Tavistock: Northcote House, 2000).

53 Maggie Kilgour, *The Rise of the Gothic Novel* (London: Routledge, 1995), pp. 3–4.

CHAPTER TWO

1 Indeed, as E. J. Clery argues, the term ' "Gothic novel" is ... mostly a twentieth-century coinage'. Clery, 'The genesis of "Gothic" fiction', in *The Cambridge Companion to Gothic Fiction*, ed. Jerrold E. Hogle (Cambridge: Cambridge University Press, 2002), p. 21.

2 Sir Walter Scott, 'Ann Radcliffe', from the *Lives of the Novelists* from the *Miscellaneous Prose Works* (1827); repr. in Ioan Williams, *On Novelists and Fiction* (London: Routledge, 1968), p. 110.

3 Ann Radcliffe, *A Sicilian Romance* (1790), ed. Alison Milbanke (Oxford: Oxford University Press, 1993), p. 1.

4 See Alison Milbanke's excellent 'Introduction' to this edition, where she provides a good interpretation of this landscape, and its subsequent uses in the novel, along the lines of nature versus culture. Radcliffe (1790), p. xxv.

5 Devendra P. Varma, *The Gothic Flame* (1957; New York: Russell and Russell, 1966), pp. 17–18.

6 Longinus, *On the Sublime*, trans. W. Hamilton Fyfe, in *Aristotle, Longinus, Demetrius* (London, 1927). See David Punter, *The Literature of Terror: A History of Gothic Fictions from 1765 to the Present Day*, 2 vols (Harlow: Longman, 1996), vol. I, p. 37, for further information on this classical source.

7 Edmund Burke, *A Philosophical Enquiry into the Origin of our Ideas of the Sublime and Beautiful* (1757), ed. David Womersley (London: Penguin, 1998), p. 86.

8 Burke (1998), p. 101.

9 Burke (1998), pp. 101–2.

10 Burke (1998), pp. 102–3.

11 David Punter, *The Literature of Terror*, 2nd edn (Harlow: Longman, 1996), p. 39.

12 Radcliffe (1993), p. 103.

13 Radcliffe (1993), explanatory notes, p. 200.

14 A. L. Aikin, 'On the Pleasure Derived from Objects of Terror', from *Miscellaneous Pieces, in Prose* by J. and A. L. Aikin (London: J. Johnson, 1773), p. 120.

15 The reference that Aikin makes to Pistol eating his leek in this section of her essay is taken from Shakespeare's *Henry V*, Act 5, sc. 1. Pistol has insulted the Welshman Fluellan by suggesting that he eats the leek that he wears proudly for St David's Day because, Pistol confesses, 'I am qualmish at the smell of leek.' Fluellan's outraged response is to force Pistol to eat the leek. Aikin's choice of this analogy is interesting: this lengthy representation of Pistol being forced to eat a leek hinges upon outraged honour and customs that are alien and not easily understood by Englishmen. If we compare this to the alien tradition of romance (as we explored in Chapter One through Reeve's work), we can perhaps argue that Aikin is defending the romance tradition.

16 Aikin (1773), pp. 123–4.

17 Charles Maturin, *Melmoth the Wanderer* (1820), ed. Douglas Grant, introd. Chris Baldick (Oxford: Oxford University Press, 1989), p. 257.

18 Aikin (1773), p. 125.

19 Alexander Pope, 'Essay on Man' (1773–4), 3, ll. 251–2.

20 Aikin (1773), p. 125.

21 Ann Radcliffe, *The Italian* (1797), ed. Robert Miles (London: Penguin, 2000), pp. 105–6.

22 Nathan Drake, *Literary Hours or sketches critical and narrative*, XV (Sudbury, 1798).

23 Radcliffe (2000), pp. 271–2.

24 These contemporaries of the 'new school' mentioned in this essay could include Richard Payne Knight (1751–1824) and Uvedale Price (1747–1829), both aesthetic theorists who warmly endorsed the concept of the 'picturesque'.

25 Ann Radcliffe, 'On the Supernatural in Poetry', *New Monthly Magazine and Literary Journal* (1826), II, pp. 149–50. A footnote accompanying the text of the essay explained

that it was not originally intended to appear as an isolated article: 'Having been permitted to extract the above eloquent passages from the author of the "Mysteries of Udolpho", we have given this title to them, though certainly they were not intended by the writer to be offered as a formal or deliberate essay, under this, or any other denomination. They were, originally, part of an INTRODUCTION to the Romance, or Phantasie, which is about to appear. The discussion is supposed to be carried on by two travellers in Shakespeare's native country, Warwickshire' (p. 145). The Romance referred to here is Radcliffe's posthumously published final novel, *Gaston de Blondeville* (1826), which was later reviewed in the same magazine.

26 See again the opening epigraph to this chapter, from Radcliffe's *The Mysteries of Udolpho*, where the Appennines are 'exhibited' in their 'darkest *horrors*' [emphasis added].

27 Steven Bruhm, *Gothic Bodies: The Politics of Pain in Romantic Fiction* (Philadelphia: University of Pennsylvania Press, 1994), p. 37.

28 Bruhm (1994), p. 40.

29 Bruhm (1994), p. 41.

30 Bruhm (1994), p. 58.

31 Burke argues in Section VII of the *Enquiry*, 'Of the sublime', that 'When danger or pain press too nearly, they are incapable of giving any delight, and are simply terrible; but at certain distances, and with certain modifications, they may be, and they are delightful' (Burke, *Philosophical Enquiry*, p. 86). This distancing that must be effected in order to partake of the more delightful aspect of pain and danger he links to self-preservation in the following sections.

32 Morris's note: 'Horace Walpole, *The Castle of Otranto*, ed. W. S. Lewis (London, 1964), p. 4.'

33 Morris's note: 'Burke includes as sublime "the idea of bodily pain" (torture), "the power which arises from institutions in kings and commanders' (tyranny), and "the last extreme of littleness" (incarceration).' See *Philosophical Enquiry*, pp. 86, 67, 72.' Morris uses the following edition of Burke: Edmund Burke, *A Philosophical Enquiry into the Origin of our Ideas of the Sublime and Beautiful* (1757), ed. James T. Boulton (New York, 1958), p. 58.

34 David B. Morris, 'Gothic Sublimity', *New Literary History*, 16 (Winter 1985), pp. 300–1.

35 Morris (1985), p. 301.

36 Morris (1985), p. 302.

37 Morris (1985), p. 303.

38 Morris (1985), p. 304.

39 Morris (1985), p. 305.

40 Morris (1985), p. 306.

41 Morris (1985), p. 307.

42 Morris (1985), p. 311.

43 Robert Miles, *Gothic Writing 1750–1820: A Genealogy* (1993; 2nd edn, Manchester: Manchester University Press, 2002), pp. 64–5. Miles makes the point that in 'Gothic Sublimity', by distinguishing between the eighteenth-century and Romantic sublime, Morris elaborates upon Thomas Weiskel's study *The Romantic Sublime: Studies in the Structure and Psychology of Transcendence* (Baltimore: Johns Hopkins University Press, 1976).

44 Miles (2002), p. 64.

45 Miles (2002), p. 65.

46 Miles (2002), pp. 74–5.

47 Vijay Mishra, *The Gothic Sublime* (New York: State University of New York Press, 1994), pp. 22–3.

CHAPTER THREE

1 See also E. J. Clery's chapter 'The Terrorist System' in her excellent study *The Rise of Supernatural Fiction: 1762–1800* (Cambridge: Cambridge University Press, 1995), and Robert Miles, 'The 1790s: the Effulgence of Gothic', in *The Cambridge Companion to Gothic*

*Fiction*, ed. Jerrold E. Hogle (Cambridge: Cambridge University Press, 2002), for further analyses of this revolutionary connection.

2 Anon., 'The Terrorist System of Novel Writing', *Monthly Magazine*, 4, 21 (August 1797), pp. 102–4.

3 William Hazlitt, 'On the English Novelists', *Lectures on the English Comic Writers*, vol. VI in *The Complete Works of William Hazlitt*, ed. P. P. Howe, 21 vols (London: Dent, 1931), p. 122.

4 Hazlitt, 'On English Novelists' (1931), p. 123.

5 Of course, as we noted in both Chapters One and Two, the Gothic romance was inaugurated long before 1790, but it enjoyed unprecedented success and attention in the 1790s.

6 Edmund Burke, *Reflections on the Revolution in France* (1790), ed. Conor Cruise O'Brien (London: Penguin, 1968). Burke notes immediately after the title-page to his pamphlet that 'the following Reflections had their origin in a correspondence between the Author and a very young gentleman in Paris, who did him the honour of desiring his opinion upon the important transactions, which then, and ever since, have so much occupied the attention of all men', p. 84.

7 Burke (1968), p. 93.

8 Burke (1968), p. 93.

9 See Conor Cruise O'Brien's 'Biographical Note' to Burke in his edition of the *Reflections on the Revolution in France*, pp. 77–81.

10 Burke (1968), p. 119.

11 Burke (1968), pp. 119–20.

12 Mary Wollstonecraft, *A Vindication of the Rights of Men* (1790), in *Political Writings*, ed. Janet Todd (Oxford: Oxford University Press, 1993), p. 8.

13 Wollstonecraft (1993), p. 41.

14 Ann Radcliffe, *A Sicilian Romance* (1790), ed. Alison Milbanke (Oxford: Oxford University Press, 1993), p. 1.

15 Burke (1968), p. 169.

16 Burke (1968), p. 170.

17 Wollstonecraft (1993), p. 60.

18 Miles (2002), p. 48.

19 T. J. Mathias, *The Pursuits of Literature*, First Dialogue (1794), 13th edn (London: T. Becket, 1805), p. 56.

20 See Chapter One of this Guide.

21 Marquis de Sade, 'Essay on the Novel', from *Selected Writings of de Sade*, trans. Leonard de Saint-Yves (New York: British Book Centre, 1954). The essay, originally entitled 'Idée sur les romans', was written in 1800 as a Preface to de Sade's *Les Crimes de l'Amour*.

22 David Punter, *The Literature of Terror: A History of Gothic fictions from 1765 to the Present Day*, 2 vols (Harlow: Longman, 1996), p. 54.

23 Maggie Kilgour, *The Rise of the Gothic Novel* (London: Routledge, 1995), p. 23.

24 Kilgour and Ronald Paulson both suggest that the remote temporal settings of the Gothic reflect the displacement of political anxieties. However, several examples of the Gothic romance in the 1790s stand apart as *not* being temporally remote. Radcliffe's *The Italian*, for example, which seemingly engages with a hostile, other Catholic continent, is quite specific about its temporal setting on the opening page. Here, we find out that the events only occurred in 1758, less than forty years before Radcliffe's publication of the novel.

25 Matthew Lewis, *The Monk* (1796), ed. Howard Anderson (Oxford: Oxford World's Classics, 1980), p. 7.

26 Lord George Gordon (1751–93), a retired navy lieutenant, was strongly opposed to proposals for Catholic Emancipation in Britain. On 2 July 1780, Gordon led a crowd of 50,000 people to Parliament to present a petition for the repeal of the 1778 Roman Catholic Relief Act. This demonstration turned into a riot and for the next five days many Catholic chapels and private houses were destroyed. Other buildings attacked and

damaged included the Bank of England, the King's Bench Prison, Newgate Prison and Fleet Prison.

27 Lewis in fact published *The Monk* in March 1796.

28 Ronald Paulson, *Representations of Revolution (1789–1820)* (New Haven and London: Yale University Press, 1983), pp. 217–18.

29 André Parreaux, *The Publication of 'The Monk': A Literary Event 1796–1798* (Paris: Didier, 1960), p. 132.

30 Markman Ellis, *The History of Gothic Fiction* (Edinburgh: Edinburgh University Press, 2000), p. 82. Ellis's good chapter on Lewis, entitled 'Revolution and Libertinism in the Gothic Novel', refocuses the discussion of *The Monk* and revolution more in relation to Lewis's career as a diplomat in the Hague in 1794.

31 Ellis (2000), p. 82.

32 Paulson (1983), p. 219.

33 Miles (2002), 'The 1790s: the Effulgence of Gothic', p. 45.

34 This is a note of caution that Miles (2002) also sounds when he argues that 'The first point to note is that the fad for Gothic romances predates the French Revolution, or at any rate, the fall of the Bastille in July 1789' (p. 45).

35 Paulson (1983), pp. 221–2.

36 Paulson (1983), p. 222.

37 Paulson (1983), pp. 224–5.

38 Paulson (1983), p. 227. See also Jerrold E. Hogle's excellent essay 'The Ghost of the Counterfeit – and the Closet – in *The Monk*', in Matthew Lewis's *The Monk*, ed. Fred Frank, a special issue of the electronic journal *Romanticism on the Net*, 8, November 1997 (www.erudit.org/revue/ron/1997).

39 Paulson (1983), pp. 231–2. Although Paulson's focus on Godwin is slightly anachronistic (*Caleb Williams* was published two years prior to *The Monk* and undoubtedly influenced Lewis's portrayal of Ambrosio), the connections that he forges are none the less important to understanding how the Jacobin novel intersects with the Gothic genre. For further explorations of the sexual nature of the Caleb/Falkland pursuit obsession, see also Chapter Six of this Guide, where I examine David Punter's chapter on *Caleb Williams* in *The Literature of Terror* and Eve Kosofsky Sedgwick's argument in *Between Men: English Literature and Male Homosocial Desire*.

40 William Godwin, Preface to *Caleb Williams* for Bentley's Standard Novels II (London, 1832).

41 William Godwin, *Caleb Williams* (1794), ed. David McCracken (Oxford: Oxford University Press, 1969), p. 4.

42 Kilgour (1995), *The Rise of the Gothic Novel*, p. 51.

43 John Thelwall, *The Rights of Nature against the Usurpation of Establishments. A Series of Letters to the People of Britain, Occasioned by the Recent Effusions of the Right Honourable Edmund Burke* (London and Norwich: H. D. Symonds and J. March, 1796), p. 15.

44 Miles (2002), p. 49.

45 Clery (1995), p. 134.

CHAPTER FOUR

1 See, for example, Montague Summers, *The Gothic Quest: A History of the Gothic Novel* (London: Fortune Press, 1938), pp. 195–6.

2 Matthew Lewis, *The Monk* (1796), ed. Howard Anderson (Oxford: Oxford World's Classics, 1980), p. 7.

3 Robert Miles, 'Europhobia: the Catholic Other in Horace Walpole and Charles Maturin', in *European Gothic*, ed. Avril Horner (Manchester: Manchester University Press, 2002), p. 84. For a further interpretation of this scene, see also my own essay in this collection, Angela Wright, 'European Disruptions of the Idealized Woman: Matthew Lewis's *The Monk* and the Marquis de Sade's *La Nouvelle Justine*', pp. 39–54.

4 Lewis (1980), p. 17.

5 Lewis (1980), p. 48.

6 Ann Radcliffe, *The Italian* (1797), ed. Robert Miles (London: Penguin Classics, 2000), p. 100.

7 Charles Robert Maturin, *Melmoth the Wanderer* (1820), ed. Douglas Grant (Oxford: Oxford World's Classics, 1989), pp. 164–5.

8 J. M. S. Tompkins, *The Popular Novel in England, 1770–1800* (1932; London: Methuen, 1969), p. 88.

9 Tompkins's note: 'v. *Critical*, March 1792, on Mrs Mary Robinson's *Vancenza*. Mrs. Robinson, who was liberal and "philosophic" in her sympathies, was very careful to make this clear in her next romance, *Hubert de Sevrac* (1796). Critics sometimes refused to accept an author's premises, if these were based on Catholic usages; thus the *Critical*, reviewing Mrs. Bennett's *Agnes de Courci* (1789), denied the enormity of a breach of celibacy. There is in some novels a mild plea for a "Protestant nunnery" (e.g. *Indiana Danby*, 1765), but the motive is not so much religious as social; such an institution would be a centre of good works and a means of disposing unmarried women.'

10 Tompkins's note: 'On the other hand, the Catholic Mrs. Inchbald dealt with the theme in *A Simple Story* (1791) discreetly and delicately. Dorriforth, though charmed, does not love till released from his vows; it is the Protestant girl, unaccustomed to associate a sacred prohibition with any man, who is enmeshed.'

11 Tompkins's note: 'A few quietly-authentic convent settings can be found, though the story they enclose is frequently improbable. This is the case with *Anecdotes of a Convent* (1771) by the author of *Memoirs of Mrs. Williams;* here the plot is concerned with a boy, bred up in a convent as a girl, and believing himself to be one; the author declares that the story is true.'

12 Tompkins (1932), pp. 274–6.

13 Marquis de Sade, 'Essay on the Novel', from *Selected Writings of de Sade*, trans. Leonard de Saint-Yves (New York: British Book Centre, 1954).

14 Leslie Fiedler, *Love and Death in the American Novel* (1960), repr. in *The Gothick Novel*, ed. Victor Sage (London: Macmillan, 1990), p. 137. Fiedler's quotation in the final sentence of this extract is taken from Horace Walpole's 1768 drama *The Mysterious Mother*, which also serves as the epigraph to chapter 1 of Ann Radcliffe's *The Italian*.

15 Radcliffe (2000), p. 6.

16 Chris Baldick and Robert Mighall, 'Gothic Criticism', in *Companion to the Gothic*, ed. David Punter (Oxford: Blackwell, 2000), p. 216.

17 André Breton, 'Limits not Frontiers of Surrealism' is discussed more fully in Chapter Five, on psychoanalysis and the Gothic.

18 Baldick and Mighall (2000), pp. 216–17.

19 Sir Walter Scott, 'Introduction' to volume on Mrs Radcliffe in Ballantyne's Novelist's Library (Edinburgh, 1821–4, 1 September 1824), in Sage, *The Gothick Novel* (1990), p. 59.

20 Baldick and Mighall (2000), p. 219.

21 Robert Miles, 'Introduction', in Radcliffe (2000), p. xxiii.

22 For more information on this, see Miles's introduction to Radcliffe (2000), pp. xxi–xxiii, and 'Members Unlimited', chapter I of E. P. Thompson's *The Making of the English Working Class* (1963; London: Penguin, 1991).

23 An excellent study of this 'crisis' at the heart of the Protestant nation in the 1790s can be found in Paul Keen, *The Crisis of Literature in the 1790s* (Cambridge: Cambridge University Press, 1999).

24 For more in-depth accounts of this historical moment, see E. J. Hobsbawn, *Nations and Nationalism since 1780: Programme, Myth and Reality* (Cambridge: Cambridge University Press, 1990); Linda Colley, *Britons: Forging the Nation 1707–1837* (New Haven and London: Yale University Press, 1992).

25 Angela Keane, *Women Writers and the English Nation in the 1790s: Romantic Belongings* (Cambridge: Cambridge University Press, 2000), p. 24.

26 For further readings of the novel vs. romance debate, see also Ian Duncan, *Modern Romance and the Transformations of the Novel* (Cambridge: Cambridge University Press, 1992).

27 Horace Walpole, 2nd 'Preface' to *The Castle of Otranto* (1764), ed. E. J. Clery (Oxford: Oxford World's Classics, 1996), p. 14.

28 E. J. Clery, 'The Genesis of Gothic Fiction', in *The Cambridge Companion to Gothic Fiction*, ed. Jerrold E. Hogle (Cambridge: Cambridge University Press, 2002), pp. 30–1. For further discussion of Walpole's two prefaces, see also E. J. Clery, *The Rise of Supernatural Fiction, 1762–1800* (Cambridge: Cambridge University Press, 1995), pp. 60–7, and E. J. Clery, 'Introduction' to *The Castle of Otranto* (1764), ed. E. J. Clery (Oxford: Oxford World's Classics, 1996).

29 Horace Walpole, 2nd 'Preface' to *The Castle of Otranto* (1764), Walpole (1996), p. 9.

30 Keane (2000), pp. 25–6.

31 Keane (2000), p. 26.

32 James Watt, *Contesting the Gothic: Fiction, Genre and Cultural Conflict, 1764–1832* (Cambridge: Cambridge University Press, 1999), p. 7. Besides Clara Reeve's *The Old English Baron*, in his chapter on the Loyalist Gothic romance Watt also discusses William Godwin's adaptation of Walpole's *Otranto Imogen: A Pastoral Romance, From the Ancient British* (1784).

33 Rictor Norton, *Mistress of Udolpho: The Life of Ann Radcliffe* (London and New York: Leicester University Press, 1999).

34 Robert Miles, 'Abjection, Nationalism and the Gothic', in *The Gothic*, ed. Fred Botting for the English Association (Cambridge: D. S. Brewer, 2001), pp. 47–70.

35 Julia Kristeva, *Powers of Horror: An Essay on Abjection*, trans. Leon S. Roudiez (New York: Columbia University Press, 1982). For other accounts of Gothic texts in relation to the abject, see in particular Jerrold E. Hogle's work on Mary Shelley's *Frankenstein* (1818) and *The Phantom of the Opera* (1911) by Gaston Leroux (1868–1927) in 'The Gothic and the "otherings" of Ascendant Culture: the Original Phantom of the Opera', *South Atlantic Quarterly*, 95, 821–46; 'Frankenstein as Neo-Gothic: from the Ghost of the Counterfeit to the Monster of Abjection', in *Romanticism, History, and the Possibilities of Genre*, eds. Tilottama Rajan and Julia Wright (Cambridge: Cambridge University Press, 1998), pp. 176–220; and 'The Gothic Crosses the Channel: Abjection and Revelation in *Le Fantôme de l'Opéra*', in *European Gothic: A Spirited Exchange*, ed. Avril Horner (Manchester: Manchester University Press, 2002), pp. 204–29.

36 Miles (2001), p. 53.

37 Miles (2001), p. 51.

38 Miles's note: 'For a print culture overview of the rise of the novel, see [James] Raven, 2000.'

39 Miles (2001), pp. 61–2. For a further excellent analysis of the first 'Preface' to Walpole's *Castle of Otranto*, see also the beginning of Jerrold E. Hogle's essay 'The Gothic Ghost of the Counterfeit and the Progress of Abjection', in *The Blackwell Companion to the Gothic*, ed. David Punter (Oxford: Blackwell, 2000), p. 293.

40 Miles, 2001, p. 64.

41 Slavoj Zizek, 'Enjoy your Nation as Yourself!' in *Tarrying with the Negative* (Durham: Duke University Press, 1993). See. pp. 54–8 of Miles's essay for a further explanation of how this works.

42 Radcliffe (2000), p. 381.

43 For further examples and explanations of the blurring of these religious boundaries in *The Italian*, see Miles (2001), pp. 66–7.

44 Mark Canuel, *Religion, Toleration and British Writing, 1790–1830* (Cambridge: Cambridge University Press, 2002), pp. 55–6.

45 Canuel (2002), p. 62.

46 Victor Sage, *Horror Fiction and the Protestant Tradition* (London: Macmillan, 1988), p. 29. Whilst Sage's book concentrates predominantly on fiction in the later nineteenth century, it also contains some interesting readings of Radcliffe, Maturin and Lewis.

47 Canuel (2002), pp. 62–4.

48 Canuel (2002), p. 72.

49 Robert Miles, in Radcliffe (2000), p. xx. Mark Canuel also reads Radcliffe's portrayal of Santa della Pietà as embodying 'an order and stability that contradicts monasticism's rigidly patriarchal authority', Canuel (2002), p. 75.

50 Radcliffe (2000), p. 348.

51 Radcliffe (2000), p. 348.

52 Angela Keane (2000), p. 38.

53 Jerrold E. Hogle, 'Introduction' to Hogle (2002). Hogle acknowledges here the arguments from two excellent essays in this collection by E. J. Clery ('The Genesis of "Gothic" Fiction') and Robert Miles ('The 1790s: the Effulgence of Gothic') which are quoted elsewhere in this Guide.

CHAPTER FIVE

1 Walpole's account of this creative process perhaps influenced the famous painting *The Nightmare* by Henry Fuseli (1741–1825) which he exhibited at the Royal Academy in 1782. In *The History of Gothic Fiction*, Markman Ellis offers a good analysis of Fuseli's painting in his 'Prologue', where he argues that 'As the title suggests, the painting represents a nightmare, but it does so in a curious way, depicting it as both a dream image and the image of a dream.' Ellis, *The History of Gothic Fiction* (Edinburgh: Edinburgh University Press, 2000), p. 5.

2 Horace Walpole, Letter to the Rev. Mason, 17 April 1763.

3 Mary Shelley, 'Author's Introduction' to *Frankenstein, or the Modern Prometheus* (1831 edition).

4 See also Susan Wolstenholme's analysis of Mary Shelley's retrospective passive account where she argues that Shelley ' "sees" herself as spectator of a dream vision', and that for her and other women who account for their novels through a dream, 'these imagined images are freighted with implications about their positions as women who write' (Wolstenholme, *Gothic (Re)Visions: Writing Women as Readers* (Albany: State University of New York Press, 1983), pp. 4–5).

5 [Anon.], 'Terrorist Novel Writing' (1798), *Spirit of the Public Journals for 1797*, vol. 1 (London, 1798), pp. 223–5. Reprinted in Clery and Miles, eds, *Gothic Documents* (Manchester: Manchester University Press, 2000), pp. 183–4. Cf. Chapter One for the quotation in full from 'Terrorist Novel Writing'.

6 André Breton, 'Limites non frontières du Surréalisme', *Nouvelle Revue Française*, 48, I (1937); translated as 'Limits not Frontiers of Surrealism', in Herbert Read, (ed.,), *Surrealism*, pp. 106–11; reprinted in *The Gothick Novel: A Casebook*, ed. Victor Sage (Basingstoke: Macmillan, 1990), p. 114.

7 Devendra P. Varma, *The Gothic Flame* (1957; New York: Russell and Russell, 1966), p. 69. Further down, Varma anachronistically confirms that 'Walpole's own method employed in his Gothic story is truly surrealistic. His manner of "telescoping" different ages, settings, and characters, his strong manipulation of "the sense of contrast", his use of dialogue and style, his story as it unfolds swiftly giving a nightmarish sensation: all these are methods of surrealism in particular.'

8 Breton (1990), p. 113.

9 Sophia Lee, *The Recess, or a tale of other times*, 3 vols (London, 1785), vol. III, p. 165. See Margaret Anne Doody's ground-breaking essay 'Desert Ruins and Troubled Waters: Female Dreams in Fiction and the Development of the Gothic Novel', *Genre*, 10 (1977). This is one of the first critical essays to discuss *The Recess* in detail. In it, Doody explores

the dreams and insanity in Lee's novel, and demonstrates how it goes on to influence a range of other Gothic novels, including those of Radcliffe.

10 Ann Radcliffe, *The Mysteries of Udolpho* (1794), ed. Bonamy Dobrée (Oxford: Oxford University Press, 1980), p. 329.

11 Ann Radcliffe, *The Italian* (1797), ed. Robert Miles (London: Penguin, 2000), pp. 329 and 330.

12 Charles Maturin, *Melmoth the Wanderer* (1820), ed. Douglas Grant, introd. Chris Baldick (Oxford: Oxford University Press, 1989), p. 502.

13 David Punter, *The Literature of Terror: The Gothic Tradition* (1978), vol. I (Harlow: Longman, 1996), pp. 74–5. It is interesting to note that the Freud passage which Punter quotes here is reminiscent of Anna Laetitia Aikin's 1775 essay 'On the Pleasure Derived from Objects of Terror', discussed in Chapter Two of this Guide.

14 Punter (1996), p. 85.

15 'Dismemberment' is a term that Maggie Kilgour also later invokes in the opening section of her monograph *The Rise of the Gothic Novel* (London: Routledge, 1995), p. 31.

16 Maturin (1989), p. 159.

17 Ellis (2000), p. 13. Ellis's claim that criticism of the Gothic has been dominated by psychoanalysis is rather unfair, as the wealth of material in the other chapters of this Guide demonstrates. In particular, the materialist accounts of Clery, Jacobs, Watt, Keane and Canuel testify to the richness of other critical interpretations of the genre.

18 For Oedipal analyses of the incest motif, see, for example, Varma, *The Gothic Flame* (1957); Mario Praz, *The Romantic Agony* (1930); Eino Railo, *The Haunted Castle* (1927).

19 Michelle A. Massé, 'Psychoanalysis and the Gothic', in *Companion to the Gothic*, ed. David Punter (Oxford: Blackwell, 2000), p. 230. Massé is quoting from Freud's 1919 essay 'The Uncanny', *The Standard Edition of the Complete Psychological Works of Sigmund Freud*, 24 vols, ed. James Strachey (London: Hogarth Press, 1955), vol. 17, pp. 217–52.

20 Freud (1955), pp. 217–23.

21 Freud (1955), p. 218.

22 Hélène Cixous, 'La fiction et ses fantômes: une lecture de l'*Unheimliche* de Freud', *Poétique*, 10 (1973).

23 Cixous (1973), p. 208.

24 Massé (2000), 'Psychoanalysis and the Gothic', p. 230.

25 See, for example, Rosemary Jackson's *Fantasy: The Literature of Subversion* (London: Methuen, 1981), p. 64, where she states that Freud's essay 'provides a clear theoretical introduction to psychoanalytic readings of fantastic literature, especially to nineteenth-century works, where the uncanny is at its most explicit'. See also Kelly Hurley's excellent *The Gothic Body: Sexuality, Materialism and Degeneration at the Fin de Siècle* (Cambridge: Cambridge University Press, 1996), pp. 39–41 in particular.

26 Terry Castle, *The Female Thermometer: Eighteenth-Century Culture and the Invention of the Uncanny* (Oxford: Oxford University Press, 1995), pp. 7–9. In a note, Castle refers the reader to John Locke's *An Essay Concerning Human Understanding*, ed. A. D. Woozley (London: Collins, 1964), Book I, 'Introduction', section 7. Castle's chapter in this study, 'The Spectralization of the Other in *The Mysteries of Udolpho*', which charts what she views as the 'haunted consciousness' which pervades Radcliffe's novel, offers one of the best and most insightful studies of this particular work.

27 Castle (1995), p. 10.

28 Castle (1995), p. 10.

29 'The Spectralization of the Other in *The Mysteries of Udolpho*' was originally published as an essay in a collection entitled *The New Eighteenth Century: Theory, Politics, English Literature*, ed. Felicity Nussbaum and Laura Brown (New York and London: Methuen, 1987), pp. 231–53.

30 Castle (1995), p. 135.

31 The most prominent complaint about Ann Radcliffe's relentless use of the 'explained supernatural' came from Sir Walter Scott, who in his essay on 'Ann Radcliffe' in *Lives of*

*the Novelists* objected, 'It must be allowed that this [the rationalization of the supernatural] has not been done with uniform success, and that the author has been occasionally more successful in exciting interest and apprehension, than in giving either interest or dignity of explanation to the means she has made use of' (Scott, 'Ann Radcliffe', from the *Lives of the Novelists*, from *Miscellaneous Prose Works* (1827) in Scott, *On Novelists and Fiction*, ed. Ioan Williams (London: Routledge, 1968), p. 115).

32 Radcliffe (1980), pp. 533–4.

33 Radcliffe (1980), p. 532.

34 As Robert Miles argues elsewhere, Freud's early work on the pleasure principle 'bears some similarity to Radcliffe's "explained supernatural": manifest absurdities (such as dreams or "slips of the tongue") turn out to have a rational explanation, or "latent meaning". But when Freud comes to analyse the "death" instinct his language turns Gothic: we are now in the realm of the inexplicable and the primitive' (Miles, *Ann Radcliffe: The Great Enchantress* (Manchester: Manchester University Press, 1995), p. 109).

35 Castle (1995), p. 135.

36 David Punter, 'Social Relations of Gothic Fiction', in *Romanticism and Ideology: Studies in English Writing: 1765–1830*, ed. Aers, Cook and Punter (London: Routledge, 1981), p. 107.

37 Freud (1955).

38 Kilgour (1995), p. 220.

39 David Punter, Review of Elizabeth Napier's *The Failure of Gothic*, in *The Times Higher Education Supplement*, 20 March 1987, p. 26.

40 Kilgour (1995), p. 221.

41 Massé (2000), p. 231.

42 Miles (1995), p. 108.

43 Matthew Lewis, *The Monk* (1796), ed. Howard Anderson (Oxford: Oxford World's Classics, 1980), p. 7.

44 Lewis (1980), pp. 11–12.

45 Robert Miles, 'Europhobia: the Catholic Other in Horace Walpole and Charles Maturin', in *European Gothic*, ed. Avril Horner (Manchester: Manchester University Press, 2002), p. 84. See also my own essay in this collection, for further analysis of the visual aspects of Lewis's opening scene: Angela Wright, 'European Disruptions of the Idealized Woman: Matthew Lewis's *The Monk* and the Marquis de Sade's *La Nouvelle Justine*', pp. 39–54.

46 Coral Ann Howells, *Love, Mystery and Misery: Feeling in Gothic Fiction* (1978; London: Athlone Press, 1995), pp. 15–16.

47 Maturin (1989), p. 257.

48 A. L. Aikin, 'On the Pleasure Derived from Objects of Terror', *Miscellaneous Pieces, in Prose* by J. and A. L. Aikin (London, 1775), pp. 123–4.

49 Wolstenholme (1993), p. 14.

50 Wolstenholme (1993), pp. 18–19.

51 Miles (1995), p. 111.

52 Ann Radcliffe, *The Romance of the Forest*, ed. Chloe Chard (Oxford: Oxford University Press, 1986), p. 7. As Miles (1995), p. 119 argues, this textual opening is both indebted and resistant to Jean-Jacques Rousseau's discourses on women's proper dress in his educational work *Emile* (1762).

53 Michelle A. Massé, *In the Name of Love: Women, Masochism and the Gothic* (New York: Cornell University Press, 1992), pp. 11–12.

54 Massé (1992), p. 19. As her footnote records, her quotation is taken from Joanna Russ, 'Somebody's Trying to Kill Me and I Think It's My Husband: the Modern Gothic' in Juliann E. Fleenor, ed., *The Female Gothic* (Montreal, Eden Press, 1983), p. 50.

55 Laura Mulvey, 'Visual Pleasure and Narrative Cinema', *Screen*, 16, 3, (Autumn 1975), pp. 6–18. Although Mulvey's essay does not directly engage with Gothic fiction, it is none the less useful in illuminating how precisely Freud's theories can be explored in relation to a great number of female images on the screen. As an early piece of criticism upon this

topic, it remains one of the most important essays to have explored the gendered ramifications of the gaze. See also John Berger's *Ways of Seeing* (Harmondsworth: Penguin, 1972).

56  Radcliffe (1980), p. 258.

57  Massé (1992), p. 40. On p. 54, Massé offers a similarly persuasive example from William Godwin's *Caleb Williams* where indeed, the lowly servant-narrator Caleb not only argues that 'curiosity' was 'The spring of action which, perhaps more than any other, characterised the whole train of my life' but also meditates specifically on how spying upon his employer Mr Falkland offers him a 'strange sort of *pleasure*'. Godwin's protagonist Caleb loves his master Falkland, but also aspires to be on a more equal footing of confidence with him. His aspirations towards equality and friendship are also about asserting himself and placing himself within the same codes of authority and feudalism that Falkland honours. Although this reading seems at first glance to go against the gendered arguments of the rest of her study, Massé is careful to point out that where the subordinate victim is male, their inequality is signified through class or paranoia. Both of these categories apply to the character Caleb.

58  Massé (1992), pp. 62–3.

59  Radcliffe (1980), p. 232.

60  Elisabeth Bronfen, *Over her Dead Body: Death, femininity and the Aesthetic* (Manchester: Manchester University Press, 1992), p. 406.

61  See, for example, Wolstenholme (1993), pp. 10–11.

62  David Punter, *The Romantic Unconscious* (New York and London: Harvester Wheatsheaf, 1989), p. 122.

63  Punter (1989), p. 122.

64  Jacques Lacan, 'The Mirror Stage as Formative of the Function of the I', 'The Symbolic Order' and 'The Agency of the Letter in the Unconscious or Reason since Freud', in *Ecrits* (1966), trans. Alan Sheridan (London: Routledge, 1977).

65  S. L. Garner, et al., eds and introd., *The (M)other Tongue: Essays in Feminist Psychoanalytic Interpretation* (Ithaca and London: Cornell University Press, 1985), p. 21. See also chapter 6 of Miles (1995), pp. 104–6, for a clear explanation of Lacan's theory of the Imaginary and Symbolic Orders.

66  Claire Kahane, 'The Gothic Mirror', in S. L. Garner et al., eds, *The (M)other Tongue: Essays in Feminist Psychoanalytic Interpretation*, p. 334.

67  When, for example, in Radcliffe's *The Italian*, Schedoni listens to the guide's story about the Barone's murder by his brother, the guide's convoluted and digressive narrative, frequently interrupted by Schedoni's impatient reflections upon his story, covers the first two chapters of the third volume in the novel. Its prominence in the novel highlights the significance of its status as narrative digression. Likewise, Maturin's *Melmoth the Wanderer*'s endless unpacking of tales-within-tales is so marked that narrative digression becomes the point of the novel, in many ways.

68  Kahane (1985), p. 336.

69  Miles (1995), pp. 106–7.

70  Miles (1995), p. 107.

71  Kahane (1985), p. 340.

72  For a full summary of Cixous's and Irigaray's theories, see the anthology *New French Feminisms*, ed. Elaine Marks and Isabelle Courtivron (Amherst: University of Massachusetts Press, 1980), and Ann Rosalind Jones, 'Writing the Body: Toward an Understanding of *L'Ecriture Féminine*', *Feminist Studies*, 7 (1981).

73  See Alison Milbanke's introduction to Ann Radcliffe's *A Sicilian Romance* (Oxford: Oxford University Press, 1993).

74  Anne Williams, *Art of Darkness: A Poetics of Gothic* (Chicago and London: Chicago University Press, 1995), p. 22. See Chapter Six for a full discussion of Williams's intervention in the debate on 'Female Gothic'.

75 Williams (1995), p. 13. See also Williams's later chapter in this study, entitled 'The Mysteries of Enlightenment; or Dr. Freud's Gothic Novel'. In this chapter, Williams criticizes the critical tendencies to read Gothic as a proto-Freudianism, and in particular the reading of Oedipal motifs and psychosexual secrets within the genre. In its place, she proposes that 'Instead of using Freud to read Gothic, we should use Gothic to read Freud. We can begin with their common cultural matrix.'

76 Jerrold E. Hogle, 'The Gothic Ghost of the Counterfeit and the Progress of Abjection', in David Punter (ed.), *Companion to the Gothic*, (Oxford: Blackwell, 2000), p. 293.

77 Hogle (2000), p. 293.

78 Hogle (2000), p. 293.

79 Robert Miles, 'Abjection, Nationalism and the Gothic', in *The Gothic*, ed. Fred Botting for the English Association (Cambridge: D. S. Brewer, 2001), pp. 47–70. See also Robert Miles, 'Europhobia: the Catholic Other in Horace Walpole and Charles Maturin', in *European Gothic*, ed. Avril Horner (Manchester: Manchester University Press, 2002), pp. 84–103.

80 Hogle, (2000), pp. 295–6.

81 Punter (1981), p. 107.

82 David Punter and Elisabeth Bronfen, 'Violence, Trauma and the Ethical', in *The Gothic*, ed. Fred Botting (Cambridge: English Association, 2001), p. 16. Punter and Bronfen's analysis here makes reference to Jean Laplanche's *Essays on Otherness*, trans. John Fletcher (London: Routledge, 1999).

83 Recent critical accounts of the Gothic which have combined both a strong attention to context and a psychoanalytical angle include the examples cited above by Punter, Castle, Williams, Hogle and Miles.

## CHAPTER SIX

1 Thomas Noon Talfourd, *Memoir of the Life and Writings of Mrs Radcliffe*, prefixed to Ann Radcliffe, *Gaston de Blondeville, or The Court of Henry III*, 4 vols (Henry Colburn, 1826), p. 12.

2 E. J. Clery, *Women's Gothic: From Clara Reeve to Mary Shelley* (Tavistock: Northcote House, 2000), p. 2. This book provides a good original analysis of these women's Gothic writing, closely linking their innovations to the theatrical innovation of one of the eighteenth century's most famous actresses, Sarah Siddons (1755–1831).

3 Clery (2000), p. 2.

4 For further information about this debate, see Paul Keen, *The Crisis of Literature in the 1790s* (Cambridge: Cambridge University Press, 1999). See also E. J. Clery's section 'The Terrorist System' in *The Rise of Supernatural Fiction*, where she discusses the Gothic rage: 'Writers and booksellers were attempting to balance profitably the need for both novelty and sameness with no comparable experience in the past to guide them; the rage for Gothic could vanish as suddenly as it had appeared, its origins were inscrutable and the only safe course was to mine a proven formula, with minimal variations, until it was exhausted' (p. 142).

5 For a good account of Gothic fiction in relation to circulating libraries, see Ed Jacobs's *Accidental Migrations* (Lewisburg: Bucknell University Press, 2000).

6 Ellen Moers, *Literary Women* (1976), introd. Helen Taylor (London: Women's Press, 1986), p. 91.

7 Moers's claim here, that 'religious fears were on the wane', is belied by the complexities of the political and national situation during the Romantic era. The Gothic's profound engagement with religion and nationalism was explored in Chapter Four.

8 Moers (1976), p. 91.

9 Sophia Lee, *The Recess, or a tale of other times*, 3 vols (London, 1785). For an early and ground-breaking analysis of the female motifs in this novel, see Margaret Ann Doody's

essay 'Desert Ruins and Troubled Waters: Female Dreams in Fiction and the Development of the Gothic Novel', *Genre*, 10 (1977), pp. 529–72. See also the chapter on Clara Reeve and Sophia Lee in Clery (2000), pp. 25–50, and my recent essay, 'To Live the Life of Hopeless Recollection: Mourning and Melancholia in Female Gothic', in 'Female Gothic', ed. Andrew Smith and Diana Wallace, *Gothic Studies*, 6:1 (May 2004).

10 Jacqueline Howard, *Reading Gothic Fiction: A Bakhtinian Approach* (Oxford: Clarendon Press, 1993), p. 57.

11 Howard (1993), p. 59.

12 'Female Gothic', ed. Robert Miles, *Women's Writing*, 1:2 (1994), and Smith and Wallace (2004).

13 E. J. Clery, 'Ann Radcliffe and D. A. F. de Sade: Thoughts on Heroinism', in Miles (1994), p. 203.

14 Here, Clery refers to three important works of feminist criticism: Nancy K. Miller, *The Heroine's Text: Readings in the French and English Novel, 1722–1782* (New York: Columbia University Press, 1980); Janet Todd, *The Sign of Angellica* (London: Virago Press, 1989); and Jane Spencer, *The Rise of the Woman Novelist* (Oxford: Basil Blackwell, 1986). She points out that Nancy K. Miller reads only male authors, and Janet Todd and Jane Spencer read only female authors.

15 Clery, in Miles (1994), p. 204.

16 Miles (1994), p. 132.

17 Smith and Wallace (2004), p. 2. See also Lauren Fitzgerald's excellent survey essay on the critical field in the same collection: 'Female Gothic and the Institutionalization of Gothic Studies', pp. 8–18.

18 Kate Ferguson Ellis, 'Can You Forgive Her? The Gothic Heroine and Her Critics', in *Companion to the Gothic*, ed. David Punter (Oxford: Blackwell, 2000), pp. 264–5.

19 Horace Walpole, *The Castle of Otranto: A Gothic Story* (1764), ed. E. J. Clery (Oxford: Oxford University Press, 1996), p. 91. This formative instance of heroines challenging the patriarchal order, however, bears testament to the fact that this is not exclusively a tradition executed in women's writing.

20 [Anon.], 'Terrorist Novel Writing' (1798), *Spirit of the Public Journals for 1797*, vol. 1 (London, 1798), pp. 223–5; reprinted in Clery and Miles, eds, *Gothic Documents* (Manchester: Manchester University Press, 2000), pp. 183–4.

21 John Sekora, *Luxury: The Concept in Western Thought, Eden to Smollett* (Baltimore and London: Johns Hopkins University Press, 1977).

22 E. J. Clery, *The Rise of Supernatural Fiction, 1762–1800* (Cambridge: Cambridge University Press, 1995), p. 101.

23 Clery also cites a further good example of concerns over female readerships which appeared in 1797: 'Novel Reading a Cause of Female Depravity', *Monthly Mirror*, 4 (November 1797), pp. 277–9. Clery (1995), p. 100.

24 Harriet Guest, 'The Wanton Muse: Politics and Gender in Gothic Theory after 1760', in *Beyond Romanticism: New Approaches to Texts and Contexts 1780–1832*, ed. Stephen Copley and John Whale (London and New York: Routledge, 1992), p. 134. Among other texts, Guest refers in this essay to Richard Hurd's 1811 *Moral and Political Dialogues, with Letters on Chivalry and Romance* in *Works*, 8 vols (London: Cadell), Thomas Warton's 1774 'Dissertation on the origin of Romantic fiction in Europe', in *The History of English Poetry*, 3 vols (London), and Clara Reeve's 1785 *The Progress of Romance* (Colchester: Keymer).

25 Clery (1995), pp. 96–7.

26 Jane Austen, *Northanger Abbey* (1818), ed. and introd. Marilyn Butler (London: Penguin, 1995), pp. 95–6.

27 Austen (1995), pp. 124–5.

28 Austen (1995), p. 150.

29 Austen (1995), p. 174.

30 Clery (1995), pp. 115–16.

31 Kate Ferguson Ellis, *The Contested Castle: Gothic Novels and the Subversion of Domestic Ideology* (Urbana: University of Illinois Press, 1989), p. xii.

32 See Clery (1995), pp. 124–6, Wolfram Schmidgen, *Eighteenth-Century Fiction and the Law of Property* (Cambridge: Cambridge University Press, 2002), pp. 164–70, and Sue Chaplin, *Law, Sensibility and the Sublime in Eighteenth-Century Women's Fiction: Speaking of Dread* (Aldershot: Ashgate, 2004).

33 William Blackstone, *Commentaries on the Laws of England*, 4 vols (Oxford: Clarendon Press, 1765–9), p. 268.

34 Schmidgen (2002), p. 166.

35 Schmidgen (2002), p. 167.

36 Mary Wollstonecraft, *The Wrongs of Woman: or, Maria. A Fragment*, in *Mary and The Wrongs of Woman*, ed. Gary Kelly (Oxford: Oxford University Press, 1980), p. 155. For explorations of Wollstonecraft's novella in relation to the Gothic, see Diane Long Hoeveler's 'The Construction of the Female Gothic Posture: Wollstonecraft's *Mary* and Gothic Feminism', in Smith and Wallace (2004).

37 Clery (1995), pp. 126–7.

38 Austen (1995), p. 163.

39 Robert Miles, *Ann Radcliffe: The Great Enchantress* (Manchester: Manchester University Press, 1995), pp. 137–8.

40 Ellis's use of 'Feminine Gothic' shifts from the biologically natural identification of sex with author that 'Female Gothic' offers to the more culturally determined category of 'Feminine'.

41 Chaplin (2004), p. 128.

42 In this particular section, Chaplin specifically compares Radcliffe's invocation of the law to Eliza Fenwick's exploration of marriage and the law in her novel *Secresy, or The Ruin on the Rock* (1795).

43 Chaplin (2004), p. 128.

44 Chaplin (2004), pp. 128–9.

45 Chaplin (2004), p. 129.

46 Anne Williams, *Art of Darkness: A Poetics of Gothic* (Chicago and London: University of Chicago Press, 1995), p. 107.

47 Williams (1995), p. 139.

48 Julia Kristeva, *Revolution in Poetic Language* (1974), trans. Margaret Waller (New York: Columbia University Press, 1984). Kristeva here detects two forces competing for expression in the language of poetry, the symbolic and the semiotic. The *Symbolic* is that aspect of language that allows it to *refer*, and is firmly tied to Lacan's notion of social order. The *Semiotic* order of language is the revolutionary force; it is the aspect that bears the trace of the language user's own body and of the mother's protolinguistic presence. It is represented through pulse and rhythm, and disrupts the Symbolic Order. The concerns of this argument have, in many respects, already been anticipated in the focus of the chapter on 'Psychoanalysis'.

49 Williams (1995), p. 139.

50 Diane Long Hoeveler, *Gothic Feminism: The Professionalization of Gender from Charlotte Smith to the Brontës* (Liverpool and Pennsylvania: Liverpool University Press and Pennsylvania University Press, 1998), p. 7.

51 Adriana Craciun, *Fatal Women of Romanticism* (Cambridge: Cambridge University Press, 2003), p. 22. While, in this particular section, Craciun is engaging with Margaret Homans's *Women Writers and Poetic Identity*, and Anne Mellor's *Romanticism and Gender*, the point also carries for the approach to feminist poetics that Anne Williams executes in *Art of Darkness*.

52 Craciun (2003), p. 111.

53 Charlotte Dacre, *Zofloya, or the Moor: A Romance of the Fifteenth Century* (1806), ed. Adriana Craciun (Peterborough: Broadview, 1997). See also Dacre's other fiction for

further examples of heroines who do not conform to the helpless passivity outlined by Williams in *The Confessions of the Nun of St Omer* (1805); *The Libertine* (1807) and *The Passions* (1811).

54 *Monthly Literary Recreations*, 1 (July 1806), p. 80, cited in Dacre (1997), p. 261.

55 *The General Review of British and Foreign Literature*, vol. I (London: D. N. Shury, 1806), pp. 590–3, cited in Dacre (1997), p. 263.

56 Craciun (2003), p. 113. Here, she cites the review of *Zofloya* in *The Annual Review*, 5 (1806), p. 542.

57 See also Craciun's review of Diane Long Hoeveler's *Gothic Feminism* in *Gothic Studies*, 1:2 (December 1999).

58 Craciun (2003), p. 146.

59 Craciun (2003), p. 147.

60 Craciun (2003), p. 147.

61 Clery (2000), p. 100.

62 David Punter, *The Literature of Terror: A History of Gothic Fictions from 1765 to the Present Day*, 2 vols (Harlow: Longman, 1996), p. 115. Punter singles out as a particular Radcliffean example of Lathom's fiction his novel *The Castle of Ollada* (1794).

63 Eve Kosofsky Sedgwick, *Between Men: English Literature and Male Homosocial Desire* (New York: Columbia University Press, 1985), p. 90.

64 Sedgwick (1985), p. 91.

65 Sedgwick remains, however, somewhat equivocal about the three writers' homosexuality: 'a case can be made about each that he was in some significant sense homosexual – Beckford notoriously, Lewis probably, Walpole iffily', Sedgwick (1985), p. 92.

66 Sedgwick (1985), p. 92.

67 Sedgwick (1985), p. 91.

68 Sedgwick (1985), p. 91.

69 Sedgwick (1985), p. 92.

70 The case for Radcliffe's penultimate novel *The Italian* is less convincing. Whilst Vivaldi's relationship with Schedoni and Nicola di Zampari borders on persecuted obsession, this is not the sole driving force of the narrative.

71 Punter (1996), p. 122.

72 Robert Miles, *Gothic Writing, 1750–1820: A Genealogy* (1993; 2nd edn, Manchester: Manchester University Press, 2002), p. 25.

73 Miles (2002), p. 25.

74 Miles (2002), p. 26. See also Punter's arguments on marriage, sexuality and gender divides in eighteenth-century Britain in *The Literature of Terror* (1996), p. 83.

75 Hoeveler (1998), p. 20.

CONCLUSION

1 The two presses to which I refer are Zittaw Books: Purveyors of the Trade Gothic, who specialize in Gothic Bluebooks, the cheap print editions that were issued and rewritten during the 1790s and 1800s, and Valancourt Books, which is reprinting many good and unjustly neglected Gothic romances from the 1790s and 1800s.

2 See, for example, Michael Gamer, *Romanticism and the Gothic: Genre, Reception and Canon Formation* (Cambridge: Cambridge University Press, 2000), and *Seven Gothic Dramas, 1789–1825*, ed. Jeffrey Cox (Athens, OH: Ohio University Press, 1992).

3 Avril Horner and Sue Zlosnik, *Gothic and the Comic Turn* (Basingstoke: Palgrave Macmillan, 2004).

# Bibliography

## GOTHIC NOVELS

Austen, Jane, *Northanger Abbey* (1818), ed. and introd. Marilyn Butler (London: Penguin, 1995).

Dacre, Charlotte, *Zofloya, or the Moor: A Romance of the Fifteenth Century* (1806), ed. Adriana Craciun (Peterborough: Broadview, 1997).

Godwin, William, *Caleb Williams* (1794), ed. David McCracken (Oxford: Oxford University Press, 1969).

Godwin, William, Preface to *Caleb Williams* for Bentley's Standard Novels II (London, 1832).

Hogg, James, *The Private Memoirs and Confessions of a Justified Sinner* (1824), ed. Peter Garside (Edinburgh: Edinburgh University Press, 2002).

Lee, Sophia, *The Recess, or a tale of other times*, 3 vols (London: T. Cadell, 1783–5).

Lewis, Matthew, *The Monk* (1796), ed. Howard Anderson (Oxford: Oxford World's Classics, 1980).

Maturin, Charles Robert, *Melmoth the Wanderer* (1820), ed. Douglas Grant, introd. Chris Baldick (Oxford: Oxford World's Classics, 1989).

Radcliffe, Ann, *The Castles of Athlin and Dunbayne: A Highland Story* (1789) (Oxford: Oxford University Press, 1993).

Radcliffe, Ann, *A Sicilian Romance* (1790), ed. Alison Milbanke (Oxford: Oxford University Press, 1993).

Radcliffe, Ann, *The Romance of the Forest* (1791), ed. Chloe Chard (Oxford: Oxford University Press, 1986).

Radcliffe, Ann, *The Mysteries of Udolpho; a Romance, interspersed with some Pieces of Poetry* (1794), ed. Bonamy Dobrée (Oxford: Oxford University Press, 1980).

Radcliffe, Ann, *The Italian* (1797), ed. Robert Miles (London: Penguin Classics, 2000).

Roche, Regina Maria, *The Children of the Abbey, a tale*, 4 vols (London: William Lane, 1796).

Roche, Regina Maria, *Clermont, a tale*, 4 vols (London: William Lane, 1798).

Scott, Walter, *Waverley, or, 'tis sixty years since* (1814), 3 vols (Edinburgh: Constable, 1814).

Talfourd, Thomas Noon, *Memoir of the Life and Writings of Mrs. Radcliffe*, prefixed to Ann Radcliffe, *Gaston de Blondeville, or The Court of Henry III*, 4 vols (London: Henry Colburn, 1826).

Walpole, Horace, *The Castle of Otranto* (1764), ed. E. J. Clery (Oxford: Oxford World's Classics, 1996).

Walpole, Horace, *The Yale Edition of Walpole's Correspondence*, ed. W. S. Lewis (New Haven, CT: Yale University Press, 1937–83).

Wollstonecraft, Mary, *The Wrongs of Woman: or, Maria. A Fragment*, in *Mary and The Wrongs of Woman*, ed. Gary Kelly (Oxford: Oxford University Press, 1980).

## CONTEMPORARY CRITICISM AND THEORIZING OF THE GOTHIC

[Anon.], 'The Terrorist System of Novel Writing', *Monthly Magazine*, 4:21 (August 1797), pp. 102–4.

[Anon.], 'Terrorist Novel Writing', *Spirit of the Public Journals for 1797*, vol. 1 (London, 1798), pp. 223–5; reprinted in Clery and Miles (eds), *Gothic Documents* (Manchester: Manchester University Press, 2000).

Aikin, A. L., 'On the Pleasure Derived from Objects of Terror', from *Miscellaneous Pieces, in Prose*, by J. and A. L. Aikin (London: J. Johnson, 1773).

Burke, Edmund, *A Philosophical Enquiry into the Origin of our Ideas of the Sublime and Beautiful* (1757), ed. David Womersley (London: Penguin, 1998).

Burke, Edmund, *Reflections on the Revolution in France* (1790), ed. Conor Cruise O'Brien (London: Penguin, 1968).

Coleridge, Samuel Taylor, 'Review' of *The Monk* (1796), in *Critical Review*, 19 (February 1797), pp. 194–200.

Drake, Nathan, *Literary Hours or sketches critical and narrative*, xv (Sudbury, 1798).

Green, Sarah, 'Literary Retrospection', the 'Preface' to *Romance Readers and Romance Writers: A Satirical Novel*, 3 vols (London: T. Hookham, 1810).

Hazlitt, William, 'On the English Novelists', *Lectures on the English Comic Writers*, vol. VI in *The Complete Works of William Hazlitt*, ed. P. P. Howe, 21 vols (London: Dent, 1931).

Mathias, T. J., *The Pursuits of Literature* (1794–7), 13th edn (London: T. Becket, 1805).

Radcliffe, Ann, 'On the Supernatural in Poetry', *The New Monthly Magazine and Literary Journal*, II (1826).

Sade, Donatien Alphonse François, Marquis de, 'Idées sur les romans', translated as 'Essay on the Novel', from *Selected Writings of de Sade*, trans. Leonard de Saint-Yves (New York: British Book Centre, 1954).

Scott, Sir Walter, 'Ann Radcliffe', from the *Lives of the Novelists* from the *Miscellaneous Prose Works*, in Ioan Williams, (ed.), *On Novelists and Fiction* (London: Routledge, 1968).

Wollstonecraft, Mary, *A Vindication of the Rights of Men* (1790), in *Political Writings*, ed. Janet Todd (Oxford: Oxford University Press, 1993).

## GOTHIC CRITICISM

Botting, Fred, *Gothic* (London: Routledge, 1996).

Botting, Fred (ed), *The Gothic* (Cambridge: English Association, 2001).

Bronfen, Elisabeth, *Over her Dead Body: Death, Femininity and the Aesthetic* (Manchester: Manchester University Press, 1992).

Bruhm, Steven, *Gothic Bodies: The Politics of Pain in Romantic Fiction* (Philadelphia: University of Pennsylvania Press, 1994).

Canuel, Mark, *Religion, Toleration, and British Writing, 1790–1830* (Cambridge: Cambridge University Press, 2002).

Castle, Terry, *The Female Thermometer: Eighteenth-Century Culture and the Invention of the Uncanny*, (Oxford: Oxford University Press, 1995).

Chaplin, Sue, *Law, Sensibility and the Sublime in Eighteenth-Century Women's Fiction: Speaking of Dread*. (Aldershot: Ashgate, 2004).

Clery, E. J., 'Ann Radcliffe and D. A. F. de Sade: Thoughts on Heroinism', in 'Female Gothic', ed. Robert Miles, a special issue of *Women's Writing*, 1:2 (1994), p. 203.

Clery, E. J., *The Rise of Supernatural Fiction, 1762–1800*. (Cambridge: Cambridge University Press, 1995).

Clery, E. J., *Women's Gothic* (Tavistock: Northcote House, 2000).

Clery, E. J., 'The Genesis of Gothic Fiction', in *The Cambridge Companion to Gothic Fiction*, ed. Jerrold E. Hogle (Cambridge: Cambridge University Press, 2002).

Cox, Jeffrey (ed.), *Seven Gothic Dramas, 1789–1825* (Athens, OH: Ohio University Press, 1992).

Craciun, Adriana, *Fatal Women of Romanticism*, (Cambridge: Cambridge University Press, 2003).

DeLaMotte, Eugenia C., *Perils of the Night: A Feminist Study of Nineteenth-Century Gothic* (Oxford and New York: Oxford University Press, 1990).

Doody, Margaret Anne, 'Desert Ruins and Troubled Waters: Female Dreams in Fiction and the Development of the Gothic Novel', *Genre* 10 (1977), pp. 529–73.

Duncan, Ian, *Modern Romance and the Transformation of the Novel* (Cambridge: Cambridge University Press, 1992).

Ellis, Kate Ferguson. *The Contested Castle: Gothic Novels and the Subversion of Domestic Ideology* (Urbana: University of Illinois Press, 1989).

Ellis, Markman, *The History of Gothic Fiction* (Edinburgh: Edinburgh University Press, 2000).

Gamer, Michael, *Romanticism and the Gothic: Genre, Reception and Canon Formation* (Cambridge: Cambridge University Press, 2000).

Guest, Harriet, 'The Wanton Muse: Politics and Gender in Gothic Theory after 1760' in *Beyond Romanticism: New Approaches to Texts and Contexts 1780–1832*, ed. Stephen Copley and John Whale (London: New York and Routledge, 1992), pp. 118–39.

Hoeveler, Diane Long, *Gothic Feminism: The Professionalization of Gender from Charlotte Smith to the Brontës*. (Liverpool and Pennsylvania: Liverpool University Press and Pennsylvania University Press, 1998).

Hogle, Jerrold E., 'The Ghost of the Counterfeit – and the Closet – in *The Monk*', in Matthew Lewis's *The Monk*, ed. Fred Frank, a special issue of the electronic journal *Romanticism on the Net*, 8 (November 1997) (www.erudit.org/revue/ron/1997).

Hogle, Jerrold. E. (ed.)., *The Cambridge Companion to Gothic Fiction* (Cambridge: Cambridge University Press, 2002).

Horner, Avril (ed), *European Gothic* (Manchester: Manchester University Press, 2002).

Horner, Avril and Zlosnik, Sue, *Gothic and the Comic Turn* (Basingstoke: Palgrave Macmillan, 2004).

Howard, Jacqueline, *Reading Gothic Fiction: A Bakhtinian Approach* (Oxford: Clarendon Press, 1993).

Howells, Coral Ann, *Love, Mystery and Misery: Feeling in Gothic Fiction* (1978; London: Athlone Press, 1995).

Hughes, William (ed.), *Gothic Studies* (Manchester: Manchester University Press, 1999).

Hurley, Kelly, *The Gothic Body: Sexuality, Materialism and Degeneration at the Fin de Siècle*. (Cambridge: Cambridge University Press, 1996).

Jackson, Rosemary, *Fantasy: The Literature of Subversion* (London: Methuen, 1981).

Jacobs, Edward, *Accidental Migrations* (Lewisburg: Bucknell University Press, 2000).

Kahane, Claire, 'The Gothic Mirror', in S. L. Garner et al., (eds), *The (M)other Tongue: Essays in Feminist Psychoanalytic Interpretation* (Ithaca and London: Cornell University Press, 1985), pp. 334–51.

Keane, Angela, *Women Writers and the English Nation in the 1790s: Romantic Belongings* (Cambridge: Cambridge University Press, 2000).

Kilgour, Maggie, *The Rise of the Gothic Novel* (London: Routledge, 1995).

Massé, Michelle A., *In the Name of Love: Women, Masochism and the Gothic* (Ithaca, NY: Cornell University Press, 1992).

Massé, Michelle A., 'Psychoanalysis and the Gothic', in David Punter (ed.), *Companion to the Gothic* (Oxford: Blackwell, 2000).

Miles, Robert, *Ann Radcliffe: The Great Enchantress* (Manchester: Manchester University Press, 1995).

Miles, Robert, 'Abjection, Nationalism and the Gothic', in *The Gothic*, ed. Fred Botting for the English Association (Cambridge: D. S. Brewer, 2001), pp. 47–70.

Miles, Robert, 'Europhobia: the Catholic Other in Horace Walpole and Charles Maturin', in *European Gothic*, ed. Avril Horner (Manchester: Manchester University Press, 2002).

Miles, Robert, *Gothic Writing, 1750–1820: A Genealogy* (1993), 2nd edn (Manchester: Manchester University Press, 2002).

Miles, Robert, 'The 1790s: the Effulgence of Gothic', in *The Cambridge Companion to Gothic Fiction*, ed. Jerrold E. Hogle (Cambridge: Cambridge University Press, 2002).

Mishra, Vijay, *The Gothic Sublime* (New York: State University of New York Press, 1994).

Moers, Ellen, *Literary Women* (1976), introd. Helen Taylor (London: The Women's Press, 1986).

Morris, David B., 'Gothic Sublimity', *New Literary History*, 16 (1985), pp. 299–319.

Napier, Elizabeth R., *The Failure of Gothic: Problems of Disjunction in an Eighteenth-Century Literary Form* (Oxford: Clarendon Press, 1987).

Norton, Rictor, *Mistress of Udolpho: The Life of Ann Radcliffe* (London and New York: Leicester University Press, 1999).

Parreaux, André, *The Publication of 'The Monk': A Literary Event, 1796–1798* (Paris: Didier, 1960).

Paulson, Ronald, *Representations of Revolution, 1789–1820* (New Haven and London: Yale University Press, 1983).

Praz, Mario, *The Romantic Agony* (1930), trans. A. Davidson, introd. F. Kermode (London, 1970).

Punter, David, 'Social Relations of Gothic Fiction', in *Romanticism and Ideology: Studies in English Writing, 1765–1830*, ed. Aers, Cook and Punter (London: Routledge, 1981).

Punter, David, 'Review' of Elizabeth Napier's *The Failure of Gothic* in *The Times Higher Education Supplement*, 20 March 1987, p. 26.

Punter, David, *The Romantic Unconscious: A Study in Narcissism and Patriarchy* (London and New York: Harvester Wheatsheaf, 1989).

Punter, David, *The Literature of Terror: A History of Gothic Fictions from 1765 to the Present Day* 2 vols (Harlow: Longman, 1996).

Punter, David (ed.), *Companion to the Gothic* (Oxford: Blackwell, 2000).

Punter, David and Bronfen, Elisabeth, 'Violence, Trauma and the Ethical in *The Gothic*', ed. Fred Botting (Cambridge: The English Association, 2001), pp. 7–21.

Railo, Eino, *The Haunted Castle: A Study of the Elements of English Romanticism* (London, 1927).

Raven, James, 'The Novel Comes of Age', in Peter Garside, James Raven, and Rainer Schöwlering, (eds), *The English Novel 1770–1799: A Bibliographical Survey of Prose Fiction Published in the British Isles* (Oxford: Oxford University Press, 2000).

Richter, David, 'Gothic Fantasia: the Monsters and the Myths – a Review Article', *The Eighteenth Century: Theory and Interpretation*, 28, no. 2 (Spring 1987), pp. 149–70.

Sadleir, Michael, 'The Northanger Novels: a Footnote to Jane Austen', *English Association Pamphlet*, no. 68 (November 1927).

Sage, Victor, *Horror Fiction and the Protestant Tradition* (Basingstoke: Macmillan, 1988).

Sage, Victor, (ed.), *The Gothick Novel: A Casebook*, (Basingstoke: Macmillan, 1990).

Schmidgen, Wolfram, *Eighteenth-Century Fiction and the Law of Property* (Cambridge: Cambridge University Press, 2002).

Sedgwick, Eve Kosofsky, *Between Men: English Literature and Male Homosocial Desire* (New York: Columbia University Press, 1985).

Smith, Andrew and Wallace, Diana (eds), 'Female Gothic', a special issue of *Gothic Studies*, 6:1 (May 2004).

Sowerby, Robin, 'The Goths in History and Pre-Gothic Gothic', in *Companion to the Gothic*, ed. David Punter (Oxford: Blackwell, 2000).

Summers, Montague, *The Gothic Quest: A History of the Gothic Novel* (London: Fortune Press, 1938).

Tompkins, J. M. S., *The Popular Novel in England, 1770–1800* (1932; London: Methuen, 1969).

Varma, Devendra P., *The Gothic Flame* (1957; New York: Russell and Russell, 1966).

Watt, James, *Contesting the Gothic: Fiction, Genre and Cultural Conflict, 1764–1832* (Cambridge: Cambridge University Press, 1999).

Williams, Anne, *Art of Darkness: A Poetics of Gothic* (Chicago and London: Chicago University Press, 1995).

Wolstenholme, Susan, *Gothic (Re)Visions: Writing Women as Readers* (Albany: State University of New York Press, 1983).

Wright, Angela, 'European Disruptions of the Idealized Woman: Matthew Lewis's *The Monk* and the Marquis de Sade's *La Nouvelle Justine*', in *European Gothic*, ed. Avril Horner (Manchester: Manchester University Press, 2002).

Wright, Angela, ' "To Live the Life of Hopeless Recollection": Mourning and Melancholia in Female Gothic', in 'Female Gothic', ed. Andrew Smith and Diana Wallace, *Gothic Studies*, 6:1 (May 2004).

## RELATED HISTORICAL AND THEORETICAL CRITICISM

Berger, John, *Ways of Seeing* (Harmondsworth: Penguin, 1972).

Cixous, Hélène, 'La Fiction et ses fantômes: une lecture de l'*Unheimliche* de Freud', *Poétique*, 10 (1973).

Colley, Linda, *Britons: Forging the Nation, 1707–1837* (New Haven and London: Yale University Press, 1992).

Freud, Sigmund, *The Standard Edition of the Complete Psychological Works of Sigmund Freud*, 24 vols, ed. James Strachey et al. (London: Hogarth Press, 1953–74).

Garner, S. L. et al. (ed. and introd.), *The (M)other Tongue: Essays in Feminist Psychoanalytic Interpretation*. (Ithaca and London: Cornell University Press, 1985).

Hobsbawm, E. J., *Nations and Nationalism since 1780: Programme, Myth and Reality* (Cambridge: Cambridge University Press, 1990).

Keen, Paul, *The Crisis of Literature in the 1790s* (Cambridge: Cambridge University Press, 1999).

Kristeva, Julia, *Revolution in Poetic Language*, trans. Margaret Waller (New York: Columbia, 1984).

Kristeva, Julia, *Powers of Horror: An Essay on Abjection*, trans. Leon S. Roudiez (New York: Columbia University Press, 1982).

Lacan, Jacques, *Ecrits* (1966), trans. Alan Sheridan (London: Routledge, 1977).

Laplanche, Jean, *Essays on Otherness*, trans. John Fletcher (London: Routledge, 1999).

Mulvey, Laura, 'Visual Pleasure and Narrative Cinema', *Screen*, 16, 3 (Autumn 1975), pp. 6–18. Collected in Laura Murvay, Virtual and other pleasures (Basingstoke: Macmillan, 1989).

Thompson, E. P., *The Making of the English Working Class* (1963; London: Penguin, 1991).

## USEFUL WEBSITES – ALL DETAILS ARE CORRECT AT THE TIME OF GOING TO PRESS

*The International Gothic Association.*   An excellent website which contains details of how to join the IGA, as well as useful links to other research-related sites.
http://gothic.english.dal.ca/

*The Literary Gothic.* A great resource for students of Gothic Literature.
www.litgothic.com/index_fl.html

*Romanticism on the Net.*   Although not devoted entirely to Gothic Studies, this excellent online journal and website contains articles on many of the authors discussed in this Guide.
www.ron.umontreal.ca/

*The Sickly Taper.*   An excellent, regularly updated bibliography of criticism on the Gothic, with very helpful links.
http://thesicklytaper.net/

*Valancourt Books.*   A small specialist press dealing in reprinting many of the out-of-print 'Northanger Novels' mentioned in Chapter One.
www.valancourtbooks.com/about.html

Zittaw Press: Purveyors of the Trade Gothic. Contains a good Gothic Literature page, as well as details of how to order the more rare eighteenth-century Gothic novels and novellas that they reprint.
http://www.zittaw.com

# Index